The Terror That Comes in the Night

Publications of the American Folklore Society
New Series
General Editor, Marta Weigle
Volume 7

The
Terror
That
Comes
in the
Night

An Experience-Centered Study of
Supernatural Assault Traditions

David J. Hufford

upp

University of Pennsylvania Press
Philadelphia

This work was published with the support of the Haney Foundation.

Library of Congress in Publication Data
Hufford, David.
    The terror that comes in the night

    (Publications of the American Folklore Society;
new ser., v. 7)
    Bibliography: p.
    1. Nightmares.   2. Incubi.   3. Witchcraft.   4. Sleep
paralysis.   I. Title.   II. Series.
BF1099.N53H83   1982   398'.45   82-40350
ISBN 0-8122-7851-8

Printed in the United States of America
First paperback printing 1989

Contents

Acknowledgments

It is impossible to list all those who have helped with the research and writing of this book. In fact, I benefited from so much advice and direction before I had any notion of where the research was leading that I doubt that I myself am aware of all the major contributions. Nonetheless, certain invididuals stand out so clearly that I must give them a special word of thanks here.

First of all my family has been crucial in this work. Not only did they frequently have to relinquish my time, but my wife, Ellin, has from the beginning helped me enormously in library research, the location and organization of materials, checking and making suggestions on drafts, and countless other tasks without which the book would still be far from finished. And all of this took place in the context of being unable to give a concise and satisfactory answer when people asked, "What is the book about?" More than any other she has shared with me the odd feeling of working on a subject for which there is no really useful English vocabulary.

Among my teachers I am particularly grateful to Anthony Wallace and Don Yoder of the University of Pennsylvania for having first made clear to me the wonderful complexity and inherently fascinating nature of belief as a subject for study; and to Kenneth Goldstein of Penn for emphasizing the profound respect and seriousness that we owe to those whom we study. Also, though I never took a course from him and did not meet him until the latter part of my career as a folklore graduate student, I count Wayland Hand of UCLA as one of my teachers, and his interest and encouragement in all of my work with belief have been invaluable.

As the topic of the Old Hag began to resolve into a subject of study, the Folklore Department and the Folklore and Language Archive of Memorial University in Newfoundland provided the only setting in which that study could have been started. Of the many friends and colleagues at Memorial who helped me with the work in its beginning stages I am especially indebted to Neil Rosenberg and Herbert and Letty Halpert for advice and suggestions. After research on the mainland had raised new questions about the Newfoundland beliefs and accounts, they continued to help by making the archive available to me for further investigation.

Help in the form of access to archival material has also been given to me by William (Bert) Wilson at the University of Utah (Logan) and Lynwood Montell at Western Kentucky University. Wayland Hand has also helped enormously in this regard by making his Dictionary of American Popular Beliefs and Superstitions files available to me. And in the use of those files Wayland's able assistants, Frances Tally and Sondra Theiderman, helped me repeatedly and continued to send me useful additional references after my visits to the files at UCLA.

Jan Brunvand (University of Utah), Roger Welsch (University of Nebraska), and Michael Taft (University of Saskatchewan) have also kept my research in mind and have not only offered encouragement but have sent me numerous references and copies of useful unpublished material.

At the Penn State College of Medicine my colleague Robert Miller has provided endless help and encouragement by reading drafts, sending a constant stream of pertinent references, and taking a great deal of time to discuss difficult points ranging from the analysis of data to the selection of appropriate vocabulary for use in this book. Finding such interest and enthusiasm, coupled with the distinctly different academic perspective of medical sociology, has been invaluable. Also at the College Arthur Zucker has been very helpful and encouraging as I have struggled with the philosophy of science issues raised by this research.

Of course the cooperation of those whom I have interviewed about their experiences has been essential. Without their willingness to take this time, and to discuss personal experiences which in many cases they had never before mentioned to anyone, this book could not have been written. They have been most generous with both their time and their trust.

To all of these people, and to all of those whose aid I have not been able to mention, I am very grateful. I hope that in this book they will find their support in some measure rewarded.

Introduction

No commonly accepted term exists in modern English for the experience that is the subject of this book. This unusual situation of language is an object of, as well as a complication in, my research. The use of such folk terms as incubus, nightmare, and witch riding, for example, has led to mistaken conclusions about the distribution of the experience that lies behind the associated beliefs. Such problems in terminology have made it necessary to investigate the academic study of belief along with the beliefs themselves. In the absence of a precise name, I have chosen a title for this book that conveys the feeling characteristic of what some have considered to be the most frightening event ever experienced by humans—the terror that comes in the night.[1]

When I began this project I expected it to take only a few months and to result in a single article.[2] Instead I have taken almost ten years to reach the present point, and I cannot claim

---

1. See, for example, John E. Mack, *Nightmares and Human Conflict* (Boston: Houghton Mifflin Co., 1974), p. 48.

2. I began the work in 1971. In 1973 I presented a paper, "A New Approach to 'The Old Hag': The Nightmare Tradition Reexamined," at the Conference on American Folk Medicine organized by Wayland Hand and held at UCLA (subsequently published in *American Folk Medicine,* ed. Wayland D. Hand [Berkeley and Los Angeles: University of California Press, 1976], pp. 73–85.) Although in the paper I suggested several of the points covered in this book, it was already clear that much more research would be required.

that the investigation is complete even now. One reason is that the topic has proved to be much larger than I could have known in the beginning. Another reason is that my subject matter has required the development of a novel approach, a fact that I came to realize gradually in the course of the work. Only when I had completed this book did I begin to see the outlines of what I now call the experience-centered approach to the study of supernatural belief. The study presented here does, however, permit a view of some of the major emphases and characteristics of the approach, and some comments about these may make the implications of the book as a whole easier to grasp. I present this approach as one that can be added to those already in use. I do not propose that it should become the only way that folklorists should study belief or that it should replace any specific alternatives, although I do believe that it can substantially supplement many other strategies.

This approach recognizes the epistemological difficulties of focusing on experience, especially when dealing with the materials of greatest interest in the folkloristic study of super- natural belief. Another's experience is always a reconstruction to be inferred rather than a "fact" to be directly observed. The data the folklorist relies on for this reconstruction consist largely of verbal accounts, and these are well known to be loaded with sources of error: faulty memories; the creative pro- cesses of oral tradition; the very processes of perception, which are generally recognized to be influenced by expectation. But the folklorist cannot consider such factors to be merely sources of error, for they are themselves important subjects of study, and the changed material is recognized as having its own integ- rity and authenticity. Some folklorists have gone so far as to say that in the study of supernatural belief the issue of whether a given belief is correct is irrelevant.[3] Given the findings re-

---

3. Donald Ward, for example, writes, "The folklore scholar . . . need not concern himself with the question of the existence or non-existence of paranormal phenomena" ("The Little Man Who Wasn't There: Encounters with the Supranormal," *Fabula: Journal of Folktale Studies* 18 [1977]:216).

Part of the problem is the simultaneous consideration of a kind of inter- pretation (paranormal) and the observations to which it refers (the phenome- na). The folklorist must often be concerned with the existence of such

ported in the present study, I must consider this to be an over-statement. For some research questions the actual connection between accounts and the objective facts of allegedly related personal experience matters little; for example, "Why does this group enjoy hearing this particular legend, regardless of their personal involvement in the events it describes?" But for other questions our ability to describe confidently the features of related experience can be crucial; for example, "Why is a particular believed narrative stable across time and space?" This question lay behind Walter Anderson's formulation of the law of self-correction and his theory of the formation of special redactions.[4] It has also been basic in the development of theories about the psychological and social functions of narratives and individual narrative elements. For believed narratives that claim repeated experience as their authority, however, the explanation of stability cannot be ultimately settled without a consideration of the alleged experiences. All explanations of the stable accounts of giant, many-tentacled sea creatures told by seafarers over long periods of time and in many different locations, for example, were called into question (to put it mildly) by the discovery of the giant squid.[5]

Because the consideration of actual experience in traditional beliefs tends to sound like an apologetic for those beliefs, I will present here an example that concludes somewhat differently from the giant squid case. A recent issue of the journal *Nature* contained an excellent article entitled "The Norse Merman as an Optical Phenomenon." The authors begin with the details of surviving medieval Norse descriptions of the mer-

---

phenomena, though not with their "paranormalness." The distinct issues of accuracy of observation and adequacy of explanation must generally be taken one at a time.

4. For a discussion of Anderson's folktale theories see Stith Thompson, *The Folktale* (New York: Holt Rinehart and Winston, 1946), pp. 437f.

5. Frederick Aldrich has provided a thorough discussion both of the history of the description and the biology of the giant squid. The historical material is emphasized in "The Giant Squid in Newfoundland," *The New Newfoundland Quarterly* 65, no. 3 (1967):4–8. The biology is stressed in "The Distribution of Giant Squids *(Cephalopoda Architeuthides)* in the North Atlantic and Particularly about the Shores of Newfoundland," *Sarsia* 34 (1968):393–98.

man. They then describe optical effects produced by "a moderate (atmospheric) inversion to total strength 7.5° C and with a thermocline at elevation 2.2m."[6] They use these figures to present undistorted drawings adapted from photographs of a killer whale "spy-hopping" and a walrus with its head and neck showing above the water line and compare these with drawings of the distorted images of each based on computer programs developed for ray tracing. The distortions are shown to conform very well with the Norse descriptions, even accounting for variations between one description and another. It is then pointed out that the necessary elevation for these effects is the same as would be obtained by standing on the deck of a medieval Norse ship and that sightings became increasingly rare as the size of Norse vessels increased. The traditional connection of merman sightings with a subsequent storm is shown to be correct because the necessary atmospheric optics are found just before storms in the North Atlantic. A number of other traditional details are also shown to fit the optical explanation. Finally, the authors present a photograph of a "modern day merman" at Lake Winnipeg, together with a photograph of the rock protruding from the water that provides the merman image when the lake conditions approximate those described in the physical model.

This systematic use of traditional features to develop a plausible hypothesis concerning the nature of the eliciting experience, followed by a reconstruction of that experience for comparison, and then finally the direct empirical support of the theory by photographic evidence is most impressive. Although no actual merman analogous to the giant squid was discovered, an improved understanding of naturally occurring atmospheric optical anomalies did result from a serious consideration of an apparently fabulous medieval belief. More germane to the concern of my study is the fact that two natural scientists were able to document with a high degree of confidence the role of accurate observations in the development of a medieval tradition, and the accurate correlation of these observations

6. W. H. Lehn and I. Schroeder, "The Norse Merman as an Optical Phenomenon," *Nature* 289 (1981):362–66; quotation on p. 363.

with impending storms, apparently achieved by properly performed inductive reasoning and empirical generalization. Furthermore, these findings allowed the scientists to provide a useful interpretation of changes in the merman tradition subsequent to a decline in Norse maritime skill, and changes in the size of ships and therefore the elevation of an observer on deck.

Although neither of these examples involved the use of the experience-centered approach as I have been working with it, they do illustrate several very important points. First, events accurately observed and reasoning properly carried out are in some cases central in the development and maintenance of folk belief, even when the beliefs appear fantastic. Also, in such cases folk knowledge is sometimes well in advance of scientific knowledge. Furthermore, an awareness of the roles of observation and reason can be essential in answering important folklore questions. The merman example also indicates that such explanatory efforts should demonstrate a high degree of correspondence with the details of the tradition in question. Explanations that require the omission of substantial quantities of traditional features or the attribution of poor observation and faulty reasoning in the development of the tradition are more speculative. For example, before the article in *Nature* the most prevalent theory about the merman had been that the sightings referred to either the dugong or the manatee.[7] First suggested in the seventeenth century, this explanation of the merman tradition was generally accepted by the end of the nineteenth century, despite its obvious shortcomings. Not only is it difficult to reconcile the actual appearance of either of these animals with the traditionally reported descriptions, but both are *tropical* animals. The sole advantage of this "explanation" was that it replaced a creature of folk tradition with an animal that had been described by naturalists. This was accomplished, however, at the cost of extreme and unsupported implications about the powers of observation, knowledge of the environment, and reasoning ability of northern sailors. Such explana-

---

7. Bernard Heuvelmans, *In the Wake of Sea Serpents* (New York: Hill and Wang, 1968), cited in Lehn and Schroeder, "The Norse Merman."

tions are not necessarily inaccurate, but empirical support for them is vital. Otherwise they tend to be circular. In the case of the giant squid, for example, it was said that superstitious sailors in their panic mistake floating trees for sea monsters; their beliefs and consequent fear prevent them from accurately observing the event or using their reason to check their superstitious conclusions; and we know that they are capable of such misperception and irrational behavior because they do such things as claiming to see sea monsters.

Such explanations also should presuppose only phenomena that are themselves subjects of empirical investigation and therefore are scientifically well authenticated. To the extent that an explanation relies on phenomena whose existence is controversial (e.g., the statement that death-announcing apparitions are merely symbolically represented telepathic perceptions[8]) or are poorly understood, that explanation must be considered speculative. In some cases there is simply a change in language that trades one unknown for another and thus is redescription or translation rather than explanation. The folk belief has been explained away rather than explained.

The search for scientific descriptions of phenomena that appear analogous to traditional accounts can be a useful step in the interpretation of folk belief. In such cases as the merman example, this procedure can at times even clarify and support traditionally reported features of a phenomenon. More frequently, though, extensive work is first required to arrive at a thorough description of both the beliefs and the associated experiences. Of major importance in accomplishing such a description has been the development of a phenomenological style of interviewing for use with those who claim firsthand experiences that support a supernatural belief. Such an interview style attempts to draw closer to the actual perceptions that lie behind the most natural modes of expression. Immediately, however, I must qualify this statement. I am not speaking here of any of the specific phenomenological schools of thought

8. For a discussion of this theory from psychical research at the turn of the century see G. N. M. Tyrell, *Apparitions,* rev. ed. (New York: Macmillan, 1963), pp. 45ff.

such as the phenomenological philosophy of Edmund Husserl,[9] but rather of the dictionary meaning of the term: "the study of . . . appearances in human experience, during which considerations of objective reality and of purely subjective response are temporarily left out of account."[10] The phenomenological schools of thought alluded to above seem to proceed very rapidly to the development of elaborate interpretations of phenomena. In fact, one gets the impression that some of them consider the straightforward approach suggested by the dictionary to be downright pedestrian.[11] To draw an analogy from the study of culture, it appears that much of phenomenology is in the position that ethnology (the study of culture) would be without ethnography (the description of culture). Many phenomenologists have apparently felt that since everyone has experience, the basic data of phenomenology are the subject of general consensus and may be taken as givens. So strong is this tendency and so frequently have I been misunderstood in my attempts to use the word in its "pedestrian" sense that I was tempted to coin a new word—phenomenography—to mean simply the description of phenomena. Fortunately, I restrained myself. But whatever the case with "ordinary" experiences, the phenomena involved in numinous experiences are in great need of careful description. This procedure does not simply remove expressive culture from the picture; it illuminates it and aids in its analysis. To some extent this method is similar to that of the psychological structuralism of such investigators as Edward Titchner. A major methodological difference is that the procedure is carried out with untrained subjects in connection with naturally occurring past events rather than experimentally presented stimuli. Its goal ís also very different in that it aims only at a

9. See, for example, Pierre Thevenaz, *What Is Phenomenology? And Other Essays,* ed. James M. Edie (Chicago: Quadrangle Books, 1962).

10. William Morris, ed., *The American Heritage Dictionary of the English Language* (Boston: Houghton Mifflin Co., 1978), p. 983.

11. For example, Paul Ricoeur calls this limitation of phenomenology to the description of appearances the word's "diluted sense" (Charles E. Reagan and David Stewart, eds., *The Philosophy of Paul Ricoeur: An Anthology of His Work* [Boston: Beacon Press, 1978], p. 75).

description of specific subjective experiences with a minimum of interference from postevent interpretation and ambiguous language, rather than a description of all elementary psychological states.

A combination of survey techniques with field work has been another useful method because knowing the distributions of both beliefs and the experiences said to support them has helped to evaluate possible sources of traditional misconstruction of events. For example, one check for the cultural shaping of certain perceptions is the determination of whether the same perceptions are found under different cultural conditions. Answering this question permits us to address the difference between the impact of culture on experience and on the description of experience. The value of knowing something about the frequency and distribution of traditional beliefs and related personal experiences calls into serious question many interpretations of folk belief carried out without this knowledge. The most common folkloristic methods of locating informants need to be balanced by other methods that give more information about the relationship between informants studied in some depth and the general population within which they live. Our knowledge of "star informants" needs to be balanced with information about those who either are unfamiliar with the traditions being studied or who may know them only slightly. Attention only to the "best" informants, or those who are self-selected through various means, can greatly restrict the number of questions that can be answered by the resulting information. One consequence of this development has been the discovery that the study of disbelievers can be as useful as that of believers in the effort to understand a particular set of beliefs. On the other hand, some questions can best be addressed by the means of selecting informants more commonly used by folklorists. For example, a better knowledge of the transmission of material along social networks can be gained by proceeding from one informant to another by referral than by surveying the entire community. I stress this point because, again, the experience-centered approach is not intended to replace other approaches but rather to be added to them. For some questions it is a necessary part of investigation, while for others it would not be relevant.

This point deserves special emphasis because of an unfortunate tendency in folklore studies to divide into academic factions seen as either unrelated to one another or as necessarily in conflict. Such divisions are those found between persons with a humanities emphasis and those with a social science footing, collectors as opposed to theoreticians, and text-oriented versus context-oriented scholars. Similar divisions, of course, occur in other fields and in the relations among different fields. Perhaps to some extent they are all a result of academic "future shock" inasmuch as the distinctions are often described as old-fashioned versus modern. Whatever the source of this trend, the resulting conflict is frequently expressed in new ways of doing things that are intended both to show the shortcomings of and to replace competing approaches. No doubt such disputes and competition are at times healthy in the effort to extend man's knowledge and understanding. But, at least in folklore, they have tended to be overdone, and I do not wish this book to be viewed as one more salvo in such a battle. I have found that the important criteria of usefulness are simply rigor of scholarship and the suitability of one's methods to the research task. In conducting the investigation presented in this book, I have made use of a great deal of work by other folklorists and scholars in other disciplines, including efforts on both sides of most of the divisions noted above. I have used archives, motif indices, and volumes of annotated collectanea. I have also used social science methods and a modest quantity of statistics. I have used materials from medicine and psychophysiology rarely if ever before associated with the study of folklore. All of this material has been necessary to the systematic pursuit of what I take to be basic questions in the study of folk belief. The present work, then, is not intended to be partisan in any sense except as it supports those who are in favor of careful scholarship.

Because I have presented the experience-centered approach as a stage of investigation that largely precedes theoretical interpretation, I must acknowledge that no approach can be truly free of theory, nor should it be. The experience-centered approach holds theory to a minimum in its attempt to provide better raw material that may be of use to analysts who subscribe to a variety of theoretical schools of thought.

The primary theoretical statement of the approach might be roughly summed up as follows: some significant portion of traditional supernatural belief is associated with accurate observations interpreted rationally. This does not suggest that *all* such belief has this association. Nor is this association taken as proof that the beliefs are true. This latter point must be stressed because much of the investigation of supernatural belief, especially since the Enlightenment, has been implicitly governed by a desire to show that the beliefs under investigation are false. The easiest way to do this seems to have been to assert that believers lack an understanding of how to separate true propositions from false ones. This has ranged from statements about a lack of appreciation for the rules of logic to assertions that the believer fails to use, at least within the domain of belief, adequate reality testing. The experience-centered approach does not seek to show that such interpretations are never accurate; rather, it is a useful means for determining when and under what circumstances they may be accurate. But the approach is in part based on the conclusion that poor observation and incorrect reasoning cannot account for all reported supernatural experience.

As I have noted in connection with the history of belief concerning the giant squid, the discovery of accurate observation and appropriate reasoning in connection with a belief has the appearance of support for the belief itself. That was one reason for using the "Norse merman" as a counterexample, but more needs to be said on this point. Perhaps because of the loose way the words "empirical" and "rational" have been used in connection with belief, there has been a tendency to overlook their technical meanings. They have developed connotations that make them almost synonymous with "correct" or "true." A brief consideration of the history and philosophy of science should be sufficient to dispel this notion. For example, Ptolemaic astronomy was empirically supported and generated accurate predictions by means of both logical deduction and inductive reasoning. It was also incorrect, even though it continues to be useful for such purposes as navigation. On the other hand, volumes could be filled with correct conclusions that have at times been supported by inaccurate observations and faulty reasoning.

I stress this point because I am well aware that many readers will wish to know whether I am engaged in the reduction of supernatural belief to physical explanations or the construction of an argument that the experiences presented in the book are evidence of a paranormal or supernatural reality. Given the sensitivity of the supernatural as a topic and the current public and academic involvement in such disputes, this is a natural question. The answer, however, is an emphatic "neither." The bulk of this book is concerned with obtaining a better description of those observations and processes of reasoning that are associated with a particular kind of widely distributed supernatural belief. As a part of that inquiry I have analyzed the observations and arguments that various academic schools of thought have employed in attempting to explain beliefs of that kind. I have also undertaken as much interpretation and explanation as can be well supported. At the present moment, however, all of this falls well short of the point at which I could bring this subject matter and my investigation of it into the debates between reductive materialism and its opponents. This is one advantage of the experience-centered approach—it allows for the development of a common ground of observations and research that is antecedent to those questions that are most culturally and emotionally loaded and therefore most difficult to approach in an unbiased manner. And yet the contributions of the approach are relevant to such ultimate questions.

This study was not conceived of as a demonstration of the experience-centered approach, as I have noted. Instead, the approach grew out of the study, and the term "experience-centered approach" will not be found within the body of this book. Nonetheless, I hope that the discussion just presented will be of use both in understanding the book and in considering some of the implications of this approach for future research.

In addition to my approach to collecting data, some discussion is needed concerning the manner in which I have presented them. The greatest part of that data appear in what I have called "cases." The focus of these cases is not the same in every instance. Some contain only a single person's description of one attack, together with contextual and background information. Others include descriptions of several attacks involving one person; still others describe more than one person's attacks. In deciding how to divide the information into cases, I have allowed its natural contours to be the major guide. If one person connected several experiences and told them in such a way that they are inextricably intertwined, I have given them as a single case. When, as in Case 20, the experiences of several people occurred in a single context and were recounted jointly, I have allowed that mass of material to stand as "a case." I have done this because I consider the cases to be data and not merely examples. Any editing of these materials has carried with it the risk of altering the data and therefore has been kept to a minimum. Obviously, I have had to select particular accounts for presentation and have been required by space limitations to perform some editorial maneuvers. The selection process has been like that performed whenever data are presented, and I have been as objective and unbiased as possible. The large quantity of material presented here should help to reduce concern that I may have given any seriously skewed impressions through a biased selection of cases.

The editing process has been done as follows. All omissions are marked by ellipses. If there are no ellipses, there have been no omissions. I have used dashes (— and ——) to indicate interruptions in the flow of speech, primarily pauses of varying length. The dashes do not indicate omissions. On the rare occasions when I have had to add a word for a sentence to make sense, I have indicated this editorial addition by putting the word in parentheses. In most of these instances, a word was either inaudible or difficult to understand on the tape recording. Finally, I have tended toward inclusiveness in the selection of starting and ending points for the extracts from transcripts. To the extent that a subject's words are not spontaneous, the effects of my questions or comments should, then, be clear from the material reproduced in the case.[12]

---

12. In some instances, the selection process may create the impression of interviewer effects and leading questions where there are none. I have occasionally asked closed questions to double check impressions given in earlier spontaneous statements by subjects. Since I cannot reproduce all

It would have been useful to employ a number of interviewers as an additional control for unintentional interviewer bias. Unfortunately, that method would have required extensive funding, which was not available. But, in addition to the full presentation of verbatim material, several of the texts presented in Chapter 5 provide an excellent means of checking for bias. The primary purpose of that section is to show how the phenomena under investigation occur in the context of various belief traditions and the consistency of the phenomena from one cultural setting to another, but it also allows the comparison of accounts collected and edited by others with those in which I am the interviewer. In several cases the materials are taken from printed sources with which I have had no personal connection (some predating not only this research but also my birth). In one extensively presented case (20), I have juxtaposed interview material collected by Lynwood Montell before he learned of my research on the topic with my own interview material gathered subsequently from one of the same informants. In this case, I have clearly indicated which materials were gathered by which interviewer, and I have at some points provided descriptions of precisely the same events, first from one interview and then from the other, for comparison. Taken together these checks should demonstrate that the major findings reported here cannot be accounted for by interviewer bias.

I have not found the experiences recounted in this book to be associated with ethnicity, religious background, or any other ethnographic variable. Nor have I found any association with those features of medical history that I could elicit using a basic illness checklist. This lack of association with obvious features of medical history has been supported by Robert Ness, who interviewed sixty-nine adults about the same kind of experiences and administered the *Cornell Medical Index* to them. He found no significant association between a history of attacks and emotional or physical illness as measured by the

---

preliminaries of each interview and have not edited out material merely to "improve" my questions, there are some points at which I may appear to have led a response.

CMI. [13] Of course, better sampling techniques and more sensitive measures may eventually establish some significant connections. However, because of the current lack of connection, I have not presented detailed personal history information with these accounts, focusing instead on the gross variable of presumptive evidence of exposure to traditional models of attacks. I have also strictly preserved the anonymity of my subjects by changing all names and disguising other personal information that might help to identify them.

Because I have treated the texts themselves as data, this book differs from folklore "collections" in several ways. Nonetheless, it contains a large number of texts, and this is a significant similarity to such collections. I hope that the result will suggest a form for the publication of folklore research that combines the advantages of collections of texts with those of theoretical works. I have not included a motif index in this book, a general and reasonable requirement for most collections of folk narratives, because I feel that at the present it would be confusing. Although many of the features of the accounts given here are recognizable as motifs, the motifs carry with them misleading connotations. For example, some features of experience that are well represented in the *Motif-Index* [14] section dealing with witches are found here in narratives that contain no references to witchcraft. The same is true for the whole gamut of supernatural attacker categories found in the *Motif-Index.* Instead of motifs, whose development has been predicated on some far-reaching assumptions about the literary nature of texts, I have provided an index of experiential features of the attacks. At some point it will be possible to cross-reference this index to the *Motif-Index,* and this will in a sense bridge the existential and the literary perspectives. This job should be saved, though, until we have a more fully developed phenomenology of the experiences that underlie supernatural belief traditions.

13. Robert C. Ness, "The Old Hag Phenomenon as Sleep Paralysis: A Biocultural Interpretation," *Culture, Medicine and Psychiatry* 2 (1978):26–28.

14. Stith Thompson, *Motif-Index of Folk-Literature,* 6 vols. (Bloomington: Indiana University Press, 1966).

Because I hope that this study will be of interest to people in a variety of fields, I have tried to avoid excessively technical language. When this was not possible, I have provided basic definitions and background information. The primary example is the beginning of Chapter 5, where I have given an introduction to sleep research. I have sought, however, to keep the book from falling into special interest sections, each standing alone. The data and the concepts from each portion are necessary for the full understanding and appreciation of all others. I trust that the advantages of this integrative approach outweigh any disadvantages. At any rate, the novelty that a psychologist will find in reading primarily folklore material or that a folklorist will experience in reading about laboratory sleep studies may be a good thing in itself.

In conclusion, this study is presented as an example of "applied folklore." I am told, and I can understand, that to the nonfolklorist this term has a comical appearance. Within folklore studies, however, the arguments that raged over the propriety and even the possibility of such a thing as applied folklore were anything but funny.[15] Very strong feelings were apparent on both sides of the question. Much of the rancor is now gone from the issue, and it is generally recognized within folklore that the concepts and methods of the field can be applied to subjects outside its immediate and traditional boundaries. What is still lacking is a consensus about which kinds of application are most promising and precisely how the applications are to be made.

From its inception, I have considered this study to be applied folklore. I saw the traditions and their underlying experiences as having potential medical and psychological significance, and I found that they had formed the basis of an extensive, though incoherent, literature in these fields. In addition to folklore questions, then, some practical questions concerning the diagnosis and treatment of illness were potentially implicated. My strategy, then, involved the development of an

---

15. For a collection of early statements pro and con on applied folklore see Richard Sweterlitsch, ed., *Papers on Applied Folklore,* Folklore Forum Bibliographic and Special Studies, no. 8 (Bloomington: Folklore Forum, 1971).

approach that would address both kinds of questions in a single undertaking. The involvement of practical questions enhanced the empirical side of the venture, and the folklore questions assured some theoretical payoff. Ideally, I feel, applied folklore can always provide such a mix: the accomplishment of results with practical usefulness as well as advancement of knowledge within the field. It can also provide an arena for genuinely interdisciplinary research. The problem focus allows for the bringing together of methods and theories from several fields strictly on the basis of their utility, rather than because of their traditional associations with one another.

1

The Old Hag in Newfoundland

The Canadian province of Newfoundland is an island in the North Atlantic off the east coast of Canada. Its 42,734 square miles provide a home for a population of only a little more than 570,000—about the same area as Pennsylvania but roughly one-twentieth the population. This sparse population, predominantly of Irish and English extraction, is concentrated on the Avalon Peninsula at the eastern end of the island, where the capital city of St. John's is located. St. John's is the only large city in Newfoundland, with a population of over 100,000. Most of the remaining people live in small villages scattered along the coast. A British colony until 1948, Newfoundland has been isolated from both the Old World and the New by a combination of historical factors, geography, and weather. In recent years that isolation has begun to yield, but culturally the island is still distinct and fascinating.

From 1971 to 1974 I lived and worked in St. John's as a faculty member in the Folklore Department of Memorial University of Newfoundland. This Folklore Department and the associated Folklore and Language Archive are ideally located because the conservative influences of isolation have left intact in Newfoundland elements of traditional culture no longer functioning in most of the English-speaking world. My work at the university included archival duties, and I was pleased to find that the rich and extensive collections included great quantities of folk belief material, my main interest. Through the archive and field work I found that beliefs and accounts of

1

supernatural lights—Will-o'-the-Wisp, Jack-o'-Lantern, ghost ships, weather lights—are very common, as are ghosts, omens of death, and many other categories. Even beliefs and accounts about the fairies can be found in St. John's and the outports, although these are much less common now than they once were. The current distribution and the changing state of such traditions appear to support the conventional academic point of view that supernatural beliefs are survivals from a naive past and must decline as "scientific thought" ascends. Newfoundland seems to have more of them than do less isolated parts of North America, and they seem to be more generally distributed. As the forces of acculturation proceed in the province, the beliefs are becoming less common, with the most rapid loss among the most acculturated portions of the population. Similar observations have been made many times all over the world for centuries and are a major part of the basis for the modern understanding of the relationships between supernatural belief, culture, and experience. I first encountered "the Old Hag" while working with these Newfoundland traditions.

Many Newfoundlanders are familiar with the Old Hag tradition and define it as did a university student about twenty years of age: "You are dreaming and you feel as if someone is holding you down. You can do nothing only cry out. People believe that you will die if you are not awakened." Brief definitions, however, are not the natural form of living traditions. In fact, they are very rarely found in this form except when a folklorist or other outsider asks questions of the "What is . . ." variety. Beliefs, like values and attitudes, normally find their expressions either in action or descriptions of action, that is, narratives. Narratives are far more easily elicited, recorded, and analyzed than are spontaneous acts, and thus they provide a convenient means of examining beliefs in their natural setting. For these reasons, my data in this book consist primarily of narratives and their accompanying conversations.

The three legends[1] that follow provide a much more ac-

---

1. The word "legend" has a variety of popular and scholarly meanings. Without entering into the pros and cons of those definitions I will here use the word to mean simply a narrative that is believed to be true.

curate, and therefore complex, introduction to the Old Hag tradition than could any number of definitions. The first two legends were received by the archive in response to a questionnaire distributed among university students in 1970 (reproduced in the Appendix). This was called the "Nightmare/Hag/Old Hag" questionnaire because the terms "nightmare" and "Old Hag," or simply "Hag," were known to be related, although the nature of the relationship was not immediately clear. Eight general questions about the Old Hag were asked, but it was emphasized that a detailed account of a single experience would be the most useful form of response. The students who received the questionnaire were free either to respond from their own knowledge and experience or to interview others. The following account is presented as submitted by two female students who collected it from a sixty-two-year-old woman.[2]

Case 1

Yes, the people of ———— did speak of having nightmares. Usually they said "I was hagged last night." To my knowledge the hag was experienced most often in the nighttime, in the person's home and it always came in human form.

I saw only one actual person who experienced the hag. It was the year 1915 and it concerns three people: Robert ————, John ————, and Jean ————. Robert was the Salvation Army schoolteacher and John ———— was just an ordinary workman. Robert was trying to date Jean who was John's steady girlfriend. About a month after this had been going on Robert began to be hagged. Every night when he went to bed, it was as if someone was pressing across his chest—it was as if he was being strangled. Robert became so sick that the people he boarded with thought he was going to die. But one night an old man suggested that Robert place a piece of board directly across his chest with an opened up pocket knife held between his hands. It was hoped that when the hag came to lie across his chest, the hag would be killed. However, in the morning when Robert got up he found that the knife was sticking into the piece of board. Only for the board

2. Memorial University of Newfoundland Folklore and Language Archive, Item #Q70B-32, pp. 1–2.

Robert would have been killed. Perhaps because the hag thought he had killed Robert that it never came back again. Robert knew that John ―――― was the person who was hagging him. He put it down to jealously on John's part. Both men were about the same age, between eighteen and twenty years old. In this case of hagging it was male against male.

Robert told the people that he stayed with the the hag was human—he could hear it coming and could recognize it but when it came he couldn't speak—he could only make throaty noises. The hag just walked in or appeared while Robert was sleeping but he woke up while he was being hagged. Robert said that he was always lying on his back and usually he was under stress. The hag was brought about by a curse. It always affected his throat most and took his breath away.

The way to call a hag, Robert later learned, was to say the Lord's Prayer backwards in the name of the devil. The only way to avoid the hag was by drawing blood or using the word of God and keeping the light on in the bedroom. Although Robert was hagged he always spoke freely about the whole thing whenever anyone asked him.

In contrasting such legends with brief definitions I was immediately confronted with a complication. In the definition, the experience is called "a dream" from which the dreamer must be "awakened." In the narrative, "being hagged" is equated with "having nightmares." To anyone accustomed to the modern usage of the word "nightmare," this suggests that being hagged is a bad dream. But the statement that "the hag was human" does not make sense if "hag" is synonymous with "dream." Dreams are generally understood to be subjective events, yet in this narrative the hagging is said both to have been done by John and to have been "brought about by a curse." This apparent contradiction does not simply indicate a difference of opinion over whether these experiences are dreams or objective, supernatural events. Rather, it is a result both of the combination of several traditions around a central core and of linguistic problems resulting from efforts to describe very difficult subjective points. I shall discuss these issues further following Case 2. For the moment, let us say that in Newfoundland "the Old Hag," and often "the nightmare," are understood to be applicable to both an experience and a feature of that experience, that is, the attacker. The experience is understood by many to be a state that is different from ordinary dreams but for which there is no good alternative word. Therefore, the use of the word "dream" does not always rule out the traditional belief that the experience is external and supernatural, although many do regard it as simply a special class of natural dream.

The next example, submitted by a male university student, was collected from an eighty-year-old man. This text was also written out by the collector and is therefore an approximation of the verbatim statement of the informant. The student's written version is presented unchanged except for the omission of unnecessary descriptive comments such as "His eyes held a unique twinkle." The words of the reported conversation are given complete with original spelling and the student's efforts to record features of dialect.[3]

Case 2

STUDENT: Do you know anything about the old Hag?

INFORMANT: Hu? No, boy, I don't.

STUDENT: The Old Hag! Don't you know anything about the Old Hag?

INFORMANT: No——hu——do you mean haggin' people? I can tell you a good one on that; I was there when it happened.

It was down on the Labrador it happened. We was fishin'. I spose it was about fifty odd year ago. 'Twas what you call a good year. We had our stages filled up with fish quicker than we could have done it fullin' 'em up with rocks. We was in the bunk house this night, and there was a fine girl, what we'd say, a bedroom girl, she was there, and one of us was tryin' to kiss her. But she wouldn't let him do it. So he said to her, 'If you don't let me kiss you, I'll hag you tonight'; now she never believed he could

3. Memorial University of Newfoundland Folklore and Language Archive, Item #Q70B-10, pp. 03–05.

do it, and she still wouldn't let him do it. Anyway he went home; and Brother, that was a night he hagged her! and hagged her good. She was that bad she was foamin' at the mouth before her father heard her. She was tellin' us about it after. Yes he give her some haggin'.

STUDENT: How did he hag her?

INFORMANT: Hu? I can't go tellin' it. 'Tis not good stuff to be tellin'.

STUDENT: Come on. If there's any sin in it, I'll take the blame. I'm writing a paper on it.

INFORMANT: Well——I'll tell you, but don't put me name on it. 'Twas like this; she went on over to her place. And as soon as she left, me buddy took off his clothes and kneeled down by the bed. I was there watchin' him when he done it. And you know what he done? He said the Lord's Prayer backwards; then jumped under the covers and took a knife from under the pilla and stuck it in the sideboard three or four times.

After awhile I put the kerosene lamp out and we all went to bunk. Every now and then we'd hear him bawl out, 'Hag, good Hag!' And that's how he hagged her.

STUDENT: Is the hag supposed to be an old woman or something? Because, who was he calling to when he said, 'Hag good Hag?'

INFORMANT: No——He, hisself must have hagged her; because she could see him standin' over her with the knife; and she couldn't move because she was stopped still with fright. The foam was even comin' out of her mouth, and her father only got her back to sense by callin' her name backwards.

STUDENT: I thought the fellow who hagged her was supposed to be in bed when all this was going on.

INFORMANT: His spirit, his spirit was what hagged her. She said after, if she'd have knowed he was really goin' to hag her she'd had a bottle ready, and finished him before he'd have hagged her.

STUDENT: What do you mean?

INFORMANT: See——if you swing at a spirit with a bottle, the spirit who is haggin' you will die. So he never hagged her no more because he knowed she had a bottle ready.

The importance of variations in terminology is illustrated by the informant's firm negative response to a question about "the old Hag" at the beginning of the interview. The topic would have been dropped if the student had not persisted. While doing a questionnaire study of my own on the subject, I found one respondent who was ignorant of the traditional meaning of "Old Hag" but who knew the term "The Hags" as a name for the experience. Another respondent, who was aware of the connection of the terms, said, "We know it as 'Hag Rogue.' One way my mother used to awaken her father . . . was to call his name backwards." Although the spelling may vary, this form often occurs, apparently a corruption of the phrase "hag rode" or "hag rid." In Newfoundland the verb "to hag" is most commonly used, with "to ride" occurring less often. Outside of Newfoundland the most common traditional expression I have found for the experience in English is "riding," although what does the riding is usually called a "witch," not a "hag." In addition to numerous variations on the words hag and ride, the experience in Newfoundland is occasionally called the "diddies" or, as noted earlier, "the nightmare." In addition to this variety of terms used in the Newfoundland tradition to describe the basic experience, each term is sometimes held to have more than a single meaning. Not only is the experience occasionally called a dream, but other types of bad dreams are sometimes classified as the Old Hag, especially if the dream involves helplessness. The broadened connotations for the traditional terms seem to result from a process of secondary generalization in which the original meaning is the experience described in the above narratives. Why and how this broadening has happened will be discussed in connection with the old nightmare tradition. This variation in terminology, especially in oral forms that can be easily misunderstood or incorrectly pronounced, is one of several factors complicating efforts to reach strong conclusions about the distribution of the tradition.

In both cases 1 and 2 there is no question of the experience being a dream, and the causal agent is said to be a living person who acts for his own reasons. In the second account, though, the means of doing the hagging are explained in greater detail. The blasphemous use of the Lord's Prayer combined with a ritual involving a knife are supposed to allow the attacker to travel as a "spirit" to the victim's bedside.

Both accounts contain a hint of ambiguity about the identity of the "Hag." In the first story, the attacks may have stopped because the hag "thought he had killed Robert." This seems inconsistent with the statement that John "was the person who was hagging him." The informant said that Robert later learned "the way to *call* a hag," (my emphasis) as opposed to "the way to *be* a hag" or "to hag someone." This question of identity is underlined by the student's question in case 2, "who was he calling to when he said 'Hag good Hag?' "

The problem of identity recurs consistently in Old Hag accounts. It is a result of the merging of two distinct possibilities that stand alone in some other traditions. The first is that the hag, or whatever the attacker is called, is a supernatural creature, not a living human, sometimes acting on its own and at other times called upon by a human to carry out an attack, as in demonic assault, vampirism, and ghosts. The second explanation is that the hagging experience is directly caused by a living human who travels as a spirit to carry out attacks or other activities, leaving its physical body behind. Witches, wizards, and sorcerers are the primary actors here. In Newfoundland the experience of hagging may be thought of as caused by an independent creature, by a human acting supernaturally, or by a combination of the two, the latter two being the most commonly held supernatural explanations.

The following example was collected by a student taking my course in Newfoundland folklore. He got the story from a twenty-four-year-old male friend, who labeled the subject "Hag-rog."

Case 3

An old lady used to wake up every night for about a month in a cold sweat, frenzy, panic, something like an epileptic seizure. She was hospitalized and treated for epileptic seizures through the use of drugs, but the drugs did not seem to be working.

The old community doctor, who served in that community for

twenty years, was called in. The old doctor found out that the old lady believed that the old lady who lived a couple of houses away was witching her. This second old lady was known for her witching by the rest of the community.

The old doctor told her how to stop this witching. She was to go home and urinate in a bottle. She was to cap the bottle and put it under her bed.

A couple of days later the second old lady came to see this old doctor, to get him to get the first old lady to undo the bottle. The old doctor told her that all she had to do was to release the curse she had on the other old lady. She agreed and the doctor told the first old lady to throw the urine away. Both of the old ladies were cured.

An interesting point is that the second old lady, the witch, came to see the doctor because she could not urinate.

My informant did not know why the first old lady was cursed by the second old lady. This story was told to my informant by the old community doctor.

Although such details as paralysis, seeing an attacker, and the means of accomplishing the attack are not given in this account, it is clearly a traditional witchcraft case. Not only is the word "witching" used to describe the act, but the remedy recommended by the doctor is a familiar one in folk beliefs about witchcraft. Initial diagnosis of the experiences as epileptic seizures may result from the fact that a physician is a major figure in the story. Firsthand accounts of such attacks presented later in this book show that both victims and physicians have occasionally noted similarities between the experience and a seizure.

These three accounts illustrate a pattern of close personal contact between the narrator and the event in Old Hag stories. One claims to have spoken with the victim of the attack, one with both the victim and the attacker, and one with the victim's physician who solved the problem. In Newfoundland and elsewhere, accounts of this experience are characteristically presented as either first- or secondhand, and the informant generally believes them to be true. This combination of immediacy with belief was one of the early reasons for considering the possibility that actual personal experiences of some kind might be involved in the accounts and, therefore, the tradition with which they are associated.

The supernatural explanations appear to be the oldest ones traditionally connected with the experience and continue to be held by many Newfoundlanders. A long-standing tradition of physical causes also exists, usually either indigestion or "stagnation of the blood," explanations that have appeared in medical literature for centuries. Galen, the great physician of the second century A.D., first explained this experience as a result of gastric disturbances.[4] The belief that circulatory problems resulting from lying too long in a single position are a cause appears in the following description of how to end an attack: "Whenever you gets the hag, you have sense enough to work your forefinger and when you works your forefinger you'll get enough blood circulating—you know what I mean—to use your arm. Once you can use your arm, 'tis all right."[5] An indication of the wide distribution of the circulatory explanation, and of the entire Old Hag tradition, is seen in the following fragment of a Newfoundland broadside composed in the 1920s by Johnny Burke, a popular local composer of such ballads.

> For her skirts were so tight around the hips, Jennie,
> It's no wonder she got the old hag.[6]

For many informants, the implication of a physical variable such as circulatory stagnation does not rule out the possible involvement of a supernatural agency. Some people take one of the explanations as exclusive; others regard a multiple cause as most likely.

The experience of being hagged as found in Newfoundland tradition, then, may be summarized as follows: (1) awakening (or an experience immediately preceding sleep); (2) hearing and/or seeing something come into the room and

4. Ernest M. Jones, *On the Nightmare,* International Psycho-Analytical Library, no. 20 (London: Hogarth Press, 1931), p. 31.

5. From a tape transcription generously made available to me by Wilfred Wareham from his own field work.

6. John White, comp., *Burke's Ballads* (St. John's, Newfoundland: n.d. [1960?]), p. 24.

approach the bed; (3) being pressed on the chest or strangled; (4) inability to move or cry out until either being brought out of the state by someone else or breaking through the feeling of paralysis on one's own. This experience is explained as caused by either a supernatural assault, indigestion, or circulatory stagnation, or some combination of these.

2

The Old Hag and the Cultural Source Hypothesis

       The general overview I received of the Old Hag tradition in Newfoundland led me to investigate the role of personal experience within that tradition. This approach was chosen because the tradition revolves around an experience reported as being fairly common and because most of the Old Hag narratives in the archive show a surprisingly close link between the narrator and the victim, the victim frequently being the narrator. The expectations that make this close narrator-victim association surprising set the primary questions for this study.

THE HYPOTHESES

Although the subject of empiricism in supernatural belief has not been dealt with extensively in academic studies of belief, there does exist a strong implicit set of understandings which may be said to form the modern point of view. Personal experience and actual observation are seen as playing a very different part in traditions involving ordinary events than in those centering on extraordinary events. Beliefs about luck, for example, are typically among the former. A black cat crossing one's path, the breaking of a mirror, or the spilling of salt are all mundane events, as are the "unlucky" things that sometimes happen afterward. For both the believer and the ethnographer, the existence of personal experience and a certain amount of accurate observation are easily accepted, but are not the main point of interest. These cases have led scholars to set about explaining· why the natural events of life come to be interpreted as being supernaturally influenced.

Beliefs that claim as their authority extraordinary events involving direct contact with supernatural agents comprise a different class. When people describe personal encounters with fairies or ghosts, for example, attention is sharply focused on the alleged experience rather than its interpretation. If an informant really had been abducted by fairies and held in fairyland for years, we would not be surprised that he expressed a belief that fairy encounters are possible and should be avoided. The greatest challenge to explanation in such traditions is the question of why people believe that they or others have had such experiences. The Old Hag beliefs obviously belong to this category of traditions involving what are believed to be direct supernatural encounters.

The most common explanations of such traditions may be divided into six categories, each involving the effect of culture in the shaping of experience and narratives about experience:

1. No first-person account exists for many such narratives in their present form, the current stories having developed during oral transmission.
2. Others are misinterpretations of ordinary events caused by the action of tradition on the imagination of the one reporting the experience (e.g., marsh gas for Will-o'-the-Wisp).
3. Some are either outright lies or errors of memory in which the one claiming the experience has placed himself in an account he at first heard involving another person.
4. Some are the experiences of those who have been victims of a hoax by someone who has used the tradition as a model (e.g., Ichabod Crane in "The Legend of Sleepy Hollow").
5. Some are actual experiences caused, often intentionally, by fasting, use of hallucinogens, or other methods

known to produce powerful subjective experiences that vary cross-culturally and are shaped by expectation.

6. Some are the experiences of abnormal individuals whose psychotic episodes are shaped by their cultural repertoire (e.g., the hallucinations and delusions of schizophrenics are known to have changed over time in keeping with the culture in which schizophrenics live).

Each of these six possibilities involves the same relationship between personal experience and accounts of supernatural events. The experiences are either fictitious products of tradition or imaginary subjective experiences shaped (or occasionally even caused) by tradition. I call this view the cultural source hypothesis.[1] Its implications vary from point to point for different traditions.

Based on the accounts given in Chapter 1, this hypothesis may be used to propose the following possibilities about the role of personal experience in the Old Hag tradition: the tradition shapes the dreams of those who know and believe it, such dreams being misinterpreted by the believer as a waking experience (explanation 2); narrators of traditional Old Hag accounts improve their stories by claiming firsthand knowledge of a case (explanation 3); hoaxes and intentionally caused experiences appear unlikely given the nature of the experience, although some culturally shaped, drug-induced experiences are possible (explanations 4 and 5); psychotic hallucinations occurring within the context of this tradition are sometimes influenced by it (explanation 6). Dreams, "improved accounts," and drug-induced or psychotic hallucinations could all be shaped by the tradition and could in turn contribute to its persistence and development (through the processes assumed in explanation 1). The hypothesis would then lead to the prediction that some first- and secondhand Old Hag accounts should occur in the tradition, although they would not be very com-

1. For a major example of such a theory about the role of cultural models in producing personal experiences associated with supernatural belief see Lauri Honko, "Memorates and the Study of Folk Beliefs," *Fabula: Journal of Folktale Studies* 1 (1964):5–19.

mon. Those who genuinely mistake a dream for reality, lie about their own role in an account, or experience psychotic hallucinations are not generally held to be numerous, and the use of psychedelic substances has not been a part of Newfoundland traditional culture. The hypothesis would further predict that all those who recount narratives of Old Hag attacks would be in touch with the tradition.

This conventional expectation renders the large number of narratives involving a close narrator-victim link surprising. The archival data do not appear to support the cultural source hypothesis on this point, although this is a "soft" prediction and might be explained in a variety of ways. Perhaps Newfoundland tradition places a particularly high value on memorates,[2] for example, which has increased the motivation for narrators erroneously to claim close personal knowledge of cases. Clearly, the predicted contact between the Old Hag tradition and the narrators of Old Hag accounts would constitute firmer evidence for the cultural source hypothesis. Both predictions have the value of being open to empirical verification.

The alternative to the cultural source hypothesis is what I call the experiential source hypothesis. This hypothesis holds that the Old Hag tradition contains elements of experience that are independent of culture. Obviously, the entire tradition could not be independent in this way. Certain parts, such as the term "Old Hag," are culturally derived by definition. Obviously, too, the cultural source hypothesis allows for some very basic elements to be culture-free. For example, the emotion of fear or the idea of attack do not by themselves require a cultural link. They may be considered universals.

The two hypotheses differ substantially concerning the level of stable complexity which could persist without a cultural source. The experiential source hypothesis predicts that recognizable "Old Hag experiences" will occur with some regularity without contact with the tradition. The cultural source hypothesis predicts instead that, in the absence of a cultural source,

2. The precise meaning of the word "memorate" has been the subject of considerable scholarly debate. I am using it here simply to mean a story told as personal experience and believed to be true.

recognizable Old Hag attacks will not occur any more frequently than any other dream, misperception, or hallucination.
The experiential hypothesis further predicts that first- and
secondhand accounts might be common, depending on the
frequency of the underlying experience. As unlikely as this hypothesis appeared at first, it was the natural alternative. The
following approach was designed to determine which hypothesis fit most consistently with available data.

THE QUESTIONNAIRE

To discriminate between the cultural and experiential hypotheses it was necessary to determine the frequency and distribution of memorates of Old Hag attacks and the connection
between these and the distribution of the Old Hag tradition
in Newfoundland. For these purposes the material already held
by the archive was not sufficient. This material indicated that
firsthand accounts exist and that the tradition has some general
distribution, but it was not specific. Much ethnographic work
on the subject of belief suffers a similar handicap as a result
of the most common approach to the field collection of traditional narratives, beliefs, and cultural materials. The ethnographer makes inquiries and sorts through the general
population as quickly as possible to locate those who are the
best bearers of the traditions in question. In this sense "best"
means those having the most complete knowledge, greatest
ability to communicate effectively, and so forth. This is a natural approach. If you wish to study cooking you look for a good
cook, for architecture you seek an excellent architect, for stories a fine raconteur. The same is true of belief. To study it
we have looked to believers.

I do not wish to criticize this method. In fact, as will be
obvious in subsequent chapters, I have employed it extensively
myself. I do, however, suggest that this approach requires sup-
plementation. The general population, including those who do
not believe in or are ignorant of a given tradition, has to be
included in some fashion. The most useful method for including the general population for the determination of frequency
and distribution is, of course, the questionnaire survey. The
original Old Hag questionnaire distributed by the archive,

however, did not record negative responses. All those who told the field worker that they were unfamiliar with the questionnaire topic were lost to the study. The new questionnaire would have to record both positive and negative responses and to ask questions with quantifiable answers.

The most accessible group for such a survey was Memorial University students. For all the same reasons that they were an attractive population for my purposes, students in general constitute one of the most frequently used groups for all sorts of study. It is widely recognized, however, that despite the practical points in their favor they are not a theoretically ideal sample for most research. Their age, life style, level of education, and many other factors differentiate them from the rest of society. In the case of the Old Hag study, the differences create a bias against folklore findings because college students are less likely to be conservators of the old ways and beliefs than would be randomly selected Newfoundlanders. Thus for most folklore purposes they will yield a conservative picture, and this was acceptable for my study.

I assembled a questionnaire that began with very general questions and became specific about the Old Hag tradition at the end. The basic form of this questionnaire was as follows:

1. Have you ever awakened during the night to find yourself paralyzed; i.e., unable to move or cry out?
2. Are you aware of anyone else ever having had such an experience?
3. Describe as many of the features of this experience as you can. (Whether your experience or that of someone else—specify.)
4. Describe the position in which you were sleeping and any other facts that might suggest a cause for the experience.
5. How long did the experience last?
6. How did it end?
7. How many times and at what age(s) did you have the experience?
8. Was it similar in any way to any other experience you have ever had? If so, specify.

9. Do you know a name or names for the experience? Please list.
10. Do you know any ways of preventing this experience? If so, please give them.
11. Is the experience considered dangerous?
12. Were you asleep?
13. Define "the Old Hag."
14. Have you known anyone who had the Old Hag?

Question 1 sets the definitive criteria of the experience: the subjective impression of being awake and the inability to move. These alone do not necessarily constitute sufficient essential features to indicate the presence of a "recognizable Old Hag experience." This structuring is intentional. The remaining features are left for the respondent to volunteer in answer to question 3, before any explicit statement of the subject of the questionnaire is made. Only questions 13 and 14 indicate that the Old Hag experience is being sought. This structure was intended to prevent any possibility of leading the respondents or the construction of misleading facetious answers. In other words, this order would reduce false positive responses and the unintentional imposition of a pattern through the questionnaire's structure. It also clearly separated information about the experience from information about the tradition, using knowledge of the term "Old Hag" as a measure of familiarity with the tradition. Contact with the tradition was also sought through question 9, which is not leading and allows for the possibility that a positive respondent might know the tradition under a less common name. Question 2 serves several purposes including allowing for the possibility of secondary contact with the tradition without actual knowledge of such details as the name or the explanations traditionally given. Of course, for these features of questionnaire design to have meaning, it had to be administered in a special way. If the questionnaire were simply distributed and then collected at a later date, there would be ample opportunity for the questions at the end to contaminate the answers to the early questions. Also, collaboration in answering the questions could not be ruled out, and the response rate would certainly be substantially less than 100 percent. Since many variables of importance to the study, such as personal knowledge of and interest in the subject, might influence willingness to respond, a poor response rate would greatly hamper interpretation of the results.

The only feasible solution to these problems was to administer the questionnaire orally to groups of students, waiting for everyone to finish writing the answer to each question before giving the next. This method yielded a response rate of 100 percent, kept the questions in order, and prevented collaboration. A total of four classes was used to yield a total of one hundred complete responses. Although these were folklore classes, they did not deal with folk belief and had not included any mention of the Old Hag. Introductory courses were used to rule out extensive academic knowledge of Newfoundland folk tradition, and none of the respondents were folklore majors. Two of the classes, yielding a total of seventy-six responses, were surveyed within twenty-four hours of each other to prevent the first group from having any extensive opportunity to discuss the project with their colleagues and influence the second group's responses. There were no important differences in the patterns of responses from the two groups, so it can be assumed that this timing was successful. The remaining twenty-four students were reached in two smaller introductory classes several months later. At that time, questions were included concerning knowledge of the first run.

Of the initial one hundred in this sample, one student in the second run disqualified herself on the basis of knowledge of the first use of the questionnaire. Six additional respondents were subsequently excluded because they were not native Newfoundlanders, the prime target of this survey. Therefore, the figures discussed here are based on a sample of ninety-three native Newfoundlanders.

THE RESULTS: FREQUENCY AND CONTENTS OF THE EXPERIENCE

The data concerning positive responses to question 1 are displayed in table 1.

Twenty-three percent of the sample—a surprisingly high figure—reported having had the minimum experience de-

TABLE 1.

POSITIVE RESPONSES TO QUESTION 1

*(Have you ever awakened during the night to find yourself paralyzed, i.e.,
unable to move or cry out?)*

	MALES	FEMALES	TOTAL
YES	12.9%	9.7%	23%
	(12)	(9)	(21)
NO	33.3%	44.1%	77%
	(31)	(41)	(72)
TOTAL	46.2%	53.8%	
	(43)	(50)	

$X^2 = .79$ with the Yates correction

$p > .4$

scribed in this first question (i.e., paralysis with the impression
of wakefulness) at least once. The difference in rates between
males and females was calculated because some informants
had suggested that the Old Hag occurred more frequently in
one sex or the other. The difference was found not to be significant, so sex was not used as a variable in the other analyses
performed with these results. Although the possibility remains
that certain features of the experience may be associated with
sex differences, the total number of positive responses is too
small to pick up such relationships.

At this point, the question arises of what constitutes a
"recognizable Old Hag attack" as discussed in connection with
the predictions of the two competing hypotheses. Paralysis
during a period subjectively perceived as wakefulness would
by itself constitute a scant base for the entire Old Hag tradition, although the number claiming the experience would be
a valuable finding. Because a great variety of additional details
could be added to such an experience, this is the kind of objectively real core experience that the cultural source hypothesis
could accommodate, proposing that additional culturally derived features are built on this foundation. The possibility also
arises that the two definitive criteria of the first question, immobility and wakefulness, have imposed order and the appear-

ance of pattern by screening out a range of more or less similar experiences. Both of these possibilities can best be dealt with by considering the answers to question 3. This is a very open-ended question, and the answers to it would be expected to show whether there is a consistent pattern of events connected with the wakeful paralysis state. If no such pattern is found, there should be considerable variety, but if there is a consistent and recognizable pattern it should show up here.

As expected, the method of administering the questionnaire did not prove to be a good means of obtaining narratives. Writing out in longhand a description of an experience while a professor and fellow students wait for you to finish, however patiently, is a very artificial situation. The resulting accounts are rushed and lacking in detail, not to mention problems of legibility. Nonetheless, each of the twenty-one positive responses was accompanied by a sufficiently descriptive account to permit some content analysis.

In addition to the impression of wakefulness and immobility indicated by the initial positive response, each was described as including the actual setting correctly perceived and a feeling of fear. These four elements are consistent with the traditionally described Old Hag attack. They are sufficient to allow the great majority of Newfoundlanders familiar with the tradition to identify the experience as the Old Hag. I call these "primary features" of the experience. The primary features do not, however, include some of the more dramatic elements found, for example, in the narratives quoted in Chapter 1. If accurately reported firsthand accounts of the experience included only these elements, a 23 percent rate of occurrence in the sample would still be surprising. But other elements are often reported in connection with the primary features. I call these "secondary features." Acquisition of a complete list of secondary features required extensive interviewing beyond the survey, and even now it is doubtful that all have been obtained. Nonetheless, the written accounts contained enough of them to expand the preliminary picture of the experience and raise important questions. Some of the most frequent secondary features stood out with great clarity, as is shown in the following quotations from two of the questionnaire responses. These cases are presented exactly as written out by the students, including punctuation, spelling, and grammar. It must be kept in mind that the writers were rushed and were not encouraged to attempt to produce excellent prose. These quotations do not include each entire response but focus on material that suggests secondary features of the experience. The omissions are indicated by ellipses.

Case 4
White Female; 27 years old

(1.) Yes. (2.) Yes. (3.) Attribute it to what we call the "Hag" with a sensation of weight on one's chest coming from external forces. Needless to say there was great fear and a need to call to someone, a fear of death. A feeling nothing but nothing is going to get rid of it.—There was a pair of rosary beads in the room which I put around my neck (R.C. background). It stayed for what seemed 7–8 hrs. There was the beginning feeling of a mass coming towards me as I was sleeping and it partially sat or enveloped my whole chest area. . . . Another time which I felt quite anxious and phoned three of my friends whom I deduced could be in need of assistance. Found out later my sister was missing. . . . (4.) back and side (6.) Each time went to sleep or tried it re-occurred. After I took the cross it leviated somewhat. By morning I was just glad it was over, but still had feeling of presence of bad psysic. (7.) 15–16 times / as a child about 9 / as a teenager 17 / at present 27 / at 22, 23 (8.) An experience which I was sure I was awake and my grandfather appeared. I was quite afraid as he walked towards me. Eventually he said, "I'm going now I'm scaring you." Age 22. (13.) Refer 3—previous answer (14.) yes

The "feeling of a mass coming towards me" is one aspect of a secondary feature that did not become clear until I had been interviewing victims of these attacks for about two years. I now call this the "sensation of presence." Victims frequently are aware of a presence but with no specifiable sensory cues. This unseen, unheard presence is not inferred to be there, but is palpably sensed. In addition to presence, which is sometimes described as overwhelming, other characteristics are felt at times, including location and motion as in the present account;

gender; intent, which is almost always threatening; and unpleasant affective qualities often characterized as "evil."

The fear that the experience may prove fatal is also found frequently. At times it seems to be a result of inferences about the nature of the paralysis (e.g., that perhaps it is the result of a stroke or heart attack); at other times it appears to be an intrinsic component of the experience.

The recurrence of the event repeatedly during a single night is uncommon but not unique. Most frequently there is a single attack, either never repeated or repeated infrequently at intervals of months or, more often, years. In other cases a series of attacks may occur frequently, even nightly, for a period of a week or two. Multiple attacks during a single night are most likely during one of these runs. A victim may experience one such run and no more, or a number of these sequences may recur separated by months or years. Least common is the individual who experiences the attacks frequently over a period of years.

The use of religious strategies, such as the rosary in this case, to cope with the attacks is common. At least in part this response seems to reflect the uncanny quality typical of the experiences. Even those who advance physical theories of causation seem to find it difficult to avoid supernatural overtones in their perceptions of and responses to the attacks, as evidenced by the present respondent's comparison of the attack to the appearance of her deceased grandfather when she was "sure I was awake." Such comparisons are often made.

Finally, the interpretation of the experience as an indication of danger to a friend or loved one is not common, although I have now heard several such accounts.

Case 5
White Female; 19 years old

(1.) Yes (2.) Yes (3.) In my experience I felt very numb and still. I do not know if I was able to move or not because I did not feel as if I wish to move. I was also lying on my back just staring in an odd fashion. Everything around me appeared to be at a distance and I felt as if I was enclosed by something. It was as if I could not touch reality, in my mind I was drifting in some peculiar realm. I was not dreaming but wide awake but as if in another realm but in fact was in my bedroom. I could see where I was, but as if I could not reach out or speak. My mother had the same experience. She could not come out of it, she was not dreaming but could not speak. She felt as if she was choking as she was lying on her back. (4.) I went to sleep on my side but awoke lying on my back. . . . (7.) About twice in my early teens; and about twice when I was about 17 or 18, and again this year, 19.

An important feature of this account is the statement that the respondent did "not know if I was able to move or not because I did not feel as if I wish to move." As with the feeling of presence, this point did not become clear until a large number of interviews had been conducted. The immobility can be perceived in a variety of ways: rigid paralysis; limp paralysis; restraint by an external force; being afraid to move; feeling one ought not to move (with or without a specific reason); not thinking of moving. The first two are the most common, but all of the others are regularly reported. Even when the victim reports having felt terrified and directly threatened, he occasionally states that he did not try to move. Although this latter feeling is surprising, it recurs too often to be dismissed as poor reporting. An important implication of these different perceptions of immobility is that they cause an unknown number of false negative responses to the paralysis question.

As in Case 4, this respondent was sleeping on her back (4 mentioned her side also). This position is very common. Of those who specified their sleeping position in response to the questionnaire, 90 percent said that they were supine. This frequency has held up consistently in subsequent research and appears to be a very important secondary feature.[3]

3. This connection with the supine position is found in widely separated traditions. The following are three of the many examples I located in the very extensive files of the Dictionary of American Popular Beliefs and Superstitions project (Wayland D. Hand, Professor Emeritus, Director) at the University of California at Los Angeles. "If you go to sleep on your back, you will have nightmares" (Richard Tallman, ed., *Belief and Legend from Northern Kings County, Nova Scotia,* a class project of II General English class of Corn-

The following outline summarizes the initial findings concerning the nature and frequency of the experience.

I. Description
   A. Primary features (definitive)
     1. subjective impression of wakefulness
     2. immobility variously perceived (paralysis, restraint, fear of moving)
     3. realistic perception of actual environment
     4. fear
   B. Secondary features (reported more than once, most experiences contain at least one, often more)
     1. supine position (very common)
     2. feeling of presence (common)
     3. feeling of pressure, usually on chest (common)
     4. numinous quality (common)
     5. fear of death (somewhat common)
II. Frequency and distribution
   A. Overall: 23 percent of sample
   B. By sex: the difference in number of positive reports is not significant
   C. Pattern of recurrence
     1. once only or once and occasionally, with intervals of months or years (most common)
     2. one or more "runs" of frequent attacks lasting one or two weeks (sometimes)
     3. frequent chronic attacks over a long period (rarely)

---

wallis District High School, Canning [Canning, Kings County, Nova Scotia, 1969], p. 56). "It is believed that one sleeping on his back will be oppressed by nightmares" (Josef Čižmăr, *Lidové lékařstoí v Československu,* 2 vols. [Brno: Melantrich A.S., 1946], 1:97). "You should not *lie flat on your back* lest: (a) evil spirits come and *overtop you* and give you bad dreams. . . . (b) your liver might be seen by the witches. . . . (c) and the witch might take away your liver " (Francisco Demetrio y Radaza, S.J., comp. and ed., *Dictionary of Philippine Folk Beliefs and Customs,* Museum and Archives Publication #2, 4 vols. [Cagayan de Oro City: Xavier University, 1970], 1:102). See also Jones, *On the Nightmare,* p. 34.

The primary features of this outline are definitive, that is, based on my initial findings I concluded that if one of these were absent I was not dealing with the Old Hag phenomenon. The conclusion that these criteria define a coherent and distinct event has been upheld by my continuing research. But these four features are not identical in their location within my research design. The impression of wakefulness and the feeling of immobility have been demanded by my method of eliciting the accounts: some form of the question, "Have you ever, while awake, found yourself unable to move?" Realistic perception of the environment and the presence of fear have not been demanded, but have been volunteered as consistent parts of the description of the experience, although realism is implicit in the impression of wakefulness. Clear and detailed recall of the experience is one means by which victims of these attacks say they have concluded that they were awake. Another is the correspondence of the setting to the victim's real setting. (These are not, however, the only criteria frequently given.) Of these primary features, fear is perhaps the most complex in its relationship to the basic attack. The development of the phenomenology of these experiences in Chapter 3 will show that this element can occur in a variety of ways, and in some cases of frequently repeated attacks the fear is reduced or eliminated over time. Ultimately, the division of fear into a series of specific varieties, each considered as a secondary feature, may prove to be a better way to deal with this element, as suggested by my separate treatment of "fear of death" as a secondary feature. As I have continued to gather descriptions of wakeful paralysis experiences, I have even found a small fraction that have not been characterized by fear at any point. Not only are these a small minority of all cases, but they are often accompanied by experiences that are substantially different in content, raising the possibility that the wakeful paralysis state may include two or more specific experiences of which the Old Hag is simply the most common (or the most freely reported). Given this possibility, it is essential that the role of the undemanded primary features, together with the secondary features and the pattern within which they occur, be understood in the delineation of the Old Hag experience as a stable and "robust" phenomenon.

The list of secondary features also requries additional comment concerning criteria for inclusion. In the close examination of all experiences, especially unusual and affectively charged experiences, it is important to distinguish between phenomenology and inference. For example, a frequent secondary feature encountered in interviews conducted subsequent to the questionnaire study has been a sound like footsteps. Technically, this is a phenomenon of the experience. On the basis of this phenomenon, the victim frequently and reasonably infers that someone is nearby. This inference would not count as the "feeling of presence." Inferences, interpretations, and other responses to the attacks must be distinguished from the experience itself. This is the reason that I have not listed here the religious strategies for protection or the interpretation of the experience as an omen. Furthermore, fear of death is sometimes a response and sometimes appears inherent in the experience itself. Very careful interviewing is necessary to make the distinction. The difficulty of expressing such distinctions is part of the reason that the hurried written accounts did not reveal more secondary features.

The answers to question 3, then, including both primary and secondary features, reveal a complex and stable experience that was recognizable as an Old Hag attack in all twenty-one cases of a positive response to question 1.

How do these findings fit with the two hypotheses? Frequent reporting of personal experience of Old Hag attack goes against the predictions of the cultural source hypothesis, especially because two primary features (fear and realistic environment) and all of the secondary features were reported spontaneously without leading questions or planned confabulation. This cluster of features includes only a relatively small number of those logically possible during a waking paralysis. For example, immobility with the conviction of wakefulness need not be accompanied by realistic perception of the actual environment. Ordinary dreams at times carry the conviction of wakefulness yet involve distant or imaginary settings. The four primary features might be expected to produce secondary features that involve a threat simply because of the helplessness coupled with fear, but a feeling of threat could as easily stem from the house being on fire, from shouts and gunfire in the street outside, from the ceiling collapsing on the victim, or from many other realistic or fanciful dangers. Yet none of those have been reported. The threat shows some variation but always seems to stem from an entity, sometimes human and sometimes not, within the house, usually within the room in which the victim is lying. It is the absence of many other kinds of features that argues that this complex experience is stable. Why this content and not others? Even though the cultural hypothesis is weakened by the frequency and consistency of first-hand reports, it can still offer the influence of tradition as the answer to this question. Now let us look at what the survey revealed about connections between the experience and the tradition.

THE RESULTS: CONNECTIONS BETWEEN THE EXPERIENCE AND THE TRADITION

Questions 1 (Have you ever awakened during the night to find yourself paralyzed?) and 3 (Describe as many of the features of this experience as you can.) were used to locate and confirm the occurrence of Old Hag attacks. Questions 2 (Are you aware of anyone else ever having had such an experience?), 9 (Do you know a name or names for the experience?), 13 (Define "the Old Hag."), and 14 (Have you known anyone who had the Old Hag?) were used to determine contact with the Old Hag tradition. The most important indicator was 13, with an accurate definition taken as evidence of contact. Question 9 was used to confirm the definition and to allow for the possibility that a traditional name unknown to the investigator might be in circulation. Question 2 allowed for a contact with the tradition in which a name for the experience was not mentioned or was subsequently forgotten.

The cultural source hypothesis predicts that, to the extent that these questions are accurate indicators of contact with the tradition, no complete, recognizable Old Hag attacks will be reported by people who have not had contact with the tradition. The experiential source hypothesis predicts that some such attacks will be reported. The crux of this difference in prediction is "some" versus "none" because the actual frequency and distribution of knowledge of the tradition in the sample, and of any experience that might be involved, were unknown before the survey. Furthermore, the experiential hypothesis must allow for some correlation between the experience and the tradition because it is reasonable to expect that one who has such an experience without prior knowledge of the tradition has some likelihood of mentioning the event. If this happens in a culture where some people know the tradition, the account may elicit discussion and thus inform the victim. Therefore, some numerical association is to be expected between the experience and my measures of contact with the Old Hag tradition. The substantial difference in predictions centers on whether sufficient numbers of recognizable attacks are reported in the absence of prior knowledge about the experience to be other than error or chance.

To interpret the results of this part of the survey, what was considered to be "an accurate definition" must be explained. I considered any definition that mentioned immobility to be accurate. I labeled inaccurate only such responses as "I don't know," "an ugly old woman," or the very general traditional usage "bad dream." This liberal scoring procedure is biased against the experiential hypothesis predictions and makes the results that much more striking.

The association between personal reports of the experience and knowledge both of someone else's attack and of the traditional definition are shown in tables 2 and 3.

These tables show that a large majority of those who reported a personal experience of the attack were familiar with the Old Hag tradition and an even larger majority were aware of someone else having experienced it. The reverse is true for those who did not report a personal experience. About 40 percent of the total sample was familiar with the Old Hag tradition. Knowledge of the tradition, then, is much more common among those who have had a personal experience of attack than among those who have not, and this difference is statisti-

TABLE 2.

ASSOCIATION OF REPORTED PERSONAL EXPERIENCE WITH KNOWLEDGE
OF SOMEONE ELSE'S EXPERIENCE

	Experience	No Experience	Total
Knowledge	16.1% (15)	22.6% (21)	38.71% (36)
No Knowledge	6.5% (6)	54.8% (51)	61.29% (57)
Total	22.58% (21)	77.42% (72)	100% (93)

X^2 = 10.52 with the Yates correction
p < .01

TABLE 3.

ASSOCIATION OF REPORTED PERSONAL EXPERIENCE WITH AN
ACCURATE DEFINITION

	Experience	No Experience	Total
Accurate Definition	15.1% (14)	24.7% (23)	39.8% (37)
Inaccurate Definition	7.5% (7)	52.7% (49)	60.2% (56)
Total	22.6% (21)	77.4% (72)	100% (93)

X^2 = 6.79 with the Yates correction
p < .01

cally significant. Given the high level of awareness of the tradition in the entire group, this strong association does not
counter the predictions of either hypothesis. That more than
a third of those who reported the experience did not know of
others having had it, and a third were not familiar with the tradition, favors the experiential hypothesis over the cultural hypothesis. The crucial test, however, comes when knowledge
and definition among those who reported the experience are
examined together. These figures are given in table 4.

TABLE 4.

ASSOCIATION OF KNOWLEDGE OF THE EXPERIENCES OF OTHERS WITH
AN ACCURATE DEFINITION AMONG THOSE REPORTING A PERSONAL
EXPERIENCE

	Accurate Definition	*Inaccurate Definition*	*Total*
Knowledge	57.1% (12)	14.3% (3)	71.4% (15)
No Knowledge	9.5% (2)	19.1% (4)	28.6% (6)
Total	66.6% (14)	33.4% (7)	100% (21)

$X^2 = 2.36$ with the Yates correction
$p < .20$

THE BEGINNING OF IN-DEPTH INTERVIEWS

About two-thirds of those who reported having had the experience had at least some knowledge of someone else's experience or familiarity with the tradition. More than half had both. About one-fifth, however, had neither. In a culture in which 40 percent of a college student sample knew of the tradition and presumably an even greater fraction of the general population could be expected to be familiar with it, the existence of four cases with no knowledge of anyone else's experience or of the tradition is striking. The brief descriptions elicited by the questionnaire were not ideal for assessing the experiences occurring in isolation, however, and it is possible that these four persons had had some contact with the tradition and forgotten it.

The next step was to conduct in-depth interviews with victims who stated ignorance of both the tradition and the experiences of others so they could give complete descriptions of the attacks and the interviewer could probe for subtle or forgotten traditional input. Locating such cases was, of course, difficult. To be most useful, the informants had to be located and interviewed without first being informed about the nature of the investigation. Also, because they were to be ignorant of the tradition, specific questions about the Old Hag would not help. The method I used then and have since employed was to ask people about strange experiences in general, while noting a special interest in those during which the victim was immobilized. This broad approach results in some false positives, but these are easily excluded. This process is similar to the most common method for searching for tradition bearers described above. It does not yield information that is useful for determining precise distribution and rates of occurrence, but it is much more reliable than a survey for obtaining clear and complete narratives. The two approaches supplement each other well.

One case located in this manner is from a university-educated man in his mid-thirties. He was born and raised in St. John's and occupied a responsible executive position at the time of our interview. I shall call him John.[4]

Case 6
White Male; 36 years old

HUFFORD: John, you told me about an experience that happened to you, repeatedly I take it, as a child. Would you give the details?

JOHN: It wasn't exactly as a child. I was a teenager at the time, you know. Well fifteen, sixteen years of age. And this happened in . . . [I have omitted the place name of a very small community to protect John's identity]. I used to go there during the summertime after school and spend the entire summer there, spend the entire summer with my grandparents. I had heard of instances of lights being in the harbour and saw them, but paid no attention to them. At that particular time and even before that, the one thing that I did like about the community was that especially at night, where there was no streetlights or anything, you'd walk in absolute pitch darkness——which didn't scare me at all. I'd not been troubled by being scared of ghosts or anything. This was completely beyond me. But . . . one summer when I was there, approximately about the age of fifteen——I used to sleep upstairs. It was a two-story house, and there was

4. For a description of my procedures for the editing of the interviews presented in this book see page xx.

one stairway going straight up. And then there was a window, and then there was a hall leading down toward the bedrooms. On the extreme right there was the bedroom of my grandparents, and then directly ahead I had the small bedroom as you immediately come down the hall. One night, everything was dark as usual and I heard footsteps on the stairs. This didn't surprise me at all——I wasn't amazed at anything. The footsteps came up the stairs. I looked around the corner, my bed was more or less in the corner and I could look out and see the stairway, and I saw a figure coming up the stairs and turned at the top of the stairway. And it was almost all white and glowing. It had a hat on. It was dressed like an elderly lady. And I watched the entire thing! I watched this figure come right down the hall and came right into the room. Of course I was, I couldn't move or say anything. Come right down the hall, right into the room. The first thing that occurred to me was that I was dreaming. When it got into the room it sat down on the floor and it looked to me like an elephant of all things! Just a blob, but white. I was—— ah——I knew I wasn't dreaming! I thought I was dreaming but I knew I wasn't dreaming! And I broke out into a sweat and was just forced onto the bed. And——closed my eyes, opened them again, it was still there. And then closed my eyes again. Practically got no sleep that night. Anyway, when I woke up in the morning——during the entire next day I didn't tell anybody about it. I never did tell anybody about it. But all during the next day I was dreading this thing of having to go to sleep again that night. But I asked my grandmother about——I told her later on in the day, I said, I said that I thought I heard somebody coming up over the stairs late at night. And she said, well——she said, "That is the canvas [local usage for linoleum]," she said, "On the stairway where during the daytime the canvas is pushed down by people walking up over it, during the nighttime it rises." But this didn't make any sense to me, because these were definite footsteps that walked up one after the other to the top of the stairs.

So anyway . . . I was so petrified during the daytime that I asked my grandmother to sleep with me that night. And she came in and slept with me. I asked her right . . . just before I went to bed again, reminded her. And she came in and slept with me, and the same thing happened! This time I didn't look out around because she was sleeping on the outside. But the steps came up over the stairway and I knew that in a minute there was going to be something in the room again. And I looked out over her and sure enough . . . there was the white blob again.

This happened several times after that until I . . . I went down to my aunt's house and spent the last two or three days that I spent for that summer, in that community.

HUFFORD: You said at one point . . . that the old woman changed into a white blob, on the floor, similar to an elephant. Did you see actual features of an elephant, like trunk and feet? Or was it just the general impression of an elephant?

JOHN: Yeah. The general impression of an elephant. What I mean by that is that there was an enormous head and down in under there was practically nothing. Just spread out, down bottom. I sort of got the vision of a trunk, you know. But the point was that I, I almost was convinced at one point that I was dreaming, you know, and then at another point I wasn't, because I knew I was awake. I could, I could——you know——it wasn't as if you were in almost a stupor.

HUFFORD: Did you actually see the transformation when the old woman sagged down onto the floor, or did you look away and then look back?

JOHN: The first time I saw, sort of, the transformation. When the figure came into the room I closed my eyes in utter fear and the next time I looked up the figure seemed to sink onto the floor——because it was definitely standing right next to my bed for a second, for a couple of seconds. . . . (Twice) I saw it walk into the room. But what I would do after that was I would close my eyes after I heard the footsteps coming and I would count them——I would even count the stairs as they came up. And I knew when it reached the top because it was a different sound. And this was what completely frustrated me about the canvas idea. Looking back it perhaps was the canvas, you know, and the whole thing. But it seemed strange at that time——I remember rationalizing the thing and knowing that it could not have been the canvas at that time.

HUFFORD: Did you get out of bed, or move, or cry out while the thing was in the room?

JOHN: No. Absolutely nothing. I just couldn't do anything. I don't know why.

HUFFORD: . . . You said at one point that you were pressed down into the bed. What did you mean by that?

JOHN: I don't know if that's through fear, or not. But it was as if you could not move. There was——ah——you know——I was afraid to turn over. Or maybe it was just——I *could not* turn over. Like, I just wanted to turn into the wall, but I didn't know what was going to happen, you know. It was a sense of utter frustration. And your heart pounds——I remember my heart pounding.

HUFFORD: Did you notice any difficulty breathing? Shortness of breath.

JOHN: Yes. But that came from just the point of being scared. You were afraid to breathe.

HUFFORD: . . . Tell me, when it first happened, the first experience, were you frightened when you heard the footsteps coming up the stairs? Or was it not until you saw that there was something of which to be frightened that you felt like this?

JOHN: I wasn't afraid of the footsteps at all, because I didn't rationalize in my own mind——I didn't know if it was, but I just thought it was strange. [Words on tape are unintelligible.] I definitely had no fear from just hearing the footsteps the first time. There was no fear whatsoever. As I say, I was not afraid of the dark. I loved the dark. I loved sleeping by myself. I loved walking at night and so on like that.

HUFFORD: When this happened were you aware of anyone ever having had a similar experience or did you know the name for the experience?

JOHN: Never, never heard it before . . . I had not told anybody of this before.

HUFFORD: Has it ever happened to you since?

JOHN: No. Never. I've never, even seen anything like that before——ever before or after.

HUFFORD: Were you satisfied at the time that you had not fallen asleep before it happened. . . ?

JOHN: I definitely didn't fall asleep. And each of the other times that it happened with my grandmother in the bed, I actually waited for this to happen. After it happened the second time, the second night, I knew it would happen the third night. And I knew it would happen the fourth night. And I knew it would happen the fifth night. . . .

HUFFORD: How did the experience terminate. . . ?

JOHN: After the experience was over, what happened was this, is that the first night I got practically no sleep at all. And then after the figure came into the room on other occasions I would close my eyes behind my grandmother——peer out every now and then and eventually it was gone. . . . I didn't have to lift my head over her really, you know, to be able to see it was there. . . .

HUFFORD: Do you remember the position, your position in the bed? Were you on your side?

JOHN: The first occasion I was on my back, simply because I couldn't turn over on my side. I sort of wanted to turn . . . because, you see, what had happened the first time——it lasted for an hour or maybe two hours, you know. It was so long and I wanted to——I was trying to rationalize in my own mind what to do. On the other occasions it was a matter of having my eyes closed all the time, practically.

HUFFORD: And you never mentioned this to anyone?

JOHN: Never mentioned it to anyone, because I was too, you know——I——I——This thing about the light across the bay and so on, which I had heard on a couple of occasions, I completely discounted as being stupid and idiotic, you know. I wouldn't dare mention that to anyone. What I had seen, you know——That would be just, to me, ridiculous.

HUFFORD: So you would have considered yourself at the time very rationalistic and not at all superstitious?

JOHN: Completely unsuperstitious. The most amazing thing that had ever happened to me. I don't know what it was. Maybe it was something I ate. I don't know.

I am sure——I am sure that there was *something* there unless there was something wrong with my mind, and wrong with my eyes at that particular point. And I'd never *ever* had anything wrong with me mentally. I am absolutely, beyond any shadow of a doubt, positive of that experience.

HUFFORD: . . . You said that it happened about five times altogether. Was that five nights in a row, or were there nights when
it didn't happen?

JOHN: No. It was every night.

HUFFORD: Every night until you moved, left the house?

JOHN: Every night until I left the house, through some excuse.
That I wanted to go down and play cards and drink cocoa until
midnight, down the other house.

HUFFORD: Did you ever sleep in that house again?

JOHN: Yes, I did. But I slept in the house on the other occasions
in a different room, which was at the other end of the hall. And
my brother was there. My brother used to come out with me at
that time, and we would sleep on the floor, almost.

HUFFORD: Was that by accident or design?

JOHN: Partly by design. Because I was——I can tell you I was
totally petrified by that experience.

This interview followed the same general plan as the
questionnaire survey. At the beginning, the informant was
given as little information as possible about the subject of the
interview. A strange paralysis experience was often the sole
basis for discussion. The informant was first asked to describe
the experience in detail. Once the initial narrative was finished, questions were asked to clarify points raised and to
probe for information not spontaneously offered. Ideally, the
probing questions are completely open. If the question suggests a response, it should be one that biases against the expected answer, as when I asked John if he was sleeping on his
side at the time of the experience. By placing as few constraints as possible on responses, an interview of this kind, repeatedly employed, should elicit the entire range of actual
experiences. Although the selection procedure does not allow
for statistical analysis, it does permit a careful investigation
and description of the phenomenology of the event and its
connection with tradition in individual cases. It is then possible to determine whether there is a stable, complex, and patterned experience or, rather, a welter of bizarre subjective

impressions from which tradition has selected only a few points in the development of one tradition or another.

John's attacks followed the second pattern described earlier, that of a single "run" lasting several nights. Despite the considerable pressure he experienced, he refused to share what was happening to him, even with his grandparents. This strong reluctance to discuss the experience is common among those who do not know of the tradition and have never heard of others having the experience. John's comments concerning "the light across the bay" leave no doubt as to the source of this reluctance. He had considered the ghost stories of others to be "stupid, idiotic . . . ridiculous," and he had no desire to make himself the target of such an evaluation by others. Such pressures against speaking of these experiences are apparently very great unless the listener can show prior knowledge and can demonstrate that an account will be heard with sympathy and respect. This attitude speaks to another question that is sometimes raised concerning people who report the attacks. Are they credulous or especially impressionable? To the extent that interview data can provide the answer, they seem not to be. The victim is frequently someone who, like John, disclaims either any general belief or interest in the supernatural and insists that he has never had any other unusual experiences.

All four of the primary Old Hag attack features are present in John's account. The strong impression of wakefulness competes successfully with an almost equally strong desire to dismiss the experience as a bad dream. "I thought I was dreaming but I knew I wasn't dreaming! . . . I was almost convinced at one point that I was dreaming . . . and then at another point I wasn't, because I knew I was awake. . . . I am absolutely, beyond any shadow of a doubt, positive of that experience."

The immobility John experienced may have included some feeling of pressure, although this is not completely clear. He says that he was "forced onto the bed," but adds that this may have been through fear. Although John did not describe the room in which he lay, it is obvious that he did not notice anything unusual in his perception of his real surroundings. In fact, his description of the location of the stairs, the corner in which his bed was located, and the door through which he saw the glowing figure enter all give the impression of clear perception of recognizable features. Also, the lighting of the room was realistic and was precisely as would be expected at night in a community without electricity.

John's comments about his fear follow a pattern that many others have since described. He felt no fear during what he later realized was the beginning of the experience. "I definitely had no fear from just hearing the footsteps the first time. There was no fear whatsoever." In some attacks fear is the first sign. In others, like John's, the fear comes later.

The secondary features John experienced included lying on his back, a feeling of pressure, and a feeling that the experience was uncanny. John also described several new secondary features that I have found in other cases. The cases discussed above include numerous references to visual contact with the environment but do not explicitly comment on control of the eyes and eyelids. John could open and close his eyes and could look in whatever direction he chose. Most informants report this ability, but the fact that a few people have described what seems to be this experience without the ability to open their closed eyes suggests that this is most safely classed as a secondary feature.

The sound of footsteps is almost as common as the supine position and the feeling of presence. The sound was very realistic to John, and he was intent on it: "I heard the footsteps coming and I would count them. . . . And I knew when it reached the top because it was a different sound."

The presence of a visual component is also common, although less so than either the footsteps or the sensation of presence. That what was seen was humanoid is typical, and that its shape was seen to shift into a nonhuman, vaguely animal form is suggestive of traditional beliefs about the powers of witches and other supernatural entities. Although such a vision is not frequently reported in firsthand accounts, I have encountered it subsequently. John's difficulty describing the figure's transformation is instructive. The language of the informant often breaks down in the effort to provide an accurate description of so many unprecedented perceptions. One common result is a heavy reliance on simile and metaphor, as when John said that the changed figure looked like an elephant. Without additional questions about his meaning, the impression would have been inaccurate and ludicrous.

Finally, John noted that "your heart pounds——I remember my heart pounding." A terrified person could be expected to make such an observation, and many informants have. Others have reported waking up drenched in sweat and experiencing other signs of autonomic nervous system arousal. These conditions have been reported spontaneously in sufficient numbers to justify their inclusion as a secondary feature.

John was a good informant both because he was certain he had never heard of the Old Hag or of anyone else ever having a similar experience and because he was not the kind of Newfoundlander who would ordinarily be expected to be strongly influenced by the island's supernatural traditions. By geography, education, and occupation he seemed unlikely to be a bearer of such beliefs. And yet he produced a complex and fascinating account of a recognizable Old Hag attack.

The next informant was even better in these respects. She was a female graduate student from the United States. She had been in Newfoundland for only a few months at the time of her experience, and she had never heard of either the tradition or my research. I shall call her Caroline.

Case 7

HUFFORD: Caroline, I know nothing about the details of what you are about to tell me, so just proceed from the beginning. Okay?

CAROLINE: Okay. Well, I woke up, or thought I woke up. And I was conscious of the room anyway. I was looking around the room and I felt like there was a man next to me with his arm underneath my back, and holding my left arm in his hand like this. Pressing it against my body. And his head was on my shoulder. And I was so scared when I first was conscious of it, you know, that I didn't——I couldn't look around to see who it was. I was just sort of thinking, you know, what——what's going on? My stars, is somebody, some man come in from upstairs or outside, you know, come into my room? . . . You know, I was just

——I was just trying to think of what, you know, what——what was going on! And, ah, I tried to move a little bit so that I could look. And when I moved it felt like he gripped my arm tighter to my body. And then he would just kind of move closer to me. And so I tried that about three times. And each time I did it, it felt like he'd grip my arm and sort of move a little closer. And I started thinking, "Now if I move again, he's going to rape me. So I better be still, you know, so he won't wake up." I thought he must be, you know, he must be asleep and I was——I could——I remembered really distinctly his smell. Like he smelled like somebody's been working out in the fields or something. All sweaty and kind of dusty. And I was really conscious of the way he smelled and that.

And then I tried to scream. I thought I'd scream and Betty [roommate] would hear me. But I couldn't get any kind of sound out. And then I don't remember what happened in between, but then he was on top of me, and I tried to look up to see who it was or something. And here it was, and I could get my head up but I couldn't move past my chest. Like it was like pressing down on my chest. And so every time I would bend my head, I could just see this——it looked like a white mask. Like a big white mask. And it kind of had a funny face on it. And it had black dots on it and a red kind of crooked mouth. And it just kind of of——I think it had some other dots on it. It was a really funny, ghastly looking kind of mask! I thought, Lord, it must be a Martian or something! (laughter) Then I said, no, then I thought, "No, it's probably somebody who just put on a mask so I wouldn't know who he was." And I kept trying to pull up, and finally I just sort of, felt sort of released, you know. And I——I could sit up, and I got the feeling there was nobody there.

HUFFORD: That was the end?

CAROLINE: That was the end. Yes.

HUFFORD: Were you aware at the end there of waking up? That is, did you feel that suddenly you had opened your eyes, or did the impression continue that you had already been awake but unable to move?

CAROLINE: I think I felt like I'd been awake. Now——I'm saying I *must* have been asleep, but I didn't have any feeling of——I mean of opening my eyes. I think I felt like they were already open. But it was more kind of hazy, you know. It wasn't real clear but it wasn't like a dream either. In that kind of darkness——Or the feeling of suddenly waking up.

HUFFORD: What reaction did you experience emotionally? What did you feel like?

CAROLINE: Well, strange. But it felt like——It gave me a bad feeling. Like I felt bad the whole rest of the day. Sort of a scared feeling, because I was so scared. And I was trapped, sort of——

HUFFORD: Is there anything else about the experience in general that occurs to you? Did you hear anything during it?

CAROLINE: Yeah. I heard him. Every time he——You know I told you when I tried to move?

HUFFORD: Yes.

CAROLINE: And he'd grip me and just kind of grunt.

HUFFORD: Oh. So it did sound like he was making a noise?

CAROLINE: Sounded like he was——not groaning, but you know how——I mean you're asleep and somebody disturbs you, you just kind of make that sound of——

HUFFORD: Yeah.

CAROLINE: And the sound and smell of him. That's all I could feel. And I could feel his head right here on my shoulder [pointing to her shoulder].

HUFFORD: Had you ever heard of it before, that kind of experience?

CAROLINE: No, I never heard.

HUFFORD: Okay, now some specific things. . . . (In what position were you sleeping?)

CAROLINE: . . . I was on my back, but I don't sleep on my back.

HUFFORD: (I understand) that you had a recurrence of it?

CAROLINE: Not exactly, really. But I had the feeling someone was in the room last night. And I was on my side and——and it——This was part of the thing that is different. In, the other one I felt like I had waked up in the middle of the night and I was conscious of seeing the whole room you know and then I felt like, something really going on. But last night it was just——I was dreaming that someone was coming up our backstairs. I think it's more of, when you, kind of——I was dreaming something that was in a situation where I was. I was dreaming someone was coming in our stairs and I was thinking of myself being in the bed asleep and being scared and thinking that I should get up and go tell Betty or get up and go lock the door because we don't keep the doors locked. But I couldn't move to get up to run. And he kept coming in and I felt like he was—— that he was coming down on top, looking down over me like he had his arms on both sides and sort of pressing down on my head and my shoulder. Just sort of leaning on me so that I couldn't get up to move and then I tried to scream and I got sort of a muffled noise in my throat and it woke, woke me up. And I did feel like I woke up that time.

HUFFORD: (Yeah, like you had been sleeping?)

CAROLINE: Yeah, like I had been asleep.

HUFFORD: Okay. And were you terrified by that? Or when you woke up did you feel all right then?

CAROLINE: I wasn't that terrified, but sort of nervous and scared. But it wasn't as real and it wasn't——It didn't last as long. Like the other one seemed to last longer, and struggling.

HUFFORD: How long did the other seem to last?

CAROLINE: Maybe ten minutes.

HUFFORD: In the other one you said that you could see things, but they didn't seem really clear. What did you mean by that?

CAROLINE: Well it's sort of like when you first wake up in the morning and your arms are so——It was the same feeling I had, I can remember now, when I was in hospital once. And I was coming out of an anesthetic and I could half open——my eyes were half open, and I looked around. And I saw everybody in the room talking, but I couldn't——I wasn't at the point where I could talk to them, and I wasn't at the point where I was completely aware of what was going on. Like it was sort of hazy. See all these people looking——and that, sort of, was like the dream. I was aware that I could see the room and what was in there, but——it wasn't perfectly clear. Like I was sort of drugged. That's what it was. It was kind of a drugged feeling.

HUFFORD: And that feeling went away quite suddenly when you finally managed to move?

CAROLINE: Yeah, when I managed to move, yeah.

HUFFORD: It was obviously an unpleasant experience, and it also obviously had sexual overtones. But were those any stronger than just the obvious? You know, the feeling that you were, maybe, in danger of being raped?

CAROLINE: No.

HUFFORD: . . . Well, very good. Thank you Caroline.

Caroline's account was the first I had collected from a non-Newfoundlander, and it was clearly an Old Hag attack. The subjective impression of wakefulness, immobility, realistic perception of the actual environment, and fear were all present. Caroline is even more explicit than John about her efforts to dismiss the attack as a bad dream when she says, "I think I felt like I'd been awake. Now——I'm saying I *must* have been asleep, but I didn't have any feeling of . . . opening my eyes. . . . it wasn't like a dream. . . ." John and Caroline clearly experienced a struggle reported by many victims. They had a conviction of wakefulness based on what the experience *felt* like, even in memory, and what the victim considers to be the only reasonable interpretation of the event, what it must have been. The dissonance created by this situation is seen over and over again in statements that vacillate between sensation and inference. Caroline's subsequent dream of the experience makes possible a useful comparison.

It comes as no surprise, of course, that this experience, like any other, can be the subject of a dream. In her description of the dream, which had happened the night before the interview and was therefore fresh in her mind, Caroline contrasted it to the original by saying of the dream, "It's more . . . I was dreaming something that was in the situation where I was." The attack, on the other hand, "felt like I had waked up in the middle of the night . . . and then I felt like, something really going on." The attack, then, felt more real, more like a waking experience, than did a realistic dream about it. Even though the bad dream left her "nervous and scared," the feeling was much less intense than that of the original attack experience.

Caroline perceived her immobility as caused by a restraint. Others have similarly reported feeling held down by an attacker, whereas some have described a more general restraint such as being covered by something very heavy. An unusual detail here is that she was able to move her head slightly. Such limited motion has been reported by others, although it is uncommon.

Although Caroline says that she "was conscious of seeing the whole room," she adds that "it was more kind of hazy. . . . It wasn't real clear but it wasn't like a dream either." She later compares the perceptions during the experience to those of coming out from under an anesthetic: "It was kind of a drugged feeling." A change in perceptual quality has been reported by others since, although more often it has been described as increased clarity. These changes may affect any of the senses. Changes in perceptual quality, then, are another secondary feature, though they are logically related to the primary feature of realistic perception of the actual environment.

Caroline's report of her fear also added a new dimension. She said that the attack "gave me a bad feeling. Like I felt bad the whole rest of the day. Sort of a scared feeling. . . . And I was trapped, sort of——" Although not common, this persistence of negative affect has been reported by others and must be classified as another secondary feature.

Other secondary features are that Caroline was in a supine position, felt pressure on her chest, and saw a humanoid attacker. The sound she heard, on the other hand, is less common than the footsteps John described. The presence of an odor is a new feature. Only four of the victims I have interviewed to date have reported an odor, but in each case the perception was as distinct as Caroline's comment about the dusty, sweaty smell. Odor, then, is a rare secondary feature.

A detail Caroline mentioned that is absent from all other

reports that I have gathered is an apparent gap in the experience. She said, "And then I don't remember what happened
in between, but then he was on top of me." Typical accounts
are extraordinarily complete and free of gaps, especially considering that they are sometimes being recalled months or
years later.

These first two in-depth interviews supported the tentative conclusion drawn from the survey that although the occurrence of the identifiable Old Hag experience is associated with
knowledge of models for the experience (either the tradition
in general or a specific other's experience), such models are
not necessary. This conclusion in turn supports the experiential source hypothesis. Although this does not rule out the possibility that a knowledge of models might influence either the
likelihood of having the experience or some aspects of its contents, it reduces any such influence to secondary importance.

This finding in favor of the experiential source hypothesis
is startling and cries out for confirmation. The obvious route
to follow in looking for such confirmation and the continuing
description and analysis of the experience involved searching
for firsthand accounts of attacks on the North American mainland. There knowledge of the Old Hag tradition is practically
nonexistent, and other traditions of similar attacks are much
less widespread than is the Old Hag tradition in Newfoundland.

3

The Phenomenology of the Old Hag[1]

THE OLD HAG ON THE MAINLAND

The two in-depth interviews discussed in Chapter 3 were carried out in the academic year 1973–74. In the summer of 1974 I left Newfoundland to accept a position in the United States. However, I did not have to wait for the move in order to begin looking at mainland accounts. Late in the winter of 1973 I was interviewed on CBC radio about my work concerning the Old Hag tradition. In the interview, I described the tradition and explained that the attacks also occur in the absence of tradition and that they do not appear to be any cause for alarm; that is, they do not appear to be abnormal or pathological. The program was heard over much of eastern Canada, and soon I began to receive letters telling of apparent Old Hag experiences. The letters were seldom detailed, but there was little doubt that they referred to the same experience. The following case is an example.[2]

1. To be completely grammatical, "phenomenology" should refer only to the study and not to the subject of that study. For ease of communication, I have accepted the prevalent extension of meaning that is basically the same as that which is current for "symptomatology." In this book, then, "the phenomenology of an experience" refers to both the study of the subjective appearances of that experience and the combined appearances themselves.

2. In these letter extracts, as in the transcripts presented elsewhere in

47

Case 8
White Female; over 60 years old

It was with great interest and considerable relief, that I listened to you being interviewed on CBC last week.

It was in Moncton about twenty years ago that I had my first experience with the "old hag." It terrified me. Since then I have had two—or three others. I am not absolutely sure of three although I think there were two during the seventeen years I lived in Toronto. There has been one since I moved to Hamilton in June 1972. They were all as you described except that I did not hear footsteps, and on one occasion only was the hag on top of me—The others, it was in bed, at my side trying to push me out.

I have never known anyone who has experienced it and when I try to explain it to my family and friends, they look at me in disbelief. . . .

The relief reported by this woman is a typical reaction of those who report an attack after hearing a discussion of the subject. People also often automatically adopt whatever term they heard me use for the attack, as in the use of "old hag" here. To adopt the term is natural because the lack of appropriate terminology is a major obstacle to discussion of the attacks in the absence of a tradition. The following letter provided more detail.

Case 9
White Female; 49 years old

I just heard you on the radio speaking of "the Old Hag." I would like to tell you that I have been experiencing this for many years on an average of once or twice per year. I never before heard of a name for it & no one that I have described it to has ever known what I was talking about, including my Doctor. I happen to be on a drug called Etrofon (an antidepressant) which I take each night at bed time & find that I'm less likely to have "the old hag" now. I've had it both in the daytime (while napping) & at night & the position I'm sleeping in doesn't make any difference as I've *definitely* had it while sleeping on my side as well as on my back.

---

this book, I have changed all names of places and other potentially identifying features. Nothing else has been altered.

I too have heard the footsteps & the strangling scene but just as I was about to be strangled I came out of it.

When we lived in Toronto I had the experience at least 3 times in one year. I could hear the footsteps coming down the hall & each time they came closer to my bedroom until finally the almost strangling.

After we moved to Quebec (we've been here 6 years) the footsteps came up the stairs—I haven't had the strangling here but a form with a very bright light in front of it. I've been paralyzed during this experience. . . .

This experience usually occurs when I'm overtired & just before going to sleep. I can feel it coming on & am completely helpless in stopping it from continuing.

It's a dreadful, frightening experience & I sometimes am almost afraid to go to sleep especially if I'm overtired as I know I'm more apt to experience it then.

That this woman experiences the attacks less frequently since she began taking an antidepressant is interesting. It has been suggested to me that depression may have an effect on either the frequency or the nature of these attacks, and the medication, which is a combination of a tranquilizer and a tricyclic antidepressant, could also have an effect. Any drug that acts on the central nervous system might have an impact on a sleep-related experience. But victims of the attacks are naturally anxious to discover a cause for them and thus tend to associate them with any unusual variable in their lives. No depression-related effect has been indicated in the information I have collected so far, and any drug effect would be difficult to establish. This almost automatic search for a cause is in itself an important part of the reactions of most victims. Regardless of the accuracy of such speculations, they have played a role in the development of traditions relating to the experience.

Upon my return to the United States, I was able to confirm and extend the conclusion suggested by these letters. Experiences clearly recognizable as Old Hag attacks occur on the mainland with considerable frequency, and here they are far less often found in the presence of a traditional model than in Newfoundland. I have not had many opportunities to repeat and extend the oral questionnaire approach initially used in

Newfoundland, and I have therefore not added much statistical data. This is partly because I have no longer had access to a population that could be conveniently used in such a time-consuming method and partly because other questions rapidly became more pressing.

Although I have rarely been able to use the full question-naire, I have carried out numerous surveys of a less formal nature centering on some form of the question, "Have you ever awakened to find that you were unable to move?" These have involved groups in Pennsylvania, Nebraska, California, and Kentucky. I have followed up with some in-depth interviews in each case. While not yielding a large amount of quantified data suitable for statistical analysis, the results of these inquiries taken together are interesting.

Depending on the manner in which the question is presented, the positive responses have varied between 10 and 25 percent of groups containing thirty-five to one hundred people. The more initial reassurance given that positive responses are not abnormal, the larger the number of responses up to about 16 percent. Response rates up to 25 percent are found when more description is given of the experiences being sought. For example, a group of ninety yielded fifteen positive responses to the bare question. I then described the attacks on the basis of my interview materials, including the fact that some victims report feeling "afraid to move" rather than "paralyzed." I then repolled the group. This time twenty-three raised their hands. This response may represent some increase in false positives, but very few follow-up interviews in such cases have revealed any experience that was not clearly of the Old Hag variety. I think it more likely that the additional explanation removes false negatives—those who have had the attacks but do not perceive their immobility as paralysis. If the presence of the tradition in Newfoundland serves a purpose similar to my more extensive description, then the 23 percent rate of occurrence there would appear to be similar to the mainland rate.

In terms of the two hypotheses discussed in Chapter 2, the frequent report of recognizable Old Hag attacks is the softer of the two means for discriminating between the two positions.

The more conclusive evidence is the presence or absence of a complex and stable pattern of experience in the absence of a model. Interviews obtained by general questions about unusual experiences, as described with the two in-depth interviews in Chapter 2, and those that have followed presentations of the topic to groups, demonstrated that such complex experiences without models occur frequently in the United States. As soon as this had become clear, I turned my attention to collecting accounts of such experiences in order to acquire a full description of their varieties, to look for percursors and sequellae, and to examine the relationship of the experiences to tradition. The demonstration that tradition is not needed either to elicit or to shape the attacks made all of these topics more important.

The common existence of these experiences, the stability of their contents, and their independence from tradition are so surprising that no quantity of summarized data is sufficient to document them. Questions of interpretation must inevitably arise. Furthermore, the variables governing peoples' ability and willingness to respond positively to questions about the experience are complicated and require study, as are the interrelationships of the various features of the experience. For these reasons, actual accounts, most of them transcribed from tape recordings, constitute the primary data of this book.

THE OLD HAG AND LANGUAGE [3]

Before presenting the specific accounts that constitute most of the remainder of this chapter, a hypothetical answer is needed to the question: How can this experience, which is well-known in Newfoundland, be widespread but practically unknown in the United States? I shall sketch here what I consider to be at least a major part of the answer to this question. The accounts that follow can then be used to check and to some extent develop this explanation.

When one has an experience and is aware that others have

---

3. I have discussed this subject in greater detail in "Ambiguity and the Rhetoric of Belief," *Keystone Folklore* 21 (1976):11–24.

had a similar experience, that knowledge is generally accompanied by the availability of words and phrases understood to describe the experience or some of its aspects. We can say, for example, "I baked a cake," and do not need to recite a long list of steps such as, "I took eggs and milk from the refrigerator, flour from one cupboard, mixing bowls and spoons from another," and so forth. Variation can be indicated by such phrases as "the cake fell," "I baked it from scratch," and so on. Such language allows a great many complex operations and experiences to be indicated quickly and conveniently. The same is true with experiences that are considered supernatural. A common current example would be the statement, "I am a born-again Christian." "Born-again" has many different connotations and carries a heavy load of meaning, but it can be made more specific by such additional phrases and terms as, "I received the Baptism of the Holy Spirit," or "I frequently speak in tongues."

In either the mundane or the supernatural example, the speaker is saved an enormous amount of effort by the availability of such language, albeit at the cost of some precision. One who was unaware that anyone else had ever baked a cake or had a born-again experience would be forced to resort to elaborate and challenging descriptions to even approximate the meaning conveyed by the words and phrases given above.

In the same way, the Newfoundlander who states, "I had the Old Hag last night," says in seven words what one who considers the experience to be unique must spend ten or fifteen minutes attempting to convey. Not only does general knowledge allow for convenient language, but the presence of convenient language indicates the presence of a consensus, which in most cases provides assurance that one's experience is not somehow monstrous.

Difficulty of expression and uneasiness about disclosing such a personal experience interact to create pressure against talking about the attacks in the absence of a tradition and lead to the use of analogy. The people who call an attack a "dream" although they are sure they were awake during the experience are using an analogy that has two advantages. It provides a convenient noun that captures some of the features of what happened: the experience is usually sleep-related and things are seen and felt that are unlike natural events in waking life. It also allows the speaker to control the extent to which the full scope of the experience is disclosed, depending on the reactions of listeners. If reactions are incredulous or negative, the speaker can allow the typically wild and unreal nature of dreams to be understood as a part of his meaning. If, on the other hand, a listener responds with a similar personal experience or other strongly supportive feedback, the speaker can disclose more intimate details.

One function of the Old Hag tradition in Newfoundland, then, is to provide both convenient language for talking about this widespread experience, and another is to indicate a consensus that it is acceptable to have undergone it. Even in the presence of the tradition there remain problems with precisely expressing some of the phenomenologically subtle aspects of the experiences and questions about consensus and disclosure concerning interpretations of the attacks. These constraints notwithstanding, the presence of the tradition allows for relatively free sharing of knowledge about the basics of the experience. In the absence of a tradition that would serve both purposes, as throughout most of the United States, the experience remains largely unshared and unknown except through the occasional use of cautious, potentially misleading analogies.

A historical effect of the role of analogy has been considerable change in the understanding of those generally distributed words in the English language which at one time had direct reference to the experience. The word nightmare, for example, originally meant specifically such an attack. Ernest Jones has summarized the basic elements of the etymology of the word:

> The word Nightmare itself comes from the Anglo-Saxon *neaht* or *nicht* (=night) and *mara* (=incubus or succubus). The Anglo-Saxon suffix *a* denotes an agent, so that *mara* from the verb *merran*, literally means a "crusher," and the connotation of a crushing weight on the breast is common to the corresponding words in allied language (Icelandic *mara*, Danish *mare*, Low German *moore*, Bohemian *mara*, Swedish *mara*, Old High German *mara*).

. . . From the earliest times the oppressing agency experienced during sleep was personified.[4]

The written record indicates that this continued to be the primary meaning of the word well into the seventeenth century,[5] and printed references to this meaning in contradistinction to the more general meaning can be found even in this century. With the passage of time, the meaning of the word was extended to include first a connotation of dreaming attached to the attack and then by analogy bad dreams in general. The *American Heritage Dictionary,* for example, gives "A dream arousing feelings of intense . . . fear" as the first meaning of the word and the more general definition, "An event or condition that evokes feelings of horror" as the second meaning. Only a small part of the original meaning is retained in the third definition, "A demon or spirit thought to plague sleeping people."[6]

A similar change may have taken place in the meaning of the word "haggard." The *Oxford English Dictionary* gives both "wild" and "anxious" or "terrified" as the main meanings in which the word is applied to people. The former is derived from the Old French *hagard,* an untamed hawk. The second is seen as "influenced by Hag . . . as if 'somewhat hag-like,' " referring to the once common usage of the word "hag" to mean "witch." The *OED* also notes a connection with the words "hagged" and "hag-ride," although it does not make a direct connection between "hag-ride" and "haggard."[7] In Newfoundland, as noted in Chapter 1, the victim of an attack is often said to be "hagrid," and this pronunciation is sometimes used (even by those who do not know the tradition) to refer to one who looks worried and fatigued in general. The

4. Ernest M. Jones, *On the Nightmare,* International Psycho-Analytical Library, no. 20 (London: Hogarth Press, 1931), p. 243.
5. See, for example, the entries under "nightmare" in Philological Society, *The Oxford English Dictionary,* 12 vols. (London: Oxford University Press, 1961).
6. William Morris, ed., *The American Heritage Dictionary of the English Language* (Boston: Houghton Mifflin Co., 1978), p. 887.
7. Philological Society, *Oxford English Dictionary.*

Newfoundland usage may represent one step in the etymology of the word, since a haggard individual is at least as much like a victim of a witch who rides as he is like the witch. The connection would most likely have been through the ungrammatical oral form "hagrid," and therefore the connection with "hagride" might well not have shown up in print. Regardless of whether this speculation is correct, the word "haggard" has been as thoroughly laundered of its original supernatural connections as has the word "nightmare."

At one time, then, there were widespread traditions in English which correspond to what Newfoundlanders know as the Old Hag, but those traditions have lost much of their currency in other parts of North America. We shall see that a number of different traditions in English have at least included these attacks among the phenomena to which they referred and that, as the etymology of "nightmare" given above suggested, such traditions are not limited to English. In fact, this experience appears to have worldwide distribution and has been a part of the empirical foundation for a great variety of supernatural traditions.

These historical developments in the meanings of such words as "nightmare" also have major importance for current field work. The Brown Collection of North Carolina Folklore, for example, lists among beliefs about "nightmares," "To sleep with a razor and Bible under your head wards off nightmares" and "To keep off nightmare, sleep with shears under the pillow."[8] Such prescriptions for preventing nightmares are common and frequently reported, but it is impossible to know without asking whether the person reporting the preventives is using "nightmare" in its general or specific sense. Many who know such methods likely have in mind "bad dreams." However, the similarity of most of the methods to those used in defending against witchcraft and other supernatural assaults (as, for example, the use of a knife in Case 1 above) suggests that some of these reports may indicate the endurance of the origi-

8. Wayland D. Hand, ed., *Popular Beliefs and Superstitions from North Carolina*, Frank C. Brown Collection of North Carolina Folklore, vols. 6 and 7 (Durham, N.C.: Duke University Press, 1961–64), 7:137.

nal meaning of the word. The connection between "Old Hag" and "nightmare" in Newfoundland seems to be another indication of such persistence.

Given this process of changing definitions, it is particularly interesting to discover that the experiences that apparently formed the basis of the traditions continued to occur even though the traditions themselves either died or changed almost beyond recognition. No doubt a part of the pressure leading to the change of meaning has come from the decreasing acceptance of supernatural beliefs in "official culture." Similar extensions of the meanings of words originally having primarily supernatural definitions can be seen in such examples as "haunt," "spirit," and "ghost." Although these words still are understood to have a supernatural reference, they are also frequently used by analogy to refer to purely natural things and events. Other factors and the exact mechanisms by which supernatural belief and language affect one another remain a fascinating and important subject for study, but largely beyond the scope of this book.

THE CASES

The cases that follow are presented both to document the existence of "recognizable Old Hag attacks" in the absence of models and to allow for the development of a more complete phenomenology of the events. I have resisted the temptation to derive a "typical pattern" and then arrange segments of accounts accordingly. The pattern is too complex and the phenomenology too difficult for such a method to be fully accurate. Instead I am presenting full accounts that in some instances include descriptions of several attacks. I have used an order that allows points raised by one account to be explored in one or more of those that follow, but each narrative is much more than the illustration of a single point. The features of the experiences, their contexts, and the reactions of victims are all among the topics these cases open for discussion. My own comments will be restricted to raising a few of the central questions posed by the material. But this presentation is intended as a beginning rather than a definitive statement, so the reader is invited to try out additional analyses and hypotheses.

The cases given in this chapter have been selected because they are representative of the varieties of the experience that I have collected and because they do not show strong affinities to specific traditions. In subsequent chapters I look both at varieties of experience that suggest additional categories (i.e., complex stable patterns that are not recognizable Old Hag attacks but show some relationship) and at those that exhibit strong links with particular traditions.

In most cases I have not treated accounts obtained from people who had some prior knowledge of my research on the Old Hag differently from those received from naive subjects (although I have indicated which is which) for two reasons: there have been no detectable differences between the accounts given by the two groups, and the total number of accounts obtained from both sources is now substantial. These two facts taken together with the Newfoundland findings appear to rule out the likelihood that either intentional fraud or unconscious shaping has had a significant impact on my interview data. In fact, the presentation of both kinds of accounts, clearly identified, provides an additional check on unintentional interviewer bias. This consistency is analogous to that found between accounts given by those with knowledge of a nightmare tradition and those without. The opportunity to make such comparisons is an important part of this investigation.

I have not, however, followed this principle of similar treatment in cases that involve the reporting of surprising or unusual features. In such cases I have only used accounts that I could demonstrate beyond a reasonable doubt to be free of any influence from my work. Some such cases will be presented in Chapter 5.

The continuing accumulation of secondary features can be confusing, and so I have provided an Index of Features to help the reader who wishes to keep a tally. And, finally, for all of the reasons discussed in the preceding section on the problems of language, I shall from this point on call the experience we have been discussing "the Old Hag." A convenient noun is necessary to ease discussion and avoid such clumsy locutions as "the experience we have been discussing," but terms that have been used by other writers (such as nightmare and incubus) have too many extraneous connotations to be used here. "The Old Hag" has the advantage of being fairly free of experiential associations for most readers while being more comfortable than a neologism or acronym. My use of the term, like that of many Newfoundlanders, refers simply and directly to the experience itself. Neither the various Newfoundland interpretations nor any necessity of a connection with Newfoundland tradition should be inferred.

The following account was received after Ron heard me give a public lecture (in Pennsylvania) about the Old Hag. As is generally the case in such situations, he felt uneasy at first in discussing his experience but was greatly reassured at hearing that others had gone through the same thing. The portion given here concerns the last of several attacks which Ron described during the interview.

Case 10
White Male; 22 years old

RON: . . . I had one last year. My senior year in college. Now these two are afternoon ones. . . . And for some reason in the afternoon I go into a deeper sleep. When I finally go into a sleep it just seems to be a deeper one. My dreams are like really, really deep.

But last year I took a nap. I'd come back from a lab of some sort, I had so many I'm not sure which one it was, and now I crashed. . . . That was approximately four o'clock in the afternoon. I was really dead tired. I was really dead tired. I fell into a very deep sleep that day. . . . I remember, you know, it was a *really* deep sleep.

But what woke me up was the door slamming. "OK," I thought, "It's my roommate," you know, my roommate came into the room. . . . I was laying on my back, just kind of looking up. And the door slammed and I kinda opened my eyes. I was awake. Everything was light in the room. My roommate wasn't there and the door was still closed, but I had just heard the door slam. I thought, "Aw, somebody looked," you know, "opened the door to look, to see if somebody was there, and then saw I was just sleeping. Slammed the door and that was it."

But the next thing I knew, I realized that I couldn't move. OK. My eyes——I was able to look around the room. And I started to feel that pressure you were talking about. And it increased, and it increased, and the next thing I knew I was like totally wiped out. I just laid there.

And——this is——this is going to sound really strange. But ——there was a murky presence there, that just kind of materialized. Remember I said I checked the room. I checked to see if somebody——I kind of like gazed over to the door and there was no one there. But the next thing I knew, from one of the areas of the room this grayish, brownish murky presence was there. And it kind of swept down over the bed and I was terrified! I mean I don't——I can't *remember* when I was this scared! It——when I say "a murky presence" I mean that it was kind of like a——a surrealistic shape. It didn't——It——I guess it had two things that I might have conjured——conjured to be the eyes or something like that. But——It was like nothing I had ever seen before. And I felt——I felt this pressing down all over me. I couldn't breathe. I couldn't move. And the whole thing ——the whole thing was that——there was like——I could hear the stereo in the room next to me. I was wide awake, you know. It was a fraternity house. I could hear everything going on all over the house. It was a pretty noisy place. And I couldn't move and I was helpless. And I was really——I was really scared. And all I could remember there was the struggle, you know. The—— you know, "Jesus Christ, I got to——I got to get out of here! What's going on?"

And this murky presence——just kind of——this was *evil!* (Nervous laugh.) This was evil! You know, this is weird! You must think I'm a——

HUFFORD: No. I've heard people say things like this a lot——

RON: [Excitedly.] This is——I'm not——I'm not——I'm not a paranoid person and, you know, I don't——I don't have any——I don't *think* I've got any, you know problems like this but——This thing was *there!* I felt a pressure on me and it was like enveloping me. It was a very, very very strange thing. And as I remember I struggled. I struggled to move and get out. And—you know, eventually, I think eventually what happened was I kind of like moved my arm. And again the whole thing——the whole thing just kind of dissipated away. The presence, everything. But everything else just remained the same. The same stereo was playing next door. The same stuff was going on.

And I asked my roommate——I said to him "Did you come in the room and wake me up earlier?" You know, "Did you slam the door?" And he said "No." And I checked around the hall. I said "Hey, did anybody come in here and see me asleep?" And everybody said "No." They——they were going about their own things. Nobody had come in, yet I *did* hear the door slam. It woke me up. Because if it hadn't——Like I said, I was in a very, very deep sleep. And I wouldn't have been aware of the stereos and everything else going on around me. [Brief interruption as tape ends.]

I can tell you something else. The——there was a continuum here. Like usually when I dream, my scenes switch rapidly. I don't know how to explain this, but like one minute I'll be somewhere, and the next minute I'll be somewhere else, next minute somewhere else. There'll be people——But everything was *constant.* The room was there. The murky presence came out of nowhere. The door was still closed. I can tell you from where it came. There was a——The way the room was set up was very much like a right angle, OK? The doorway was at the 90° portion of the angle, where the two walls came together. In this portion over here were closets, and the bed was right here. So from where I was laying in the bed I could at one angle see the door, and at the other angle see the closets. The closets . . . had a wall adjacent to them which was like an out-pocketing. It was in such a way that light coming through the window would shine off the door. But the closets would be back in a little darkened portion of the room. Because another wall would be blocking the window, like. OK? That's from where the murky presence came.

It approached toward the bed and as I said it——It kind of stood over me with a glare. That's——that's really why I said it was evil. Because it just sort of stood over me with a glare. I don't know what else to call it. And then——and then it started to envelop the bed. And as I said I finally moved and that seemed to stop the whole thing. I——I——When it was all over I was breathing heavy, however, I don't remember breathing at all when this whole thing was happening. I think I just laid there ice dead, you know.

HUFFORD: Did you feel like you were suffocating?

RON: No. I didn't feel like I was suffocating. I just felt——I felt terror. It was more like I couldn't swallow. OK? I mean like I was just——I was *completely* immobile, and——There was something else I wanted to point out, and that was that——I said I went to sleep at four o'clock, and as this whole thing was——as I——as I looked around to the door and everything else, my clock was right next to the bed and I read the time and it was about ten to five. OK? This whole thing happened and when it was all over it was only about five minutes to five. Only five minutes had gone by. So, it kind of——it kind of reassured me that to myself I was awake. Because if I had been asleep, then I would not have noted the time on the clock, and I wouldn't have known that it was five minutes later. Do you follow my reasoning?

HUFFORD: Yeah. You noted the time when you heard the door slam?

RON: Right. You know. Right. Exactly. You know, I said "How long have I been asleep anyway?" You know, when you've been asleep for a nap, and you've got things to do or whatever, you ——The first thing you do is kind of glance at the clock to see how long you've been asleep, you know. To see is it time to get up? The door slammed. "OK, I'm awake now, let's see what time it is." So I did note the time and only about five minutes had passed. This whole thing——was when this whole thing occurred. That's pretty much it.

HUFFORD: How about the pressure. You say you felt pressure this time. How would you describe where it was?

RON: It was very much as if somebody put me in one of those, those junkyard things that are made to crunch cars. You know, they make little squares out of a two ton mass? And there's the process where the big thing comes slamming down on you, OK? Bam! To flatten the whole thing out. That's what I felt like I had on top of me. And it was uniform. It wasn't like one particular area was being pressed more than anywhere else. It was just that, if you can imagine being pressed against the mattress. You know, the mattress providing force up and something providing force down, and I just seemed to be pancaked in between. And I think this was part of the reason why I couldn't move. It seemed to me that it was because of the pressure that I couldn't move. You know, it was——like it felt as if I was being held down. But it would be as if there were a zillion tiny arms all over me holding me down. But not like, say, one here, one here, so that part of my arm could come up but my wrist was being held down. It was everything uniformly.

HUFFORD: Did you struggle against it?

RON: I think so, yeah! I tried to——sure.

HUFFORD: . . . If you could go back there and see yourself while it was happening . . . would you expect to find yourself kind of rigid, straining against this, or limp?

RON: I'd say probably rigid. Probably rigid.

HUFFORD: OK. Can you describe visually the murky presence?

RON: Well, I will——I will try to paint this as well as I can. By the time it took form——And when I say take form it's because it was like a blob, a blob of nothing. I would say it was almost kind of gaseous——but *not* gaseous in that it didn't have the transparency that a gaseous kind of thing would have. A gaseous thing you would see right through. OK? This was opaque. I could not see right through it. The color was very much like your tape recorder case. It was brown. OK? Very much like that. A grayish brown. It was an off, weird color. There was——There was——As I recall I couldn't really make out a face *per se,* but I could see two holes that would——that would seem to be eyes. But they were dark too. I couldn't see right through those.

HUFFORD: The same color but darker? Or a different color?

RON: They were the same color but darker, OK? The same color but darker. That would be a good way to put it. The——the overall shape of the thing was like a rectangle that you laid on top of a water trough, and as the waves would come through, the rectangle would move. And that's very much what it was like.

HUFFORD: . . . Were the edges sharp or fuzzy?

RON: The edges were pretty sharp. That's the thing. That's why I say it wasn't like a——They were pretty sharp.

HUFFORD: Did they have corners? Were they——were the corners sharp like a rectangle?

RON: Not quite. Not quite. Slightly rounded off. Slightly rounded off.

HUFFORD: Now, you said that this "appeared." Did it just suddenly look like that, or did it flow into that shape, or——?

RON: It flowed into that shape. That's——that's what I meant by it——it——it *formed.* That's why I said it was *almost* gaseous

in nature, but not gaseous in nature, in that it did kind of flow
——it seemed to be, like as if it was coming from the area of
the closets. From the darker area of the room. Out to the——to
the more lit area. Because there was——there was light coming
through the window, with these blousy curtains hanging down.
But the whole top part of the window was uncovered. And——
and the thing kind of flowed into that. That happened very
quickly, and I——It would be very hard for me to describe that
further. But that happened, you know. [Snaps his fingers.] Bam!

But as the thing formed it came closer and closer to the bed.
And then, as I said, it started to enwrap me. And by that I mean
that the rectangle acted like a blanket in a way.

And it had a glare——A glaring stare to it, which was a——
which was a strange thing, for a thing that had no real face and
couldn't make any facial expressions. For some reason I got a
feeling of a real cold stare from it, OK? Really terrifying! . . .
People, people would think I'm nuts!

Although the majority of attacks take place at night, the
number occurring during daytime naps is disproportionately
large considering the fraction of total sleep hours represented
by such naps. As in Ron's case, these daytime attacks are not
reported primarily by those whose work schedule requires that
they do most of their sleeping during the day. More often they
are experienced by people who take an occasional nap because
of fatigue. The fatigue reported by Ron is also a common finding, although it is not always present, and it is clearly not a necessary condition. It will come up again, however, with sufficient
frequency to suggest that it may play a role in the etiology of
some attacks.

The sound of the door that seemed to awaken Ron is the
second most frequently reported sound, following footsteps.
Not infrequently the two are heard during a single experience.

Seeing a nonhuman attacker is less frequently reported
than seeing a human one but is not rare. In all visual cases,
whether the attacker is humanlike, animal, or something else,
the detail most frequently commented on is the eyes. As in
Ron's case, the eyes are not only noticeable, but they elicit a
strong emotional response. Further examples will appear in
following cases.

The word "evil," or one of its analogs, is very often chosen to express the victim's reaction not only when eyes are mentioned but in most of the accounts that involve an attacker that is seen, heard, or "sensed." As with all secondary features, though, this is not universally true.

The use of analogy to describe many parts of the attack, as discussed above, is well illustrated by Ron. He used at least five analogies: the mechanical compacter for the pressure; the "zillion tiny arms" for the restraint; gas for the nature of the "murky presence"; the rectangle on the water trough for the manner in which the presence moved; and a blanket for the way the thing "enwrapped" him. Ron used these analogies, some of them rather fantastic, in an attempt to clarify a description that must include many features he had never experienced in any other context. The incomplete correspondence characteristic of analogies then required him to go back and eliminate some of the qualities suggested by his choice. For example, the opaqueness and sharp edges and angles of the "murky presence" struck Ron as not being consistent with the comparison to a "gaseous thing."

Ron had never told anyone about his experience before our interview. In addition to his difficulty describing its features, he leaves no doubt that part of his reason is that "people would think I'm nuts!" In fact, in the midst of the interview he showed great concern for what I would think of him despite the assurances I had given him. His insistence that he is "not a paranoid person" makes clear his assessment of what most would think if he spoke freely about his attacks. The depth of emotion he felt at that point in the interview was obvious in his voice and demeanor and is illustrated in the difficulty he had in composing and saying his sentences.

This combination of difficult expression and self-consciousness often prevents people from speaking of their experiences. Only after I have indicated that they are not necessarily pathological and that I know enough about them to understand even the difficult points do most victims begin to verbalize their experience freely.

In describing his attack, Ron goes to great length to document his certainty that he was awake. He describes his awakening and his initial reasonable thoughts that what he heard must

have been his roommate and then that it must have been someone who left before he opened his eyes. He gives details about
the real sounds he heard during the attack and subsequently
notes that all those sounds continued when the experience
ended. He makes a great effort to describe the ways he sees
the texture of this experience as differing from that of his
dreams. Finally, he notes that his observation of the time before and after the experience suggests wakefulness. Similar evidence and more has frequently been given by victims in an
attempt to "prove" that they were awake during the attack.

Although such proof is almost impossible, these frequently repeated observations call into question any effort to
dismiss these experiences as merely one variation amid the
great variety of bad dreams. Some dreams occasionally seem
to take place in the sleeper's real surroundings. These are
"false awakening" dreams, but they do not generally fool the
sleeper for long, at least not after the real awakening takes
place. Sounds in the real environment are sometimes incorpo-
rated into dreams as "protectors of sleep,"[9] but not typically
in a realistic way. But perhaps the greatest challenge to the
dream hypothesis is the persistent pattern, discussed previously, which will become increasingly evident in additional cases.
Why should a class of dreams present such a consistent pattern
in the absence of a model, and why should they be so over-
whelmingly characterized by the impression of wakefulness?
Eventually we shall consider the possibility that these attacks
involve an altered state of consciousness other than dreaming,
although perhaps related to sleep.

At this point, enough evidence has been presented to
question the manner in which proponents of the cultural
source hypothesis have used the notion of "dreams mistaken

9. The incorporation of environmental stimuli into dreams has long
been recognized; see, for example, the numerous examples discussed by
Havelock Ellis in *The World of Dreams* (Boston: Houghton Mifflin Co., 1922;
reprint Detroit: Gale Research Co., 1976), pp. 71–93. For the integration of
this knowledge with the psychoanalytic theory of wish-fulfillment in dreams
to yield the sleep-protecting function, see Sigmund Freud's *The Interpretation
of Dreams* in *The Basic Writings of Sigmund Freud,* trans. and ed. A. A. Brill, Modern Library (New York: Random House, 1938), pp. 209–11.

for reality" to explain some alleged experiences. In *Leviathan* (1651), Thomas Hobbes stated, "From this ignorance of how to distinguish dreams, and other strong fancies, from vision and sense, did arise the greatest part of the religion of the Gentiles in time past, that worshipped satyrs, fawns, nymphs, and the like; and now-a-days the opinion that rude people have of fairies, ghosts, and goblins, and of the power of witches."[10] This view was not new when Hobbes made the statement, and it remains current today. Part of the argument is that ignorant people with weak and untrained critical faculties can be more easily fooled into thinking that a dream was a waking experience than can those who are more sophisticated. This idea seems supported by the fact that sophisticated people rarely report such bizarre occurrences. The evidence of the Old Hag, however, indicates otherwise. As in Ron's case, a large number of well-educated people clearly consider the possibility that they are dreaming and then expend considerable critical effort to determine whether or not the dream hypothesis is tenable. After the experience, Ron asked his roommate and his fraternity brothers whether they had entered the room while he napped. Victims of these attacks commonly take such actions to try to find a plausible natural explanation for even a part of their experience. Such concern is another indication of the strength of the subjective impression of wakefulness that sets this experience apart from ordinary dreams. None of this evidence, of course, proves that these are not a special class of dream or a dream-related state, but it does demonstrate that gullibility and a lack of formal education are not required to explain the impression that such experiences occur during wakefulness. Furthermore, the lack of reports from the sophisticated seems to be much more a function of their unwillingness to expose themselves to ridicule or psychiatric diagnosis than of their superior critical faculties.

In the next case the dream analogy was used intentionally to prevent personal disclosure. The case also demonstrates how the decision to speak, even guardedly, about the subject

10. Thomas Hobbes, *Leviathan,* ed. Michael Oakeshott (Oxford: Basil Blackwell, 1960), p. 12.

can suddenly alter the appearance that one's own experience is unique, even among those to whom one is close.

The woman whose transcript follows heard me address a group of college students about my work and subsequently offered to tell me of her experiences.

Case 11
White Female; 24 years old

JOANNE: (After your lecture) I went home and I started thinking about these things that happened to me. And . . . there were two people that are very close to me and I said "Well, I don't care what they think of me. I'm going to just kind of mention it and see what happens."

The one was my girlfriend and roommate. And she said "Oh, well!" And she was very happy to tell me what happened to her. And she said that she had experienced astro [sic] projection three times in her life, and she studied it and knows all about it. OK, so she told me about those and I said, "Wow, that's neat." And this was three o'clock in the morning at a restaurant, we were talking about this.

The next person was my boyfriend. And I was studying in Williamsport at his house when this thing happened at the library, [an attack she later described]. But what happened——I just kind of mentioned, "Gee, a strange thing happened to me in the library." And he said, "What?" And I said, "Well, I had a strange dream." I told him it was a dream because I didn't want him to really know what I thought happened. [During her subsequent description of the attack she said, "I think there's a possibility that it could have been some kind of spiritual visitation."] But then I started thinking——So one night I told him about this and he said——and this blew my mind——he was so cool about it. And he said, "Well, if you want to know the truth, let me tell you what happened to me." And I said, "Oh no, not another one!" I couldn't believe it like, you know.

He said he stayed at a house in Chester, Pennsylvania, with three other guys while he was going to school near there. And one night everybody was in bed. And he went to bed. And he heard the door open and he felt his bed go down. And he said he was just paralyzed. He couldn't——He was so scared——He didn't know what it was. But his eyes——He kept looking and looking and he didn't see anything. And then the thing got up and he didn't you know, hear anything or see anything——no other movement, he said. He rolled over and tried to go to sleep and it happened again. This time he did hear steps, but he didn't hear the door. And it went down right beside his shoulder, just like someone was sitting on the mattress. . . . and he said the same things that you talked about. He opened his eyes, he couldn't see anybody, but he felt a presence, mostly around his head, and then he felt something touch his shoulder, and that's basically all he said.

But I thought it was really interesting that, you know, here immediately I found two people that had experienced this. And probably had I never mentioned it, we would have never talked about it. And I thought that was interesting.

(My own experiences at first happened) when I was a child, very frequently. And I remember this so vividly, very frequently when I was a child about——actually I was probably about 12 or 13 years old, in adolescence, I had what I would have considered frequent visits. I mean twice a week. And just always so extremely paralyzed. Never saw anything. Never heard the footsteps. But I was always asleep, and then awake and just frozen. And I knew someone was there, and I was so afraid. And so I just couldn't move, and fought and fought to move. And finally what I would do is just eventually roll over and cover my head with the sheets and fall asleep. And it would go away. But this happened two or three times a week.

And I don't know if it's the same as these other people, but I think it is. Because I remember exactly how my body felt. I could not move. I did look around. My eyes were open. But I never saw anything and I really never heard anything. But that happened very frequently and at one point I really thought there was something wrong with me because it happened so often. But at that age I never spoke to anyone about it.

HUFFORD: . . . When was the last one?

JOANNE: Well, I'd say it went on for about two years. That's why I was really afraid that there was something wrong with me. . . . And then nothing happened again——The next time was on campus here. I lived——I lived in the dorm and I was very fatigued. I mean, so tired——You can imagine, I worked sixty or seventy hours a week. And one day I came home from school, it was in the winter——say it was five-thirty, and it was dark. And I laid down and went to bed. And I'll tell you——this was probably the most severe experience!

I was sleeping. I know I was asleep, and I awoke. And immediately when I awoke I was afraid and scared, and I wouldn't dare move because I just thought something was going to get me if I moved. And *they* knew I was there. And I opened my eyes and there was just a face. You know, I really believed it was my imagination. I thought, "Joanne, you are nuts!" But if you believe it's your imagination you usually can go like this and rationalize and get rid of it. Really if it's your imagination you have some control, which I believe anybody does. I believe I do. Well, it wouldn't go away and I couldn't get rid of the feeling that I was so scared and couldn't move. And to tell you the truth, this was just last winter. . . . I . . . remember that I forced myself to turn on the light and get up. And I did a very strange thing, which I hadn't done before, which was to go through the house, and I had the feeling that I had to walk around. I had to look. I had to see if anything was strange in the house.

Joanne was candid about her defensive use of analogy to reduce disclosure. When telling her boyfriend, she began with a cautious mention of "something strange." When he asked her to be more specific, she intentionally used the word "dream" because she did not want to tell him that she believed her experience might have been a supernatural one involving a "spiritual visitation." Joanne's case is also valuable because it contains a description of three people, each with one or more unusual experiences of interest to the others, who had never revealed the experiences even to such intimate friends. It seems reasonable to postulate a strong similarity between the way my lecture precipitated this sharing of experience and the way that traditional knowledge functions to ease such discussions.

Joanne and her roommate's equation of the Old Hag with "astral projection" is a connection that has consistently been made by a small fraction of those interviewed. At first I felt that it was fully explainable by the reference of both to bizarre personal experiences, which occur more frequently than is generally recognized, but I later found additional connections, which will be discussed in greater depth in Chapter 5.

Joanne's boyfriend's feeling of the bed moving as if someone sat on it has been reported by others, and additional examples will be presented later in the book. The sensation of being touched is also occasionally reported. Less common, though not unique, is the fact that he had two experiences in a single night. His inference that something invisible was with him involves a distinct set of perceptions and should not be confused with the sensation of presence in which the perception is independent of such cues as footsteps and the motion of the bed.

The sensation of presence is clearly represented in Joanne's early attacks. She says that she "Never saw anything. Never heard the footsteps" but she "knew someone was there." Such descriptions have come from many people in interviews about the Old Hag. Another example is the following, from a written questionnaire response, received from a white female, twenty-seven years old, born in St. Louis, and raised "many places": "I was awake during the night with the feeling that something strange was in the room. I was frightened but could not move or cry out. Finally I was able to move but felt very apprehensive." In the simple form described here, the impact with which many sufferers experience this sensation is difficult to grasp. The next case, however, includes a particularly eloquent description of this part of the experience.

The great frequency of attacks experienced by Joanne as a youngster is rare, although I have spoken with a few others who describe a similar pattern. Her fear that these experiences were an indication that something was wrong with her is a common reaction among those who have repeated attacks. Whether this fear leads the sufferer to speak to a parent, physician, or other potential source of help seems to depend largely on whether the relationship with such a person is sufficiently close and trusting.

Joanne noted the presence of fatigue. She also attempted to discount the experience even as it was going on. She insisted that it must be "imagination," and then she discovered that it could not be made to conform to the normal conditions of imagined events. Joanne could not "rationalize" the face away. The fact that she saw a disembodied face is unusual, but another example occurs in Case 15.

The next case is taken from William James's important work *The Varieties of the Religious Experience.* [11] I present this nar-

11. William James, *The Varieties of Religious Experience: A Study in Human*

rative because it recounts so powerfully and in such detail the "sensation of presence" feature of the Old Hag attack. As interesting as the account itself is the fact that James clearly was not aware that this description, from one whom he calls "an intimate friend . . . one of the keenest intellects I know," represented a whole class of similar events. Given James's interest in the phenomenology of such experiences, this is further evidence of how well kept a secret the Old Hag experience is.

Case 12
White Male Adult

I have several times within the past few years felt the so-called "consciousness of a presence." The experiences which I have in mind are clearly distinguishable from another kind of experience which I have had very frequently, and which I fancy many persons would also call the "consciousness of a presence." But the difference for me between the two sets of experience is as great as the difference between feeling a slight warmth originating I know not where, and standing in the midst of a conflagration with all the ordinary senses alert.

It was about September, 1884, when I had the first experience. On the previous night I had had, after getting into bed at my rooms in College, a vivid tactile hallucination of being grasped by the arm, which made me *get up* and search the room for an intruder; but the sense of presence properly so-called came on the next night. After I had got into bed and blown out the candle, I lay awake awhile thinking on the previous night's experience, when suddenly I felt something come into the room and stay close to my bed. It remained only a minute or two. I did not recognize it by any ordinary sense, and yet there was a horribly unpleasant "sensation" connected with it. It stirred something more at the roots of my being than any ordinary perception. The feeling had something of the quality of a very large tearing vital pain spreading chiefly over the chest, but within the organism—and yet the feeling was not pain so much as abhorrence. At all events, something was present with me, and I knew its presence far more surely than I have ever known the presence of any fleshly living creature. I was conscious of

---

Nature (New York: Longmans, Green & Co., 1902; reprint New York: Modern Library, Random House, n.d.).

its departure as of its coming: an almost instantaneously swift going through the door, and the "horrible sensation" disappeared.

On the third night when I retired my mind was absorbed in some lectures which I was preparing, and I was still absorbed in these when I became aware of the actual presence (though not of the coming) of the thing that was there the night before, and of the "horrible sensation." I then *mentally* concentrated all my effort to charge this "thing," if it was evil, to depart, if it was not evil, to tell me who or what is was, and if it could not explain itself, to go, and that I would compel it to go. It went as on the previous night, and my body quickly recovered its normal state.

On two other occasions in my life I have had precisely the same "horrible sensation." Once it lasted a full quarter of an hour. In all three instances the certainty that there in outward space there stood something was indescribably stronger than the ordinary certainty of companionship when we are in the close presence of ordinary living people. The something seemed close to me, and intensely more real than any ordinary perception. Although I felt it to be like unto myself, so to speak or finite, small, and distressful, as it were, I didn't recognize it as any individual being or person.[12]

Many who have had this sensation have attempted to express, as James's friend has done so clearly, that the perception is far more certain than that which is ordinarily felt in the presence of others. Again, the perception can include more than simply the fact of presence. The fact that the "something" was felt to "come into the room and stay close to my bed" indicates that motion, direction, and location can also be a part of the sensation. Such additional "direct sensations" were also mentioned in Case 4. The clarity of this perception is reinforced here by the statement that the second time the subject was not aware of "the coming."

The "vivid tactile hallucination of being grasped by the arm" on the night before the arrival of the presence is intriguing. Unfortunately, not enough detail is given about this event to indicate its phenomenological relationship to the two "pres-

12. Ibid., pp. 59–60.

ence" episodes. The reaction of getting up to search for an intruder is a familiar one, however, suggesting that the term "hallucination" was applied on the basis of an inference about what it "must have been" as opposed to the subjective quality of the experience. The speaker's use of the analogy to pain to describe the feeling of "abhorrence," along with a shrinking from whatever is present in the room, is often mentioned in cases of a sensed presence as well as those in which the visitor is seen or heard.

The following case is from an interview I conducted in California after a lecture on the Old Hag tradition.

Case 13
White Female; 24 years of age

HUFFORD: You're going to describe now your experiences that were called to mind by my talk on the nightmare.

PAT: OK. I can first remember having something akin to it after the age of seven or eight. And what used to occur was, I would be on my back in bed with my arms on top of the blankets. And I always used to feel that the bed was moving. The bed was rocking up and down, back and forth. And I used to see it happening. And nothing in the room was changing. My sister was in her bed next to me. But the bed would constantly rock and it would frighten me until I started to enjoy it. Until I started to enjoy the feeling of this thing happening to me. And that went on periodically. I don't know how many times I had it. I never told anybody.

And the first time I recall ever having any visual component to the experience was when I became a teenager, and I was about thirteen. I remember that it was late. I was in bed. It was very late at night. I was on my back and I heard a "snurfling" sound. And I——I always called it "snurfling." It would be "snurf, snurf, snurf." And I was aware——there was nothing that I saw. But whatever it was I thought it was male. And . . . I just felt an incredible weight on my chest, as if somebody put a large boulder there. And somebody had their hand up against my throat. And I was terrified. And the second time it happened I was fifteen. And I could have sworn that I didn't see anything come into the room. But I remember looking at something that looked like an ape. And I always associated it with masculine——

And I remember that it was dark and it had red eyes——And it was always the feeling that there was an incredible amount of pressure against my chest. And I had a soft mattress and at the time I always used to feel that I could——that I was sinking in so deep that I could feel the mattress come up on either side of me. And almost——I was always afraid that I'd be pushed into the mattress so deep (laughs) that they wouldn't be able to find me. And——after the second time it happened I was no longer frightened of it. . . .

And I spoke to my mother who took me to a doctor who said that it was primarily nerves and the fact that I was going through normal adolescent identity crises and——That was——that happened at the time that I was having a lot of what was termed ESP sensations. So I figured that it was just my body, you know, reacting to psychic activity. Because I was being tested for ESP at the time. And——I think the period that I had——I remember having one period in my life when I had them every month for about a year. But they didn't frighten me. As a matter of fact I began to enjoy them. I enjoyed——I began to enjoy the sensation of losing control. And I remember——I couldn't move. And the way I used to——If it started to last what was an inordinately long time . . . I would try and move my fingers. And I remember I used to really——It was a painstaking chore to sit there and try to move that finger. And once I moved it I could feel myself falling out of the sensation.

It was always at night. It was always in a dark room. I was always on my back. And I remember the rocking. The bed rocking experience stopped when I started having this sensation that there was a presence entering the room. And I haven't had any of these experiences since I was about eighteen. And I always assumed it was because I had gotten myself together.

HUFFORD: OK. Do you feel, and did you feel, that you were awake during all of these?

PAT: I was *always* awake. I'm *sure* of it. I know my eyes were open. I can remember just having laid down. I know I was staring at my closet door. And I was always staring at it. And I could see the——If the door was open I could see the clothing. Everything was in order.

HUFFORD: OK. The rocking of the bed. Was it smooth or bumpy? Like was it as if it were suspended, or was it like it was bumping up and down?

PAT: I don't——I can't recall. I really can't recall. I think it was both. I——It's——It didn't frighten me so maybe that's why I think it might have been smooth. And the first time, because it frightened me, I may——I may conceive of it as bumpy, but I really can't recall that.

HUFFORD: How did the bed-rocking experience terminate?

PAT: . . . I think I just rode it out and it would just gradually—— —It would get less. The rocking or the bumping would cease. . . .

HUFFORD: Did you go to sleep while it was still rocking? Did they ever end that way?

PAT: No.

HUFFORD: You lay there awake until it stopped?

PAT: M-hm. And I would go to sleep then.

HUFFORD: Did you ever move while it was happening?

PAT: No. I was afraid I'd roll off the bed. . . . The rocking sensation I associate with a period from like eight years old to thirteen. After that I no longer got periods of rocking. Instead I got distinct impressions that somebody was walking in the hall. And the "snurfling" sound was, I thought, a breathing sound of somebody breathing.

HUFFORD: When you say snurfling, that's like a snorting, nosy kind of breathing sound? . . .

PAT: It wasn't a sniffing sound. It was a soft sound. Something that I would almost associate with——water. A watery sound. Like as if——Like when you put your foot down in a puddle, and——it makes that kind of "whoosh-squish" sound.

HUFFORD: Right. OK, did the ape snurfle? Or when you saw the ape was the snurfling gone?

PAT: No. I think the snurfling was gone when I saw the ape. But I always assumed, you know, that it *was* the ape. I only saw the ape once.

HUFFORD: Oh, that was just once?

PAT: It was just once and . . . the rest of the times I always felt the presence of something.

HUFFORD: Did you have the feeling of pressure when you saw the ape?

PAT: Yes. It stood by the side of the bed. . . . The ape then kind of disappeared and I felt the pressure get more and more intense. And I——This was the only time I was really scared, because I remember seeing the ape and thinking how strong it was, and how long its arms were. And I felt my esophagus being—— pressed out. I assumed (by) the ape, (although) the ape itself was no longer there.

HUFFORD: The pressure started after the ape disappeared?

PAT: No. The pressure was there, but it got more intense after the visual image of the ape disappeared. . . . (It felt like) a stricture all around. Not just on the windpipe. And I was always afraid that my breastbone was going to cave in.

HUFFORD: You said that you were being tested for ESP. At what point in this? . . .

PAT: Well let me just put this into some kind of sequence: the rocking of the bed I associated with eight to thirteen; then from, like, thirteen to sixteen, sixteen and a half, I remember having this presence that would always press against my chest; and I started being tested for ESP around sixteen. Because of a number of separate experiences I had had.

HUFFORD: How old were you when you heard the snurfling, would you guess?

PAT: About thirteen.

HUFFORD: That was about thirteen.

PAT: Yeah. There was——It was always accompanied by some kind of, um, snurfling sound. And I used to joke about it, that the snurfler came around.

HUFFORD: Right. And how old would you say you were when you saw the ape?

PAT: Fifteen.

HUFFORD: Fifteen. So following that you were being tested for ESP, and you had just the pressure. Is that right?

PAT: M-hm. And I stopped having this around seventeen, eighteen.

HUFFORD: Do you feel that the rocking of the bed was connected? That this whole thing represents a unit of some kind that developed, rather than separate things?

PAT: Looking back on it . . . yes. Because I remember . . . the physical feeling of not being able to move, and how I would try and wake myself out of either experience by trying to move my hands. And I remember that my eyes were always open, during both experiences.

HUFFORD: You mentioned that the ape had red eyes. Did they seem to glow or were they just plain red?

PAT: No, they glowed. I'm fairly sure that they glowed with something. . . . I made up an extensive set of, you know, rules for myself whenever this occurrence happened. I always used to think that if I were to ever cry out, out of fear, that whatever it was that was pressing against my chest would, you know, kill me. And so if an experience lasted too long, or I began to get frightened, rather than crying out I would just try and wiggle a finger. But I used to——I had made up an entire fantasy in my head that something was visiting me——ghosties.

HUFFORD: Did you talk much to other people about it?

PAT: Not really. Not really. Because I didn't think that other people would understand it. I spoke to my mother only because at the time I'd been having a——a set of different experiences in which I was communicating with a grandmother who was dead. And who was giving me information that I could not have known otherwise. And so my mother was willing to agree that whatever it was I experienced was unusual. And she would never laugh.

One of the most striking features of Pat's account is the violent motion of her bed during the early experiences. Although in the same general class as the feeling reported by Joanne's boyfriend that something sat on his bed, this is obviously a distinct sensation, involving continuous motion of the entire bed. Pat is certain that this motion was perceived visually as well as being felt, "And I used to see it happening." As do features of many Old Hag descriptions, this visual perception suggests a complex set of perceptions involving more than one sensory component.

Pat's report of having become accustomed to the experiences and learning to "enjoy the sensation of losing control" is unusual, but she obviously did not always feel enjoyment, and at times considerable fear was present. For example, during the episode with the "ape" Pat says, "I was really scared, because I remember seeing the ape and thinking how strong it was. . . . And I felt my esophagus being——pressed out." In each group of experiences, Pat's ability to relax and enjoy the odd happenings seems to have been the result of learning that physical injury would not result. Some people with repeated attacks have reported the same learning effect, but others have not. For example, a man who reported attacks once each week to ten days since childhood (the most frequent and consistent that I have found to date) stated: "I've been trying for maybe ten years to overcome the panic, because I think that if I can get myself to the point where I can overcome the panic, I can understand it. OK now, I can't totally understand what happens because consciously I'm afraid of nothing and when that occurs, that experience occurs, I'm in total absolute panic. There's no way out of it."

Both reactions—learning to enjoy the experience and continued fear—have been reported, and the difference seems to be the result of something inherent in the experiences rather than the number of attacks and the opportunity for learning. In some experiences, fear seems to be a natural response to potentially threatening perceptions. This was true, for example, in Case 6 above, in which the initial hearing of footsteps was not accompanied by any fear. John first felt fear when he saw the glowing figure enter his room. Although John did not overcome his fear during subsequent attacks, his reaction is similar to Pat's in that for both fear was experienced in a manner consistent with that of normal consciousness. The same was true in Case 10 in which the door closing initiated the experience. The example just quoted, on the other hand, in which ten years of constant effort had resulted in no diminution of fear during the attack, appears to indicate that fear can itself be an intrinsic feature. That victim went on to explain that though the apparitions he saw were not always ugly and did not always seem to be trying to do anything to him, his fear was still overwhelming. He said that he often wondered after an attack what the content of the experience held to elicit fear. This second pattern, the presence of fear as an intrinsic feature, seems to be somewhat more common than overcoming fear. But, since most cases involve infrequent attacks, and the perceptions are often threatening from the beginning, it is usually difficult to be certain which variation is present.

In Pat's case, as in most others, a lengthy effort was necessary to clarify the chronology, and parts of the phenomenology defied clarification. In comparing the results of such efforts to the greatly simplified accounts received secondhand, such as Joanne's description of her boyfriend's attack, it is evident that the latter lose an enormous number of nuances and complexities of detail, leaving a recognizable but impoverished description. This streamlining is, of course, a natural part of the process of oral transmission. The example of Old Hag accounts, however, suggests that some narratives have more to lose in this process than others. Those referring to bizarre and phenomenologically complex personal experiences, which means many of the events associated with supernatural belief, can lose details that could scarcely be guessed after the fact.

The "snurfling" noise stands out in Pat's account, and the analogy she uses to describe it—the watery "whoosh-squish" sound—is similar, though not identical, to some of the sounds mentioned in the remaining cases in this chapter.

The "ESP testing" that Pat describes and connects with the experience of communicating with her "grandmother who was dead" is intriguing. Such experiences are not frequently found juxtaposed to Old Hag attacks, and Pat separates them from the attacks she described in this interview. Nonetheless, two important questions arise: does her ESP experience indicate that Pat represents a special class of informant whose account should be treated separately; and what was its role in leading her to discuss her Old Hag attacks with her mother?

In Chapter 2, I noted that victims of Old Hag attacks frequently disclaim any general belief or interest in the supernatural and state that they have never had any other unusual experiences. But for those who have such interests and experiences a discussion of the Old Hag may lead into other weird topics just as my Old Hag interviews have occasionally led informants to volunteer descriptions of other peculiar experiences. In Case 4 above, for example, the respondent mentioned having once seen and heard her deceased grandfather. The interpretation of these occasional associations must largely proceed from an estimate of the distribution and significance of such experiences and beliefs. My own work and that of other investigators[13] suggest that experiences and beliefs of this kind are much more common than generally thought and that they are not connected in any compelling way with psychopathology or social deviance. This is true for the young and the well-educated as much as for the more isolated groups conventionally held to be the prime bearers of supernatural belief. Although the precise distribution and significance of various categories of experience and belief are not known with sufficient precision to allow a final consideration of their relationship to the Old Hag cases presented here, they do not seem to come up in this connection with disproportionate frequency. The greatest importance of these connections lies in what they reveal about the mechanisms governing the disclosure of such beliefs and experiences. Personal disclosure of this kind requires a minimum of trust and shared understanding, as well as an appropriate context. Furthermore, personal experience and belief must be called to mind in much the same way that jokes or any other category must be. Once all of these conditions have been met, a great variety of material, much of it related only remotely, will emerge. But, of course, it is relatively rare for all of these conditions to be met in most modern situations. The context of "psychic" or supernatural belief in Pat's case clearly made it much easier for her to discuss the experiences with her mother. "My mother was willing to agree that whatever it was I experienced was unusual. And she would

13. Jan Brunvand provides a useful discussion of the wide distribution of supernatural beliefs and a review of surveys on the subject in "Superstitions," a chapter in *The Study of American Folklore* (New York: W. W. Norton & Co. 1968). To date the best survey of such experiences is Andrew Greeley's *The Sociology of the Paranormal: A Reconnaissance,* Sage Research Papers in the Social Sciences, vol. 3, series no. 90-023 (Studies in Religion and Ethnicity) (Beverly Hills: Sage Publications, 1975).

never laugh." Her mother's acquiescence served the same function in allowing Pat's disclosure that the Old Hag tradition serves in Newfoundland.

The following case was received following a lecture to a group of medical students in the Pittsburgh area. In this case the reported attack took place after my talk, and I was fortunate enough to be able to get back to the student quickly for an interview. One point of particular interest here is the connection between the Old Hag attack and the preceding dreams. This informant used the term "incubus" because that is the term I had mentioned in the lecture.

Case 14
Black Male; 24 years of age

GEORGE: It happened last Thursday between 6:30 and 7, and it happened on the second floor of the library, which is unusual. And I've been studying. I've been preparing for a microbiology exam. And I've been putting in a lot of late hours, and I was tired and getting about four hours of sleep a night. Three hours sometimes and I was really very fatigued. And——I'd been studying up in the library for about three hours. And then I decided, "Well, I think you should go and lay down before you fall out. Because you're really tired," you know. I went to a sofa that's on that floor and I thought, "Well, I'll lie down on the sofa." And sofas being sofas I could really only lie down on it on my back, which was a bad choice. (Laughs.) So, I was lying on my back and had my hands across my chest, and I had a series of about three or four very quick dreams which to me made no sense, because they really didn't pertain to anything that—— that was familiar to me. They were very obscure episodes. I——I can't even describe them. But I know each one of them shocked me into waking suddenly. And I had the impression that they only lasted for about fifteen seconds apiece. And I know when I finally woke up from the last one I said, "Well, come on. Stop," you know. You know, "Why are you—your mind is just racing. Just relax and lie down. You'll be OK." So, I laid back down. And I closed my eyes, and hands folded across my chest——

And I had the impression that I could hear someone coming behind me. But I said, "Well, I don't——" You know, "They'll pass by." And I could hear the footsteps, and I said, "Well, they're going to pass on by me, and I hope they don't mess with me, whoever they are. I hope it's not somebody who comes by and messes with me." And the next thing I know I heard a female voice and——The voice wasn't really familiar to me. But the voice addressed me like she knew me. Or *it* knew me. And it said, "You knew that I would come." Something like that. And—— then there was a lot of talk about her——her face. Or her appearance. And she didn't want me to look at her or something, because of her face. And all this time I remember I had my eyes closed, and I kept thinking, "Well, who *is* this? Who's playing this——Who's who's talking?" And the next thing I know, my ——The pressure——on my arms. And I couldn't move. I couldn't move anything. And it was at that point where I said, "Hold it. Wait a minute. Who's messing around with me?" And I could still hear her talking, but I couldn't make out the words too clearly. But I'm saying, "Who's messing around? Let me see who's messing around. Let me see who's messing around with me."

And while I could still feel the pressure, I looked up and there was nobody there. But the pressure was still there. And that *scared me!* And I closed my eyes immediately again. And I was saying, "Oh, God, what's happening?" And I said, "I——don't believe——What's going on?" And I was trying to move and I could feel myself struggling to move. And I even——I was trying to scream. . . . I could feel this trying to scream. And——it still kept talking. And I——and I could still feel the pressure. And I opened up my eyes, and I tried——and I looked again. But all I could see was the library, and the books and the stacks, and I was trying to bend my head back to see, but I couldn't move my head at all. And that's how come I really knew I was awake. Because I could see the books. And I could see the library and everything that was around me there. And I know I could move my head from side to side, I could see the peripheral things. But I couldn't look back.

And finally I closed my eyes again. And the pressure was still there. And I said, "God, this is an incubus." And I——It surprised me that I was rational about it. About, you know, finally got around to being rational about it. And I said, "This is an incubus. Now you have to try to move." And then I figured, "Well the best thing for you to do is relax, and then try to move. And maybe that'll throw 'em off." So I relaxed, and the first thing I moved was my left hand.

And as soon as I moved all the pressure was gone, and I sat

up. And there was nothing there. And it——it was over. And I just sat there. And I thought about it and I thought, "Oh God, man, that was——that was an incubus." I said, "I can't believe that just happened." And I sat there for about fifteen minutes. And I've been very careful not to sleep on my back since then. And it still bothers me because I'm—I guess that I'm still afraid to sleep on my back now. And I'm even afraid to get into any position where I'm on my back, like sometimes I'll lie on my bed with my stereo, and I'll put on my headphones. And I'm afraid that I'll fall asleep on my back, listening to the headphones. And that something like that'll happen again.

But I couldn't——I couldn't understand the fact that it—— like I said, it spoke to me like it knew me. Like it was familiar. But the voice——I couldn't recognize the voice. And like I said, I tried twice to see who it was. And I couldn't even see anybody's hands or anything. But the pressure was there.

HUFFORD: And the pressure felt like hands?

GEORGE: Felt like hands. Yeah.

HUFFORD: How about, did you feel any pressure on the rest of your body? Or was the rest of your body just paralyzed?

GEORGE: It was just paralyzed. It was like my legs——Because the pressure was all in here [indicated chest area]. . . . And it was all pressing down. And I know I tried to move my midsection. And my legs. But they were just paralyzed. And like, I couldn't move. And then my head was like it was immovable. . . . My heart was really pounding. . . .

HUFFORD: The footsteps. What did the footsteps sound like?

GEORGE: I was trying at the time——It sounded like they were walking on linoleum rather than carpet [the library floor is carpeted in that area]. Which was——

HUFFORD: It was a kind of sharp sound?

GEORGE: Yeah. A *very* sharp sound. But you know, I didn't, I didn't even really think about that at the time.

HUFFORD: So it sounded like somebody with hard soles on their shoes walking on a hard surface?

GEORGE: Yes.

HUFFORD: And did it sound at all as if the feet were scuffed or anything like that? Or just clear, sharp single sounds?

GEORGE: No. Very clear. And it sounded——It sounded like a woman's shoes. Like almost maybe like heels.

HUFFORD: . . . Right, OK. Now the dreams that you had before, that shocked you into wakefulness. They were unpleasant? Is that right?

GEORGE: Yeah.

HUFFORD: So they were unpleasant. Frightening? Or ugly? Or what kind of affect did you get from them?

GEORGE: They were semi-frightening. But——It was more an effect of, "Why was I dreaming that?" You know, "Why was this on my mind?" You know?

HUFFORD: Yeah. Can you remember any of the details of the dreams? . . .

GEORGE: *Yeah.* There was *violence.* There was violence——I know at least one of them had to do with an animal. What kind of animal, I don't know. It was a very strange type of animal. But that was also, you know, "Why would I conjure up this unusual animal?"

HUFFORD: So, it was unusual?

GEORGE: Yeah, it wasn't anything *normal.*

HUFFORD: Do you remember whether it was big or small?

GEORGE: It was *big.*

HUFFORD: So——A big unusual animal, OK, that was being violent and frightening. That's really interesting.

GEORGE: And like I said, you know, I had those dreams right away [Snaps fingers.] And then I kind of said to myself, "Calm down. You're just going to relax. You're thinking about a lot of things." Because I don't know what it is about the library, but whenever I try to sleep in the library, I always have unusual dreams. And because I used to, last year, take breaks and go relax in those chairs on the first floor near the windows. Those big brown lounging chairs. And I'd sit in those chairs and stretch my feet out and lie with my head back. And I would have some very strange series of dreams. And they ——It would always happen.

HUFFORD: Would they always be unpleasant, or similar to these dreams?

GEORGE: Yeah. The majority of them. It was like——(Laughs.) I almost thought it was the library. You know, it *could* be the library and me. I don't know. . . . Every time, every time I've slept in the library I've always had unusual dreams.

HUFFORD: But never the rest of this?

GEORGE: No. Never. Not this incubus. And it was the first time, too, I'd ever fallen asleep on the second floor.

HUFFORD: How about the woman's voice now? . . . Young voice? Old voice?

GEORGE: Young voice.

HUFFORD: Young voice. High pitched? Low pitched?

GEORGE: Very calm. Not excited. And not harsh or anything.

HUFFORD: Soprano or alto?

GEORGE: Maybe soprano. Second soprano, maybe. It was not really *very* high.

HUFFORD: Any accent?

GEORGE: No. . . . I'm trying to think now if she said, "You knew I'd come," or "You knew I'd come back." Because that's been playing with me too. Because I've been really trying to recapture the whole moment, and to think about it. And I keep saying, "Now did she say, 'You——you knew I would come,' or 'You knew I would come *back.*'" . . .

I couldn't understand the thing about the face either. That scared me more than anything else. The fact that it was saying, "I didn't——I didn't want you——I don't want you to see my face," or "I didn't want you to see my face." And at that point it was like, "I'm not going to open my eyes and see what this is, because I don't want to see it." And then it got to the point where I said, "Oh, God, I've got to see what this is." And then that's when I opened my eyes for the first time. And there was nothing there, but there was the ceiling of the library and the books, and everything. And that's when I knew it was something other than somebody playing a trick on me.

In this case again, the informant was fatigued and took an afternoon nap. Here, however, another precursor is added—the dreams immediately preceding the attack. Such dreams occur as frequently as does fatigue and are present often enough to suggest a connection. There is, of course, the possibility that in cases in which a preceding dream is not reported it has been forgotten either before awakening or between the attack and the interview. Nevertheless, some connection between a preceding dream and subsequent Old Hag attack must now be considered. The only relationship that can be indicated now aside from the temporal one is the fact that the dreams tend to be frightening and violent. Violence is the most frequently mentioned descriptor and along with fear seems to be consistent with the nature of the Old Hag attack. One other point mentioned by George and others is that preceding dreams are generally incongruous: "They really didn't pertain to anything that . . . was familiar to me. They were very obscure episodes."

The fact that George heard a voice speaking to him is unusual but not unique. It is a feature that allowed George to show how much detail characterized his recollection. He specified that the voice was that of a "second soprano, maybe" and then expressed uncertainty that hinged on a single word, "You knew I would come," or "You knew I would come *back.*" Recollection of such fine details is common in these narratives.

In describing his approach to ending the attack, George says that he first relaxed and then struggled in an effort to "throw 'em off," suggesting that during the experience he believed that something was being done to him by an external agency and it was not a purely subjective experience. When he succeeded, he moved his hand. A majority who can recall exactly what they moved at the end of an attack have reported fingers, hand, or arm.

George's continued fear of sleeping on his back or even listening to his stereo in a supine position is a measure of the impact of the experience on him. Such effects on subsequent behavior are frequently reported. They are similar to the reaction of getting up and checking the house or searching for an explanation as behavioral indications of the motivating force of the experience.

Finally, George reports that he always has strange dreams in the library, although the connection with a place may not be as strong as George's comments suggest. Perhaps he has odd dreams when he naps, and most of his naps take place in the library. Even stronger connections with a single place are reported in Chapter 5, some of them involving more than one person. Such locations may indicate the presence of an external variable in the causation of the Old Hag attacks.

I was unable to tape record the next case, but it is illustrative of some major points. The events are described from my notes. This informant was unaware of my work or any other information relating to Old Hag attacks.

Case 15
White Female; 19 years of age

This young woman was in traction at a nearby hospital, being treated for a herniated disc. A physician who knew of my interests called me to suggest that I visit her to discuss a frightening experience she had had the previous day. The physician knew only that she had been badly frightened and had been given a sedative as a result. I immediately went to visit Sharon, who described the following events.

At about four in the afternoon she had decided to take a nap. Since this was in late summer, the room was still fully lit by sunlight. Because she was in traction she was, of course, lying on her back as she had since her admission about a week before.

Shortly after she closed her eyes she heard the door to her room open. She opened her eyes, but the rooms in this hospital have an "L" shape, which does not allow one lying in bed to see the door to the room. She then heard footsteps coming into the room. Sharon said that, as odd as this seems, her first thought was that several nurses were coming in with their shoes off. It sounded as if several pairs of feet were approaching in nylon stockings, shuffling across the room's wall-to-wall carpet. This footstep sound proceeded into the room and began to move around her bed, although no one was visible. Naturally this alarmed her, but when she attempted to reach the call button to ring for the nurse she found that she could not move. At this point her fear became intense.

Then she suddenly saw a bearded, male face suspended in mid-air in the vicinity of the short hallway to the door. It was totally unfamiliar to her, and it struck her as being malevolent.

It was staring intently at her. As she looked at this threatening face, she felt a very intense pressure forcing her head down into her pillow. She described this force as violent and painful. She continued to try to move in order to call the nurse but was unable to overcome the paralysis in spite of her terror.

Next she described the feeling of being lifted from her bed. She felt that she was at least two feet above the bed when she heard the door open again, and a nurse came in. The moment that the door opened the second time she felt herself dropped back onto the bed with considerable force, and all other features of the experience disappeared. She became hysterical at that point, and it required a real effort on the part of the nurse to calm her.

When Sharon had finished this basic description I asked her whether the feeling of pressure forcing her head into the pillow had ended when the lifting began and she replied, surprisingly, that it had not. I then asked whether she had felt that her legs and body had been lifted at an angle, leaving her head at bed level, and again she said that this was not the case. She stated that she had felt as if she were being lifted parallel to the bed while her head continued to be pressed into the pillow. She recognized that these sensations were contradictory, but insisted that this was how it had felt. I asked her whether her sheets had been in disarray following the experience and she replied that they had not. In fact, they had still been tucked in, and she recognized that this was also contradictory, but insisted that the perceptions still seemed absolutely real. She also mentioned that when she felt herself dropped back on the bed it had hurt her back and that the pain from that was still present, a day after the experience.

The rest of Sharon's hospital stay was uneventful.

The only variable at this point that seems consistently to indicate a substantially increased risk of Old Hag attack is the supine position. For those who do not ordinarily sleep on their backs, prolonged periods in this position may increase the likelihood of attacks, especially if the transition into normal sleep is delayed. In addition to patients in traction, I have found some evidence that systematic relaxation training or meditation in a supine position (as in the "corpse pose" in yoga) can produce a disproportionate number of attacks. I have no statistics on such populations at present, but the number of times that these contexts have been reported in this general investigation is suggestive. Sharon's experience is illustrative of this pattern.

Sharon's description of the peculiar footstep sounds aids in clarifying that feature. Through the first several years of interviewing people about these attacks, I simply accepted the term "footsteps" as self-explanatory and did not ask for further elaboration. Sharon's spontaneously offered details have led me to ask about the precise nature of the sound. In Case 14, George described a hard and distinct sound despite the presence of carpet in the area where he was taking his nap. Others have described such distinct footsteps, sometimes in settings that would naturally allow for such a sound and sometimes not. However, the kind of shuffling sound described by Sharon is much more common. Two other women, patients in the same hospital, described very similar sounds in connection with their own experiences. Both involved a "visitor" whose footsteps were heard. One said spontaneously that she heard "funny, 'whooshy' footsteps." When I probed, she was unable to clarify her meaning. The other woman simply noted that she heard footsteps. When she had difficulty elaborating, I asked her to make an analogy. I asked her to imagine how she would reproduce the sound if she could use whatever materials she wished. She thought for a few moments and then said that it was like "the sound of a block of wood being rubbed repeatedly over a piece of velvet."

In some instances this sound, which is usually but not always interpreted as footsteps, occurs in the midst of an attack that has other sensory features, as in Case 15 above. At other times the sound seems to accompany the "sensation of presence," as in the following case recalled from the age of "twelve or fourteen" by a white male, twenty-three years of age.

I remember waking up flat on my back. Paralyzed. . . . Terrified
beyond anything I'd ever experienced before. . . . Sensation of
pressure on my chest. The *terror!* The terror was both from
being paralyzed and I knew there was something in the room.
. . . Somewhere between me and the back door, quite close to
the room my parents were sleeping in was something. I don't
remember really seeing anything. . . . But I did hear something
between shuffling footsteps, heavy breathing, that kind of low
frequency, not regular, pulsating noise. That was very, very real.
Seemed to be coming toward me.

The quotation is from a description of this person's first experience. He described several others, and this sound occurred
in each. By the time of this interview, I had already obtained
the previous examples so I told him of some of those descriptions and asked whether they seemed like the sound he had
mentioned. In response to "stocking feet shuffling across the
carpet," he replied, "Yeah. It's not as if they're stepping. It's
more of a shuffle." But he considered wood on velvet to be
"too soft. It's not a harsh enough sound." I then asked him
about "something soft being dragged across a hard floor." He
said, "(Yes.) That's pretty much what I would think of in terms
of stocking feet on the rug."

This last analogy I had drawn from a composite description of an attack of the Swedish "mara" written by the folklorist
Carl Herman Tillhagen. All of the basic features of the mara
attack correspond to those of the Old Hag attack. The sound
of the approach is given by Tillhagen as follows: "The mara
could be heard coming. There was a click in the lock, there was
a patter crossing the floor, and there was a sound as if something soft were being hauled across the boards. Sometimes a
'sshh, sshh,' or some similar indefinite, weak sound could be
imagined."[14] The similarity of these sounds is striking, as is the
fact that even in the Swedish tradition they are often preceded
by a sound at the door or window.

14. Carl Herman Tillhagen, "The Conception of the Nightmare in Sweden," in *Humaniora: Essays in Literature, Folklore and Bibliography Honoring Archer
Taylor,* ed. Wayland Hand and Gustav Arlt (Locust Valley, N.Y.: J. J. Augustin, 1969), p. 317.

Perhaps the most important point about these sounds is that the discovery of a pattern required serious attention to phenomenological detail. As long as I allowed the term "footsteps" to suffice, only a general level of correspondence could be established. But reaching more specific levels of detail in experiences that are so unlike most others is not a simple matter, and I have found that the intentional use of analogy is helpful. I both request the subject to attempt an analogy and elicit reactions to the analogies of others. The victims of the attacks can, after all, be expected to be better at decoding the language used by other victims than the investigator can be. Analogy is helpful in the interview process, of course, for the same reason it is so often used spontaneously in the description of these events. No other resource is available for attempting a description of unshared subjective experience.

Another important feature of Sharon's account is her feeling that she was being simultaneously pressed down into the pillow and lifted off the bed. Such contradictory statements are not rare in Old Hag narratives, and they do not usually indicate poor reporting but rather represent phenomenological categories outside normal experience. Sharon's contradiction is a good case in point. Statements indicating impossibilities of location and/or motion have occasionally been reported from the beginning of this investigation. One description of the paralysis experience from my Newfoundland questionnaire study included the following: "very cold, dead weight—great fear with no apparent reason, couldn't move anything, only open eyes—had feeling of looking down at myself from separate place. . . . Perception of room unusually clear." A more recent questionnaire response from Pennsylvania stated: "At night I woke up and felt very tired, but not able to move, felt weak. Didn't seem like I was in myself." Although the clarity of the reference varies from one account to another, it seems reasonable to place all such statements under the technical headings of "distortions of body image" or "depersonalization." In more popular language these sensations seem to refer to at least incipient "out-of-body experiences."

The nature of the relationship between the Old Hag and out-of-the-body sensations is not yet clear, but it seems to be important. Some events in which the out-of-body experience is more completely developed, in the presence of Old Hag features, will be presented in Chapter 5. Unlike the accounts discussed there, Sharon's is one in which the sensations seem not to have been intense enough to lead her to conceptualize an actual separation or dual location. The rudimentary nature of the experience coupled with a lack of awareness of out-of-body feelings as a possible phenomenological category results in descriptions that sound confused and contradictory and further illustrate the problems of language presented by experiential features having no precedent in the knowledge of the subject. It also suggests that some of the other apparent contradictions in such narratives refer to incipient or rudimentary stages of other kinds of perception that may at times be presented in more easily expressed forms.

I have already discussed the problems of interpretation presented by the use of the word "dream" as an analogy to describe the Old Hag. In connection with Case 10 I went into some detail concerning the subjective features of the attacks which seem unlike ordinary dreams. In the next case an objective feature creates further difficulties for the dream-state hypothesis. The subject of this interview is a medical student who volunteered following a lecture that I gave to a class at his school.

Case 16
White Male; 23 years of age
JACK: Like I told you I think I have had this experience probably around a dozen times, and I think it started when I was probably an early teenager or something. It always occurred when I was just about either ready to fall asleep or shortly thereafter. I usually always sleep on my side. If not, I sleep on my stomach. But on occasion when I have slept on my back, that has been the only time that this has occurred.

Let's see——OK, terror. This is one thing, the fear, the *terror* that I would experience . . . because of the presence of someone else in the room. And me just being afraid to move or budge whatsoever. And my eyes could move and no other part. But I was sometimes afraid even to move my eyes, you know, for fear of the person, object or whatever it is, either being there, or——

You know, just looking down at me where I couldn't see him, or the few times——I think only two or three times I actually saw the image of a person.

HUFFORD: What did the image look like?

JACK: OK. When I *did* see it, it was a person not with any kind of a glow or radiance [a feature he had heard mentioned in my lecture]. In fact, that is just the opposite. It was very dark and shadowy, you know. Just like a silhouette. But it did have, like, a cape. A very transparent, like dark, cape, you know, that just hung down. . . . The face wasn't a clear face, but what it did have——and what scared me and made me not want to move ——was two very dark eyes. You know, piercing eyes looking at me. . . . I could make out distinct features of the eyes.

HUFFORD: It was like a normal eye except very dark?

JACK: Very dark eyes. They were piercing. They were just looking at me. It wasn't just like two dots. They were eyes and it sent a chill up my spine——tingling, you know, shivering type of sensation. . . . I didn't want to breathe or move in any way. I felt this hardness on my chest, you know . . . pressure was there. . . . An interesting thing is that I would think I was breathless, you know, and I just couldn't move. But in the first couple of times this did happen when I was thirteen——fourteen years old, I was still sleeping in a bed with my brother because then we only had one bed for the two of us. And he told me one time that I was breathing very heavily. And in fact one time he said, "What's the matter with you?" And when I looked over to him and moved my head, everything went, you know. And then my eyes were wide open. And I said, "Well, I just had a bad dream or something." And he says, "What's the matter," you know. And like I didn't know what to say to him. He said, "You were breathing really heavy and just staring straight out into space," you know.

HUFFORD: So your eyes were open?

JACK: They were open, and he turned to look at me and he *saw* my eyes were open. And I was just staring, you know. And I thought I was breathless, you know, and he said I was breathing. And then I scratched my head and——whew! It was over, you know. . . . He actually did nudge me, you know. And said, "What's the matter with you?" or something. And that's what brought me out of it. But before then I thought I was stock still and just staring at this thing. That was one of about four times out of twelve that I actually saw this person. . . . I did sense it coming into the room . . . like footfalls, you know.

HUFFORD: Did you see any motion from the figure?

JACK: Yes it moved across. That thing moved.

HUFFORD: Did it seem to move smoothly?

JACK: Smoothly, gliding even though there were footfalls, you know. Which didn't make sense, but it *wasn't* like a walk. It was a smooth glide across. . . . About the second or third time that I had seen this, the object or person did actually come along side me, and I was afraid to look up at it. I was afraid to look into those eyes, you know. And so I didn't move anything. I wanted to jump right out of bed or something. I was trying to figure out a fast way of getting away from it, but I just felt that it had more of a fix on me than I had on it, and I was just scared to do anything then. I did twice try to jump out and I *couldn't*. I just couldn't move.

HUFFORD: What kind of height?

JACK: Tall. Another reason why I didn't want to move.

HUFFORD: Yeah. Normal tall?

JACK: Well. I'm six one, and it seemed that if I jumped out of bed it would still be above me——closer to seven feet. It was *tall*. And I was paralyzed.

There was one funny thing when I was in college. This was just a couple years ago. This was one of the times when I saw the person right at the foot of my bed. And this is one of the only parts of the room that is illuminated, like, you know. At first, now, the thing is right behind the foot of my bed. There is a cupboard which can be open sometimes, and I can see darkness. And a couple of times I thought that was it, you know? But it wasn't because those times I would just look up and I'd say, "That ain't it! That's not it!" But I knew it when it *was* there! I mean, this was no cupboard or anything! I could see the shadow of the veil, and *everything*. And there are no trees at this part of the house, so it's not a tree rippling effect. I checked that, you know, the following night. You know, to see if it could be just leaves or something going through a street light. It wasn't that. . . .

(That time) when I was in college a couple of years ago I tried to project myself away from my body where I could sneak around this person or something, you know. Because I was afraid to move. I figured, "If I move, he's got me," you know.

I didn't know whether it was a man or a woman because I couldn't see any other features other than very plain, but very piercing, dark eyes. And it seemed like it had a hat or something, and long hair, you know. Brown hair, not black. That was strange. Like everything else was dark except brown hair, you know. So this all made me think that I was actually seeing something instead of just a silhouette. And I tried to project myself out this one time, so I could see him . . . you know, where he's just looking down at me or something. Maybe scare him away and get him out of there. But it turned out I was even afraid to do that for fear that this person would sense that, you know.

HUFFORD: Have you ever had any out-of-body sensations that gave you the impression that you could do that?

JACK: No. I've tried to do that, you know, just in playing around sometimes at night. But just when I'm laying there sometimes I can't get to sleep. So I will just pretend like I'm getting really relaxed. Stuff like that.

HUFFORD: Had you ever done that at the time you had the first experience?

JACK: That wasn't the case at that time. . . . The first time it happened I think I was just falling asleep. And I was in a supine position. And I opened my eyes. And I looked around. And someone was there, and I couldn't really see. And I noticed the stiffness coming over my body, and it just getting stiffer, and *stiffer,* and I just became stock still!

HUFFORD: So you were not immediately paralyzed the first time? You felt it as a progressive thing?

JACK: Right. . . . It's like I opened my eyes and everything was OK. And then, "No it isn't," you know. "Everything is *not* OK!"
. . . Sometimes I just try and scare it away, but I couldn't, you know. And I tried psyching it out or something by just looking at it, but I couldn't because those things are staring back at me too hard! The image would just go sometimes. And a lot of times I would still be afraid to move for fear it didn't really go——it just moved.

HUFFORD: Sometimes the image would move out of sight while you remained paralyzed?

JACK: That's right. That's right.

HUFFORD: Were there times that it didn't move, but then simply disappeared when you were suddenly able to move?

JACK: Right.

HUFFORD: . . . Does it dissolve? Does it simply blink out? Or what?

JACK: . . . It, like, senses that I'm going to move, that I'm ready to do something, and then it will turn and move away. Just when I'm really at the height of my anxiety, so to speak, you know. Just when I'm ready to jump but I haven't actually moved. I can't say that I was moving or anything when the thing just took off. It was like "I *am* going to do something," you know.

HUFFORD: So it was your decision to do something that led to its going away?

JACK: Right.

HUFFORD: Have they all terminated with your getting out of it? Or have you ever gone to sleep from it?

JACK: It's tough to go to sleep that way. Nearly every time when they've left I've stayed awake for nearly the rest of the night. And I generally did fall back to sleep, but it wasn't for an hour or so afterwards. . . . Walking around the house checking every-thing's OK, you know——the door is locked.

HUFFORD: . . . Have you ever told anyone else about it?

JACK: No. No. I haven't.

HUFFORD: (Could you describe the figure further?)

JACK: It was a human figure, and the outline of the silhouette of the human figure was there beneath this sheer, very dark veil.

HUFFORD: You could see the entire outline like arms and legs?

JACK: Right. A lot of times I was just focusing on those eyes, wondering what it was going to do and that was it.

HUFFORD: . . . Now with the face all you could see was the eyes? Was there any covering over the eyes or the face?

JACK: No. No. OK, now this is the reason why I see it like this. There is a street light that comes in and projects a shadow like this——like a 45 degree angle. And where its trunk and upper body are . . . is relatively dark compared to the lower half. And when this——he or she——would, like, move to the side of my bed——it's happened about three or four times——I could see like the outline of the whole face. It wasn't like there was just eyes, and then nothing and then the trunk. I could see the whole face, but I never really could say I could see the mouth, you know. I could see a nose outline as it turned sideways. But the thing did gaze away from me as it would walk around to the side, and I was figuring it was up to something, you know. . . . But I didn't know what it wanted, you know. . . . I never thought it was going to attack me, but that's the whole thing. I wasn't in fear of my life, but I was in fear of, "What is this and what's going to happen?" you know. "What's going to happen next?" Never in fear of my life.

HUFFORD: You'd never heard of this happening to anyone else?

JACK: That's right.

HUFFORD: (Can you think of anything that may have caused it?)

JACK: No. I can't say that it was before or after a period of stress, you know. After I had studied a lot . . . or something like that. This was just something that in fact, if anything, was when I was in a good mood, and nothing spectacular was going on at that time when this would happen.

HUFFORD: . . . OK. Do you feel that you were awake when it happened?

JACK: I was awake. I was awake! . . . There is no way that anyone can convince me that I wasn't. But this was no dream, like, because I can recall a lot of dreams, you know. . . . But this is nothing like that. This is something where I opened my eyes and I saw it, you know. I sensed its presence and I looked and I saw it. Or I sensed its presence and I didn't look, but I knew it was there. . . . It was something that was *real* and if I could have been able to go over and tackle it or something——I wanted to do that, but I found myself unable. If I could reach out it would be tangible.

One of the most striking details in this description is that the subject's brother saw that his eyes were open during the experience, as he states clearly several times. Several others have reported the same observation. Most attacks do not come to the attention of a second party while in progress, but some do. In each of these that I have found, the other person has been alerted by unusual breathing sounds. All second parties I have spoken with have either said that the victim's eyes were open or that they did not notice the eyes because of the darkness of the room and the shortness of the interval before a normal state was achieved. These cases do not rule out the possibility that some attacks take place with eyes closed, and a very few victims have stated that they were either unable or unwilling to open their eyes during the attack (for example, George's temporary decision to keep his eyes closed in Case 14), but they suggest that some victims are correct in their subjective impression that their eyes were open during the attack. And this in turn is another major difference between the Old Hag and ordinary dreams.

The brother's observation that Jack was breathing heavily during the attack has also been supported by others who have seen the end of someone else's experience. A man in Newfoundland who has suffered frequent attacks told me: "My vocal cords are paralyzed, but I've got my wife conditioned so that when I start to hyperventilate, she'll reach over and shake me." Enough such observations have been reported to justify the tentative conclusion that some cases of presumed suffocation are in fact instances of hyperventilation. Hyperventilation gives a subjective feeling of suffocation, and the overbreathing is often not noticed. In other cases, however, both objective and subjective reports suggest either apneic episodes[15] or la-

15. The possibility that apnea (transient suppression of respiration) may occasionally be involved is further supported by some of the descriptions of sleep apnea in the literature. See, for example, Christian Guilleminault et al., "Sleep Apnea in Eight Children," *Pediatrics* 58 (1976):23–30; and Christian Guilleminault et al., "Sleep Apnea Syndrome Due to Upper Airway Obstruction: A Review of 25 Cases," *Archives of Internal Medicine* 137 (1977):296–300. The possible presence of apnea is also connected with the complicated relationship between the Old Hag and stage 4 night terrors discussed in Chapter 4. See, for example, Henri Gastaut and Roger Broughton, "A Clinical and Polygraphic Study of Episodic Phenomena during Sleep," *Recent Advances in Biological Psychiatry* 7 (1965):216.

bored or strangled breathing. And a large number of the reports indicate that the victim was not aware of anything unusual connected with respiration. The safest conclusion is that two or more patterns may be present in cases involving unusual respiratory sensations, but that respiration can be totally unconnected in a sizable fraction of attacks.

Jack's description of his visitor's eyes is dramatic and compares with Ron's description in Case 10, for example, Jack's statement that "what scared me and made me not want to move——was two very dark eyes." At another point he says that he was "afraid to move. . . . sometimes afraid even to move my eyes," and again, "If I move, he's got me." These statements illustrate the perception of immobility as intentional because of fear rather than as a result of paralysis, as noted above in connection with the problems of designing a phenomenologically adequate questionnaire about the Old Hag. In this case, however, Jack goes on to give descriptions that indicate that he was unable rather than unwilling to move, for example: "I did twice try to jump out (of bed) and I *couldn't.* I just couldn't move," or "I wanted to (go over and tackle it) but I found myself unable." Similar is his statement that he "noticed the stiffness coming over my body, and it just getting stiffer, and *stiffer,* and I just became stock still!" This sounds more like the onset of a paralysis than a product of fear. Jack's is also one of the few descriptions I have received that showed a progressive onset of immobility. This evidence suggests that perceptions of immobility can vary not only from one case to another but also within a single case. As with the varying descriptions of respiratory interference, these may indicate not merely differing perceptions of a single phenomenon, but rather genuine differences in the event. However, more data are needed to reach a conclusion or to attempt an interpretation of these differences.

Jack describes the sound of "footfalls" in an apparent "smooth glide." He spontaneously remarks that this combination "didn't make sense, but it *wasn't* like a walk." This feature invites comparison with the descriptions of footsteps in George's (14) and Sharon's (15) cases, although it raises questions rather than answering them. Close attention must be paid to the descriptions of accompanying sounds in future investigations of these experiences.

In connection with Ron's attack (10), I discussed his repeated and serious attempts to determine whether he had been dreaming. Such efforts are a characteristic response. Jack made similar efforts to explain his experience as a misperceived cupboard door in a dark room or "a tree rippling effect." Consideration of natural hypotheses, followed by attempts to verify them, shows up repeatedly in such narratives. This reaction is very different from the popular stereotype of "supernatural experience." As mentioned in connection with Hobbes's dream explanation, the record of Old Hag attacks demonstrates that we must not make assumptions about the critical faculties of informants who report bizarre experiences.

In describing his efforts to "project" himself to a point behind his visitor, Jack at first appears to be speaking as one who has cultivated "astral projection" but then says that he had only "pretended." This interview took place before I realized that out-of-body sensations were consistently, though infrequently, described in Old Hag accounts. Had I considered the possibility of any connection at that time I would have pressed Jack on the point. In retrospect, I wonder if he was avoiding a full discussion of his beliefs and experiences in this connection. This was one of the suggestive bits that eventually led me to consider the possibility of a major connection between these two forms of experience, a topic that will be dealt with in more detail in Chapter 5.

Jack makes no connection between his Old Hag attacks and either stress or fatigue, even saying that the experiences were more common when he "was in a good mood." This example does not mean that stress, fatigue, or depression may not play a role in some experiences but, with similar statements by others, it indicates that they are not necessary ingredients in what is almost certainly an event with multiple causes.

Finally, not only does Jack's impression that he could "scare it away" seem incongruous, given how frightened he was, but it provides some insight into Jack's feelings about what may actually have been happening. Certainly one does not attempt to scare away a hallucination. This impression of reality is further indicated by his statement, "It was something that was *real* and if I could . . . reach out it would be tangible." Although Jack was a well-educated, middle-class young man, who had never told anyone else of his attacks or ever heard of anyone else's, he was nonetheless left with the conviction that his visitor was real and external. The difference between a hallucination and an objectively real experience is, at least on the face of it, a matter of interpretation, and we tend to consider such decisions culturally provided. Here, however, a person made an interpretation that seems to run counter to his culturally provided expectations and did so without outside guidance or social support. His allusions to "projection" may, of course, indicate a hidden connection with a subculture that provided guidance and support. This is plausible, but considering the entire run of accounts, it is hard to avoid the impression that most victims share the conviction of reality. This is the significance, for example, of the act of getting up and checking through the house after an attack. Even when victims are unprepared to express their strong impression of objective reality verbally, their behavior often eloquently indicates its presence. Such experiences, then, can be more intrinsically realistic than we are at first likely to imagine. I must add, though, that this level of "realness" is not always present.

The next account further describes the difficulty of articulating the perception of immobility in the Old Hag. The woman in this case had never heard of my work and was not familiar with the similar experiences of others. She is one of the subjects I have found by simply talking to anyone who wishes to discuss an "unusual" or "supernatural" experience. The initial contact was made through her adult son on the basis of what the family considered to be a poltergeist. They repeatedly heard a door open and close when no one was apparently near it, the sound of footsteps in the hallway, and occasional knocking sounds on the walls. All members of the family (mother, father, and two children) had heard these sounds frequently from the time they built the house until after the children were grown and had left home. They had not heard them "recently." They thought it unusual that a new house should have such phenomena associated with it, but this was tentatively explained by the possibility that the house had been built over "an Indian grave," as had been suggested by a neighbor.

The transcript presented here picks up just as the discussion of the "poltergeist" finished. The third party in this interview is the adult son.

Case 17
White Female; in mid-fifties

BILL: How about your experience the other——a couple weeks ago?

JEAN: Somebody standing by the bed?

BILL: Yeah.

JEAN: That——I don't know what it was. Felt like it was a woman. I didn't see anything. I was lying on my side, and felt something touch my side lightly. And I woke up and I could feel someone watching me, beside the bed. And it felt like, to me, that it was a woman. And I wanted to call your Daddy, Bill. See, we have the twin beds. But I couldn't, you know. I just——And it just felt like they were standing there, quite awhile. And they just went out of the room. I didn't hear anything either, but they were there! Somebody, something was there. ——You think I'm goofy, I bet.

HUFFORD: No, no, I've heard lots of people——

JEAN: *Something* was there! Something or someone was standing there.

HUFFORD: And you said you tried to call?

JEAN: I wanted to, but I couldn't. I was afraid to. I really was.

HUFFORD: You felt something bad would happen if you did?

JEAN: I didn't know. I just felt maybe it would be better just to be quiet, you know.

HUFFORD: Did you turn over, or move at all?

JEAN: Not then. Not till later.

HUFFORD: Why not then? Did you try to turn so that you could see?

JEAN: No. It was dark in there. But something was there!

HUFFORD: Were you afraid to move then? Or did you——

JEAN: I was afraid. Yeah. I was. And even afterwards I was afraid.

BILL: You told Dad about it then?

JEAN: In the morning. Yeah, I told him.

HUFFORD: What did he say?

JEAN: He said, "Why didn't you call me?" I said, "I couldn't."

HUFFORD: That really interests me because some people consistently will say that they "couldn't," but other people say that they were "afraid to" (move). And I'm very interested in knowing the difference.

JEAN: I don't know. I *didn't* move, but whether I could have, I don't——I don't know. I really don't know. I *didn't* anyway.

HUFFORD: . . . How long did it last?

JEAN: Oh——maybe five or six minutes I stayed like that. I really don't know, but just an idea.

HUFFORD: Yeah. Then as soon as it left, did you move then?

JEAN: No. I was afraid. I stayed still quite a while. And then I was afraid to go back to sleep.

HUFFORD: For fear of what?

JEAN: That it would come back, whatever it was.

HUFFORD: OK, did you feel anything else other than that it was something watching you?

JEAN: No.

HUFFORD: You said that you felt that it was a woman?

JEAN: Yeah. And I don't know why. But I just felt that it was.

HUFFORD: Did you have any——

JEAN: And staring.

HUFFORD: Staring?

JEAN: *Staring!*

HUFFORD: And that it was not moving?

JEAN: Just standing there staring.

HUFFORD: . . . You didn't feel necessarily, then, that she wanted to injure you?

JEAN: No——No.

HUFFORD: So that wasn't the reason for the fear?

JEAN: But I was frightened anyway. I——I'm getting goose-pimples just talking about it. I didn't feel I was in danger, but I still wasn't taking any chances. I was afraid.

HUFFORD: . . . OK. You said that sometime before that something else had happened.

JEAN: Three——three or four years ago, I'd say, I was lying in bed and I felt the covers being——the cover and the sheet—— being pulled slowly down. Not to the side. Not slipping off the bed, but pulling straight down till I was not covered at all. I felt it going, and I reached down and pulled it back. Then I felt it again, and it went straight down to the bottom of the bed. Then I *didn't* reach down and pull them back. I heard nothing. I was afraid. I couldn't move, and I did *not* go back to sleep that night at all! Because it went straight——It wasn't as—— You know how something will slip off to the side. It wasn't— —It went *straight* to the bottom of the bed and it was winter-time and I was *cold,* but I would not reach down and pull it back. . . . Went down to the bottom, you know, just pulled straight down into a pile.

HUFFORD: How were you lying?

JEAN: On my back, and I don't usually lie on my back. But that night I was.

HUFFORD: How long did it take the covers to get all the way down?

JEAN: Well——they went slowly. Maybe three or four minutes, you know. It was very slowly, but it was *straight down.*

HUFFORD: . . . About the same length of time both times?

JEAN: I would say that. Yeah. That was *really* scary. That never happened before or since. But it *really* scared me.

HUFFORD: . . . Did you have the feeling of someone being there?

JEAN: Oh, someone *had* to be.

HUFFORD: . . . In the more recent one that you told me about it wasn't that you felt someone *must* be there. It was that you just felt that someone *was* there.

JEAN: *Was.* Right.

HUFFORD: Did you have a sensation like that the first time, when the covers were taken down? Of a person being there?

JEAN: I knew someone was there. I didn't *feel* them being there, but I knew that someone *had* to be there.

HUFFORD: Because of the covers moving.

JEAN: Right. Right.

HUFFORD: . . . Let's see, now, you were able to move this time for sure, because you did reach down and pull the covers?

JEAN: The first time. I pulled the——And *why* I did it I don't know, you know. It's just a reaction.

HUFFORD: Were they hard to pull?

JEAN: No. No. Came right back up——But they went right back down again.

HUFFORD: Went very slowly?

JEAN: Yeah.——*That* was scary!

HUFFORD: Did they go all the way off your feet at the end?

JEAN: Right. I'm short. I don't go clear to the bottom of the bed, and they were in a pile below my feet.

HUFFORD: Do you recall what the pile was like? Was it——

JEAN: Just——Just as if you would have done it yourself, you know, pulled them down. Without folding them.[16]

16. Traditional accounts of ghosts pulling the covers off sleepers are common, as indicated by the fact that two numbers are given to the subject in the *Motif Index:* "E279.3. Ghost pulls bedclothing from sleeper" and "E544.2. Ghost pulls off blanket from sleeper." Louis Jones, in "Ghosts of New York," *Journal of American Folklore* 57 (1944):249, reported, "One of the commonest activities of ghosts is the pulling of bedclothes off the living."

Old references to this are also easy to find. For example, in 1588 the Capuchin author Father Noel Taillepied stated, "A Spirit will sometimes suddenly draw and switch away the quilt and blankets from a bed, linen and all"

HUFFORD: . . . And after they went down the second time, what did you do? Anything?

JEAN: Just stayed there. Just stayed still.

HUFFORD: With your eyes open?

JEAN: Eyes open. Yeah.

HUFFORD: How long did you stay like that?

JEAN: I stayed like that till morning. I couldn't go back to sleep.

HUFFORD: But you didn't get up? And you didn't call out?

JEAN: No. No, I was afraid to get up too.

HUFFORD: And afraid to call out, too?

JEAN: Yeah.

HUFFORD: Then as it started to get light in the morning, what did you do?

JEAN: Then I got up. I get up usually around quarter of six, and in the winter it's usually dark then.

HUFFORD: . . . You've talked about the covers being pulled off with your husband? Did you tell him about that? What did he say about that?

JEAN: I don't believe he said anything. I don't think he believed me, or thought I imagined it. . . .
   Now I don't know whether this would have anything to do with it or not. But I set the clock every night. And quite often in the morning, just when the clock's ready to go off, I hear my name. And I reach over and turn off the clock. It didn't go off yet——I hear, "Jean."

HUFFORD: . . . Does it sound like someone in the room, or does it sound like a voice in your head?

JEAN: I'd say it was a voice in the room.

(*A Treatise of Ghosts,* trans. and ed. Montague Summers [London: Fortune Press, n.d., reprint Ann Arbor: Gryphon Books, 1971], p. 78; originally published in Paris in 1588.)

HUFFORD: . . . Well, that's very interesting. You've got several really interesting accounts there.

JEAN: Well, they happened. At least *I* believe they happened.

This family's "poltergeist" provided the basic context for my interview with Jean. Since the family takes the haunting of their house seriously enough at least to consider the possibility that it was caused by building on an Indian grave and since Jean considers her experiences to be in some sense real, it would have been reasonable for her to have considered the two bedroom visits another manifestation of the basic haunting. But she did not insist on such a connection. In fact, at one point during the interview we had the following brief discussion of the relationship between the first experience (having the covers pulled off) and the second (being "watched"):

> HUFFORD: Does that one seem to you connected to the other one? The one you had more recently where you thought someone was in the room?
>
> JEAN: Not necessarily. It's been quite a long time, you know, in between.

Jean has had several experiences, then, which she considers supernatural or paranormal. And at another point during the interview she said, "I believe that there are spirits." Nonetheless, she was cautious in interpreting the specifics of her own experiences. This primacy of observation over interpretation has been common among individuals whose world view is fairly general about the paranormal. Only those who are firmly a part of a strong tradition that speaks directly to such experiences as the Old Hag seem prepared to make highly specific statements about their meaning, beyond the very common conviction that they are somehow real. This is another indication that the impression of reality is not in these cases dependent upon the expectability or even acceptability of the attacks. In fact, the impression of reality is strong even in those instances in which the victim, unlike Jean, had previously considered paranormal experience to be impossible. Once again it

appears that the conventional notions of the relationship between supernatural belief and observation are too simple and
are based on too many untested assumptions.

Jean's description of her experience of being "watched"
provides an additional example of the complex impressions
sometimes reported in connection with the sensation of presence. Jean says that she could "feel someone watching me.
. . . and it felt like . . . it was a woman." She states explicitly
that she did not see or hear anything, but she *felt* a presence,
its gender and its activity. Her strong impression of "staring"
is similar to the statements of Ron (10) and Jack (16) except
that each of them clearly saw the eyes of their visitors whereas
Jean could not. The repeated descriptions of such direct perceptions underline the phenomenological complexity of these
events and the need for a cautious approach to the analysis of
feelings when they occur in the presence of possible causes.

The way Jean reported her immobility is also complicated.
She spontaneously used both "couldn't" and "afraid to" to describe her failure to move or call out. Then when I asked her
to explain exactly which she meant, she could be certain only
of the fact that she "didn't." When her covers were first pulled
off, she reached down and pulled them back. After they were
pulled down a second time, not only did she not pull them
back, but she lay in the cold and dark "till morning." In cases
such as this in which there is some movement at the beginning,
followed by immobility that may or may not be voluntary, we
cannot rule out the possibility of a false positive, that is, that
the phenomenon was not actually an Old Hag attack. But
Jean's account is included here because all four of the primary
features of the Old Hag are present.

The experience of hearing her name called in the morning does not have any necessary connection with the Old
Hag. I have quoted that part of her account here because,
first, it indicates the sort of associations that Jean herself is
considering as she endeavors to integrate all of these experiences into her understanding. As I have already noted, the
topic of the Old Hag attacks commonly brings up other bizarre subjects. I have also included it because reports of
"spectral name calling" appear in Case 20 below in which the

Old Hag turned up in the presence of an intense series of other frightening phenomena.

The next case, the last one for this chapter, raises one final sensation that has been reported with sufficient frequency and intensity to make it intriguing. This is what those who mention it most often call "tingling." The woman who described this experience is a colleague from another university. She had heard me lecture about the Old Hag several years before this interview.

Case 18
White Female; 33 years old

BETTY: There was the one that happened to me on the airplane. I was very certain that I was awake then. I was lying across at least two, if not three, seats on a plane. I was buckled in. I was tired. . . . It was a long cross-country flight. And——I strapped myself in and I lay down. And that one and the other I just told you about were unique in that those were the only two in which I was on my side. [She was on her back in all the others.] This one I was on my side. I was lying on my side, and I had one arm touching the armrest and possibly the edge of the plane by the window. And my feet were touching the armrest at the other end. And I woke up, and there were flashes and I thought we were in a thunderstorm. . . . I looked up at the ceiling of the plane, and it seemed to me that the light was flickering. And now I realize it wasn't the——It couldn't have been the light in the airplane because it was a big round light that was flush with the surface of the plane. I don't think any airplanes have that kind of light. But that light, that was flickering.

And I felt this——tingling in my body, and I was——I was very scared because I thought it was electrical. It felt like a mild electrical shock. And I had the idea that somehow I was completing part of a circuit, and the fact that one hand was touching the side of the plane and the other——my feet were touching the armrest, that there was electricity moving through that. And I couldn't move, and I was sure that something terrible was happening. I thought I was being electrocuted, that's what I really thought.

And I wanted to get the attention of another passenger. And I could see the person across the aisle from me . . . (but) I couldn't talk and they weren't responding to my distress. And

I kept trying to move. I was really sure that that was——I had to get one of my arms out. But I also felt that it was "glued" by the electrical current. And finally I moved this arm, the arm my head was lying on, and it stopped.

HUFFORD: . . . Do you still feel that you were awake during it?

BETTY: Yeah . . . I do.

HUFFORD: . . . Your feeling of fear.——Did you have that from the moment you awoke?

BETTY: Yes.

HUFFORD: . . . Was the fear entirely the result of thinking you were being electrocuted?

BETTY: It was that and the fact that I couldn't move. I felt that I was going to die. I was very certain that I would die.

HUFFORD: Because you thought you were being electrocuted? Or just, you also felt you were going to die?

BETTY: Yeah. *Both.* I thought that somehow I was not going to breathe anymore.

HUFFORD: Were you having trouble breathing? Did you feel suffocated?

BETTY: I don't——I have to think about that——I'm not aware of feeling suffocated——I felt, I felt the paralysis strongly, and I felt that that was going to keep me from being able to breathe. . . . It was more than just the electrical activity that was concerning me, because that wasn't really painful.

HUFFORD: . . . Describe the electrical feeling more now.

BETTY: . . . It was going from one place to another place. It was going from my head to my feet. And it felt——It felt a lot like ——Once when I was a child I climbed up on the kitchen sink and either it was poorly grounded or it was damp, and I pulled a metal chain on a lamp. And I got . . . a fairly strong shock. And I couldn't let go of the chain. And that's exactly what this felt like. I felt frozen to the seat.
    . . . (And there is) something else that I remember about this. And that was that it did not feel like a surface tingling. It felt like a *deep* tingling. Not even a tingling——It was more like a

vibration than a tingling. . . . Not like it was on the surface at all, or anything. It was right in my *bones!*

Others have reported seeing a light float into the room or a light connected with a figure, and Betty's description of the flickering light in the ceiling of the plane is similar to many of the former, although in her case the light did not move. She saw it flickering against the ceiling of the plane and at first believed it to be a fixture. An extensive discussion of its appearance (not given above) revealed that she saw no fasteners, frame, or other hardware features, only a smooth, "very even . . . sort of a warm light. It was round and it was flush with the ceiling." She subsequently checked and learned that there was in fact no such light source in the plane, nor has she ever seen one on another plane. All other features of the environment, though, were the same during and after the experience.

The most important part of Betty's description for our present purposes is her account of the "tingling" or "vibration." Although this is not a frequently reported feature, it has recurred consistently and the sensation always appears to be clear. However, it does not seem always to be experienced in exactly the same way. In the following example, the perceptions are similar to Betty's. The person reporting the experience is a twenty-three-year-old male medical student.

> I guess it was about——somewhere in this past year. I was lying on my back in bed, and I was, you know, getting ready to go to sleep. And I closed my eyes and, I don't know how long after that, I was sort of awakened by a tingling feeling all over my body. And it was like, kind of the sort of tingling feeling you get when your limbs are asleep. But my whole body felt this way. Felt like electricity. And I couldn't imagine what it was, and it became really intense. And I felt as if I——my body was being lifted. Or my body was staying still, but I felt like——as if, you know, I was moving away from my body. So . . . I figured, "I'm dying."

The use of the word "tingling," the reference to electricity, and the impression that he was dying are similar to Betty's report. The following example involves a similar but not identical sensation. This description came up in connection with a paralysis attack that occurred while the subject was sitting in a chair reading. This account was given by the twenty-four-year-old female whose other experiences were reported in Case 11 above.

> JOANNE: Something forced me to close my eyes again . . . and I felt the tingles on my shoulders. And then I felt two people. And I know they were men and they were young . . . and they were fooling around with my shoulders and tickling my ribs. And then the one had his hand around my neck. And it was at a funny point because it tickled me——around my ears and neck. . . . I was so afraid.

> HUFFORD: Did they seem either friendly or unfriendly? Evil or good?

> JOANNE: Friendly at first . . . (and) then I became afraid.

> HUFFORD: . . . Then what did you begin to feel?

> JOANNE: Something evil, but I didn't know what. Not necessarily sexual, either, (even though) they were touching me.

> HUFFORD: OK. You said you felt a tingling on your shoulders. Was that throughout the experience?

> JOANNE: No. It was in the beginning. . . . It was——pleasurable, and it was very light. Like when your foot goes to sleep, but it felt better than that. Because when your foot goes to sleep that really annoys you, but this wasn't really annoying. It was more pleasant than that.

This description shares with the preceding one a reference to the feeling of a limb being asleep, but it differs in that the sensation was pleasant and that it seems to have been less intense. The precise connection with the feeling of being tickled would be interesting to know, but Joanne was never able to clarify it. These may have been two different perceptions, or they may have been two aspects of the same perception. The tickling sensation was probably what gave Joanne the possible sexual interpretation. Although she discounted any conscious sexual component, that possibility remains.

Any possibility that the reports of tingling resulted from an actual shock is ruled out by the varying circumstances in which they are reported and the absence of any subsequent observation of the sensation after the paralysis episode ended. The possibility that the sensation is in fact due to a limb "falling asleep" does not fit with the fact that the sensation is usually felt all over the body and that unlike the "sleeping limb" sensation this tingling ends completely and suddenly when the paralysis is terminated. These two analogies are almost always the ones used to describe this feeling and can therefore be considered useful descriptors, although they are not acceptable as explanations. This point is mentioned here because of the natural tendency to look for individual explanations for discrete features of such dramatic experiences. The consistent presence of a stable pattern in Old Hag attacks, however, will require a comprehensive explanation.

These three examples are representative of the accounts of "tingling" that I have received. The sensation can vary in intensity and may be either deep or superficial. It may be either pleasant or unpleasant, and the difference seems at least in part determined by intensity. Tingling has sometimes been reported in connection with distortions of body image as in the second example quoted here ("I was moving away from my body."), but each does frequently occur in the absence of the other.

The representative cases presented and discussed in this chapter comprise a sketch of the phenomenology of Old Hag attacks occurring as culturally isolated events. This sketch is not necessarily final, and many of its components are far from clear, but it is as accurate and systematic a picture as is currently possible without forcing any preconceived pattern on the data. These cases also make it abundantly clear that recognizable Old Hag attacks of great complexity can and do occur in the absence of explicit models. Also, the victims have supported the hypothesis that a combination of cultural constraints and difficulties of expression have played a major part in keeping the existence of this body of experience hidden when it is unaccompanied by a connected tradition. But, however adequate this explanation may seem for popular ignorance of the experience, it is not sufficient in the case of science. The question then naturally arises as to whether any of the sciences that touch on human experience have recorded the existence of the Old Hag.

4

The Psychological Dis-
Interpretation of the Old Hag

The failure of the cultural source hypothesis to accommodate the Old Hag data has made the present chapter the most difficult one of this book both to write and to explain. If culture had been found to supply a source, a review of psychological literature could have been restricted to the selection of a theoretical mechanism by which source material becomes experience. But if the source is not in culture, both a source and a mechanism must be sought in psychology. For centuries at least this has been the natural order of events in dealing with unnatural and unacceptable entities such as the Old Hag.[1]

In the absence of a cultural source, the availability of an adequate current psychological explanation must determine whether the phenomenon is a novel and challenging one or whether its interest is restricted to its wide distribution and role in folk tradition. A thorough search of relevant psychological literature has demonstrated that no such explanation is available. If another explanation were at hand, and if I had a strong argument to advance for what the Old Hag "really is,"

---

1. For example, the Church explained many of the alleged experiences of witches as dreams for hundreds of years before the time of the witch hunts. George Kittredge dates one authoritative church document on this point as having been written well before A.D. 906 (*Witchcraft in Old and New England* [New York: Russell & Russell, 1929], p. 244).

this statement might practically stand by itself. My explanation of what the experience is would nicely take care of what it is not. Unfortunately, I have no such explanation to advance.

Also unfortunately, the absence of an adequate psychological explanation does not mean that no psychological explanation has been attempted. Assuming the existence of a cultural source, psychologists have made of it a Procrustean bed that has offered the Old Hag rigorous hospitality at best. The occasional firsthand Old Hag account has been accounted for in a great variety of ways by a long series of authors. The effect has been to explain the phenomenon away while discouraging the development of a thorough description of it. To maintain the existence of the Old Hag experience as an important object of study, it is first necessary to rescue it from this ill treatment. If we cannot say all of what it is, we must continue the job begun with the consideration of the cultural source hypothesis and say what it is not. And given the natural human discomfort at being asked to remain in suspense indefinitely, this statement must be thorough and careful if it is to be accepted. In addition to bringing the Old Hag into sharper focus for observation, this process will raise questions about the adequacy with which other complex cultural and experiential data have been treated via the combination of cultural source with psychological mechanism.

The accommodation of bizarre experience in culture source terms has required a leap of faith. An entire class of beliefs and alleged experience represented in all cultures and at all times has had to be assumed prima facie to be the product of errors and then divided up for explanation among the various modern disciplines. As anthropologist Weston La Barre recently put it in a book on hallucinations, "The schizoid seer doubtless knows his id-self far better than do we normals. But what advantage is it to gain one's soul in eternal dream, yet lose the whole waking world? . . . Let no one denigrate the dream. But let everyone be epistemologically tidy about the location of these various realities: the supernatural is wholly housed in the subconscious."[2]

2. Weston La Barre, "Anthropological Perspectives on Hallucination and Hallucinogens," in *Hallucinations: Behavior, Experience, and Theory,* ed.

Those involved, however, have tended to assume that one or another psychological theory can be applied to a question of belief in the same way that a hammer is applied to a nail. There has been very little genuine give and take between the psychological theorizing and the richly complicated products of culture and experience. The Old Hag challenges this approach. The failure of the cultural source hypothesis to account for the phenomenon leaves it intact in all of its complexity.

At this point, I must repeat that I am not attempting to argue for any particular class of explanation for the Old Hag experience. Neither am I arguing against the development of cultural and psychological hypotheses about the Old Hag. By removing the excessively simple culture-plus-psychology strategy for avoiding a real explanation, we may move toward a richer theoretical understanding of the connections between culture and normal psychology. I shall provide several psychological hypotheses concerning the Old Hag at the end of this review. They fall short of what ought to be required of an "explanation," but before any respectable explanation can be suggested, the Old Hag phenomenon must first be recognized as a class of interesting, observable events not reducible to various categories chosen from existing psychological knowledge. For this we must hold onto the data already presented, both the subjective accounts and the quantified questionnaire results, and use that information to find out what the Old Hag is not.

In the literature, to the best of my knowledge, no psychologist or psychiatrist has ever used in print the words "Old Hag" as I am using them. To use anything in the scientific literature as a comment on the Old Hag, then, we must first connect the Old Hag with something that has been studied and discussed in print. I have already discussed the case for the relationship between the Old Hag and the original meaning of the word "nightmare."[3] The word "nightmare" frequently occurs in both the medical literature and the basic science litera-

---

Ronald K. Siegel and Louis Jolyon West (New York: John Wiley & Sons, 1975), p. 18.

   3. See pp. 53-54.

ture on sleep. Although there are important differences between these two literatures, I will not attempt here to analyze
or account for them. They are both basically "psychological"
in the technical sense and, although there is a great methodological difference between clinical observation and laboratory
investigation, they are frequently cited together and influence
one another.

As I have already noted, the word "nightmare" has undergone a great deal of development over the past several centuries, both in oral tradition and in the academic world of print,
and it continues to develop. Much of this development through
the beginning of the twentieth century has been very well summarized by Ernest Jones; so my review of the literature begins
with Jones's work. The review of twentieth-century writings is,
however, a complex and at times confusing undertaking. To
provide the reader with some solid ground to stand upon during the process, I shall first give a summary of current scientific
thought on sleep and the four sleep-related phenomena that
have been used to explain the "nightmare" in its old sense. This
summary is not controversial at the moment, but neither can it
be easily arrived at by a perusal of the most obvious literature.
Although it does put the cart before the horse, this procedure
will be helpful in reviewing the problems encountered by investigators attempting scientifically to observe, analyze, and explain a basically folk category. It should also provide a useful
starting point for those students of belief who are interested in
pursuing the subject beyond the confines of this book.

SLEEP PHENOMENA

The Stages of Sleep
Before the development of electroencephalography by
Hans Berger in the late 1920s, there was very little study of
sleep that could be properly called scientific. The EEG, however, allowed the systematic observation of measurable
changes correlated with brain activity, including differences
between waking and sleeping. Within ten years, investigators

using the new technique had shown that sleep is not simply a homogeneous state, but rather that it is made up of several more or less distinct stages that are cyclic in nature.

Rapid eye movements (REMs), the subject of a report by Eugene Aserinsky and Nathaniel Kleitman in 1953,[4] were the next major discovery of measurable correlates of sleep. REMs were found to be associated with an EEG pattern similar to that of sleep onset, and in 1957 William Dement and Kleitman reported that subjects were more likely to report dreams when awakened during REM sleep than when awakened during any other stage of sleep.[5] The combination of these observations led to systematic laboratory study of both sleep and dreams. An important consequence of that study has been the continued refinement of sleep into specific stages. The following is a condensed outline of currently recognized sleep stages.[6]

A. Stage NREM. Sleep without rapid eye movements (REMs). This is a composite made up of four separate stages varying in "depth" of sleep, which refers to both the intensity of NREM physiology and, in humans, difficulty of arousal.

1. Stage 1. The sleep stage that follows directly from the awake state. Normally constitutes 4 to 5 percent of total sleep time.

2. Stage 2. This stage is characterized by an EEG record that differs more from a normal waking record than does stage 1. Normally constitutes 45 to 55 percent of total sleep time.

3. Stage 3. With stage 4, this stage constitutes "deep

4. Eugene Aserinsky and Nathaniel Kleitman, "Regularly Occurring Periods of Eye Motility and Concomitant Phenomena during Sleep," *Science* 118 (1953):273–74.

5. William Dement and Nathaniel Kleitman, "Cyclic Variations in EEG during Sleep and Their Relationship to Eye Movements, Body Motility, and Dreaming," *Electroencephalography and Clinical Neurophysiology* 9 (1957):673–90.

6. This summary is condensed from Sleep Disorders Classification Committee, Association of Sleep Disorders Centers, "Diagnostic Classification of Sleep and Arousal Disorders," *Sleep* 2, no. 1 (1979):128.

sleep." It has been difficult to document physiological differences between stages 3 and 4, and they are sometimes combined as stage 3/4, or "slow wave sleep." Normally constitutes 4 to 6 percent of total sleep time.

4. Stage 4. Very similar to stage 3, differentiated by the predominance of high-voltage, slow EEG waves. Normally constitutes 12 to 15 percent of total sleep time.

B. Stage REM. The EEG record of this stage is similar to stage 1[7] and also to the normal waking EEG. This stage is also characterized by the suppression of muscle activity and the presence, by definition, of rapid eye movements, that is, eye movements that are more rapid than the slow, rolling movements typically found in stage 1. Because of the combination of intense central nervous system excitation and inhibition of motor activity, this stage has at times been called "paradoxical sleep." It normally constitutes 20 to 25 percent of total sleep time.

The alternation of these stages follows a fairly consistent pattern in most individuals. Normally a sleeper passes through stages 1 to 4 and then returns to stage 2. About ninety to one hundred minutes after falling asleep, he passes from stage 2 into REM and from REM back to stage 2. Some returns to stage 2 are followed by periods of stage 3/4, but these become less frequent as time passes and usually do not occur after the first third of a night's sleep. Normally a healthy sleeper will enter REM only from stage 2.[8]

In some sleep literature what I have called "stage 1" is called "stage 1 descending" because, metaphorically, it occurs as one goes "down into sleep." When this term is used, stage

7. Laverne C. Johnson, "Are Stages of Sleep Related to Waking Behavior?" *American Scientist* 61 (1973):328.

8. Ibid., p. 329.

REM is called "stage 1 ascending" or "emergent stage 1." The question of whether to separate or combine stages is still under consideration, and opinions vary. The outline above represents recent thought.

In addition to these stages, the literature contains references to the period immediately preceding sleep as the "hypnagogic" period. The time from the termination of measurable sleep to genuine wakefulness is called the "hypnopompic" period. These states have been studied less than has sleep. What attention has been given to them has dealt more with hypnagogic than hypnopompic phenomena, and the word "hypnagogic" has sometimes been used to cover both states.

A consideration of both historical developments and current thought suggests four distinct phenomena related to sleep which have been used to explain the Old Hag experience under various names including "nightmare." One of the problems I shall consider in this review of the literature is the confusion of terms that involves all four of these phenomena; so I shall label them here with terms that are as neutral and uncontroversial as possible. These are bad dreams, night terrors, sleep paralysis, and hypnagogic hallucinations. Now I shall briefly describe each and place them within the scheme of sleep-related events just given.

Bad Dreams

The definition of "dream" has not proved as simple for sleep researchers as it at first seemed. Some reports of psychological content have been obtained from each of the stages of sleep, as well as from the hypnagogic and hypnopompic periods. However, the most complex, heavily visual, and easily recalled content has consistently come from stage REM. The content from other stages is simpler, sometimes described as more like "thoughts," and is subject to rapid forgetting. Taking complexity and the presence of visual (or other sensory) content without clear consciousness of one's real environment as a definition, it can be said that "bad dreams" are primarily a phenomenon of REM sleep. They can vary in intensity with the most severe leading to awakening.

Night Terrors

Night terrors (NTs) are spontaneous awakenings from NREM sleep and have the following characteristics: they are often initiated by a loud scream; the subject shows signs of extreme fear; laboratory findings indicate great autonomic arousal (for example, tachycardia and heavy perspiration); the subject is difficult to rouse to full wakefulness and may even run from the room in which he has been sleeping; some scant psychological content may be retrieved with effort immediately following the attack, but the following morning subjects tend to be amnestic for the entire episode. Night terrors have been shown to occur primarily as arousals from stage 4 sleep, although similar but less intense arousals from stage 2 have been observed.[9]

Sleep Paralysis

Sleep paralysis (SP) is a period of inability to perform voluntary movements, either when falling asleep or when awakening, accompanied by conscious awareness. This condition has been ascribed both to the hypnagogic and hypnopompic states and to an atypical state in which REM occurs during stage 1. Part of the reason for this ambiguity is the difficulty in clearly distinguishing the drowsy period immediately preceding sleep onset from stage 1. Sleep paralysis is more frequently reported in connection with falling asleep than with awakening.

Hypnagogic Hallucinations

Hypnagogic hallucinations (HH) and, more rarely, hypnopompic hallucinations (which I shall also call HH) are simply hallucinations that occur just before (or upon awakening from) sleep. They are also sometimes described as occurring during sleep-onset REM in connection with sleep paralysis. Dreams are also hallucinations in a technical sense; so HHs must be distinguished from dreams. This distinction is rarely made explicit but tends to be done in one of two ways: (1) HHs occur-

9. See, for example, Charles Fisher et al., "The Nightmare: REM and NREM Nightmares," in *International Psychiatry Clinics*, vol. 7: *Sleep and Dreaming*, ed. Ernest Hartmann (Boston: Little, Brown & Co., 1970), p. 183.

ring before sleep, during the actual hypnagogic state, are defined by their location before stage 1; (2) those occurring during sleep-onset REM are defined by their association with SP, which is experienced as wakefulness and, therefore, different from normal sleep.

The possibility exists that HHs, defined as they are by their timing rather than their content or specific physiological characteristics, do not represent a single phenomenon. If the two distinctions just described do in fact refer to separate entities, then the second variety may be said to resemble the nightmare and the Old Hag.

All four of these states—bad dreams, night terrors, sleep paralysis, and hypnagogic hallucinations—have certain elements in common with the Old Hag. Now I shall consider how these similarities have been dealt with in the sleep literature of this century. Because the word "nightmare" and associated terms such as "incubus" and "night terror" have been used with such varied definitions, this review can be confusing. To help the reader keep the material in focus, I have provided in table 5 an outline of usages by various writers. The sleep states that have been most often connected with both the "classic nightmare" and sleep-event-related explanations of supernatural traditions are listed down the left side of the table. HH with SP as a REM event is a synthesis of several recent findings reported in the sleep literature, and stage 4 night terrors were not known as such until the publication of Henri Gastaut and Roger Broughton's findings in 1965, elaborated by Broughton in 1968. In these categories, therefore, I have made connections with earlier writings on the basis of the identity of clearly stated features, for example, Jones's awareness that the nightmare could occur during wakefulness. The three categories of "bad dream" are derived from the writings analyzed in the review that follows. "Overwhelming bad dreams" and "bad dreams with 'oppression' and 'helplessness' " sometimes overlap. Each of the first six graphically presented usages are here linked with major representative examples from the literature, but the table is not intended to be exhaustive for these, and several items briefly discussed in my review are not given here. The seventh usage, however, identifying the classic nightmare of tradition exclusively as hypnagogic hallucinations with sleep paralysis, is given here with the only five papers with which I am familiar that have made this connection. Of course, such a tabular representation involves simplification, and for the comparisons offered here to be fully understood this table must be considered along with the review that it supplements.

NIGHTMARE, INCUBUS, AND NIGHT TERROR

In 1931 Ernest Jones, a psychoanalyst and biographer of Freud, published a book entitled *On the Nightmare*. [10] Part I of this book, "Pathology of the Nightmare," had been published in the *American Journal of Insanity* in January 1910. Part II, "The Connections between the Nightmare and Certain Medieval Superstitions," had been separately published in German in 1912. Part III, "The Mare and the Mara: A Psycho-Analytical Contribution to Etymology," had been in preparation when the work was interrupted by World War I. Only a brief concluding essay and the indexes were new when the book was published in English in 1931. The first printing was popular enough to be followed by a second impression in 1949. In 1951 a new edition was published, changed only by the addition of a three-page preface by Jones.

In this book Jones attempted to use psychoanalysis to explore problems in anthropology, history, religious studies, and language, as well as abnormal psychology. It was a prodigious effort, and the result is a remarkable piece of scholarship. He left no doubt as to his estimation of its importance when he explained his reasons for publishing in 1931 a book composed of material written more than twenty years previously: "For the true significance of the Nightmare to be properly appreciated . . . would in my opinion entail consequences, both scientific and social, to which the term momentous might well be applied. What is at issue is nothing less than the very meaning of religion itself."[11] He reiterated this position in his preface to the second edition twenty years later.

10. Ernest M. Jones, *On the Nightmare,* International Psycho-Analytical Library, no. 20 (London: Hogarth Press, 1931).
    11. Ibid., p. 20.

USAGES OF "NIGHTMARE" AND RELATED WORDS ASSOCIATED WITH SUPERNATURAL TRADITIONS

	JONES (1931)	CASON (1935)	HADFIELD (1971, orig. 1954)	BROUGHTON (1968)	MACK (1974, orig. 1970)	HERSEN (1972)	LIDDON (1967) SCHNECK (1969) HUFFORD (1974 & 1976) NESS (1978)
HH with SP (Sleep onset or postdormital REM)	�meshed	▒					▒
Stage 4 Night terrors		▒		▒	▒	▒	
Stage REM "Bad dreams" — Bad dreams in general							
Stage REM "Bad dreams" — Overwhelming bad dreams		▒	▒		▒	▒	
Stage REM "Bad dreams" — Bad dreams with "oppression" and "helplessness"	▒						

Jones used the word "nightmare" in a restricted sense that he believed matched its old folk usage. His extensive discussion of the etymology of the word and its relationship to other traditional beliefs such as the incubus and the vampire indicates that he was well aware of the variety of folk traditions that have been related to the nightmare experience. From these sources Jones arrived at "the three cardinal features of the malady . . .: (1) agonizing dread; (2) sense of oppression or weight at the chest which alarmingly interferes with respiration; (3) conviction of helpless paralysis."[12]

Jones called the state in which these features occur a distressing dream. He recognized that this experience was less common than the general run of distressing dreams and blamed the impression that nightmares are very common on "an unduly wide conception of Nightmare."[13] In this connection, he particularly takes to task J. R. Jewell's findings in a questionnaire study reported in 1905. Jones was keenly aware of the multiple meanings of the word "nightmare" and the effects of that multiplicity on studies of the subject. Unfortunately, his warnings on this point have generally been overlooked by subsequent researchers.

Jones's interpretation of the nightmare is what would be expected from a student of Sigmund Freud. He said that it "is a form of *Angst* attack, that it is essentially due to an intense mental conflict centering [sic] around a repressed component of the psycho-sexual instinct, essentially concerned with incest." He states that "agonizing dread" is an emotion consistently found associated with pathologically repressed sexuality and notes that "it has been a generally accepted opinion that Nightmare is more likely to attack a person who is sleeping on his back." He connects this observation with the commonness of the supine position for women in sexual intercourse and by the same association explains the "weight at the chest." He further bolsters this interpretation with a statement that in his experience it is most often the repression of the "feminine or masochistic component of the sexual instinct" that results in

12. Ibid., p. 52.
13. Ibid.

the nightmare.[14] The "helpless paralysis" is by implication connected with the conflict between repressed incestuous desires and the conscious rejection of them.[15] Given this interpretation of the nightmare, it is not surprising that Jones insists that the presence of nightmare is always shown by psychoanalytic investigation to be connected with *Angst* neurosis even in the cases of those "who pass as being mentally normal."[16]

Following this psychological explication of the nightmare, Jones reviews a variety of supernatural belief traditions, focusing especially on incubi, vampires, werewolves, the devil, and witchcraft. Using the nightmare as a prototype, he finds all such beliefs to be expressions of repressed sexuality and draws direct connections to the nightmare experience when possible, as with vampire traditions. If the features of a belief do not show strong resemblances to his three definitive features, he settles for more subtle and symbolic links. He then ascribes to formal religion the function of controlling these repressed influences, a function symbolically worked out in the suppression of, for example, witchcraft and devil worship. Unlike most authors who have subsequently quoted him, then, Jones describes an experience (the repression of sexuality), especially in its nightmare form, as a source for a wide variety of cultural material. He believes the features of the nightmare proper are sufficiently explained by the psychological events he considers universal. We might call this a psychological source hypothesis, as opposed to the cultural source hypothesis.

At the time that Jones wrote, of course, nothing was known of the stages of sleep. From our modern vantage point, it is possible to see that his definition of the nightmare allowed the inclusion at least of bad dreams and hypnagogic hallucinations. Because he did not make the impression of wakefulness a definitive characteristic he included ordinary bad dreams if they involved fear, oppression or weight at the chest, and helpless-

---

14. Ibid., pp. 54, 27, 53.
15. Sigmund Freud had argued this point in *The Interpretation of Dreams.* See *The Basic Writings of Sigmund Freud,* trans. and ed. A. A. Brill, Modern Library (New York: Random House, 1938), p. 360.
16. Jones, *On the Nightmare,* p. 53.

ness. These features are occasionally present together in a wide variety of settings in bad dreams, especially since "oppression" is such a general term. An example of this inclusion of what are clearly REM dreams is found in his quote from R. Macnish's *Philosophy of Sleep*. [17] "He can neither breathe, nor walk, nor run, with his wonted facility. If pursued by any imminent danger, he can hardly drag one limb after another; if engaged in combat his blows are utterly ineffective."[18]

Jones was also aware, however, that his definitive characteristics could be accompanied by the conviction of wakefulness. He said that nightmares "may not only occur but may run their whole course during the waking stage."[19] The nightmare experienced during wakefulness corresponds to the Old Hag and includes the features of SP with HH. Jones's combination of this state with bad dreams helped to pave the way for major confusion in sleep literature in the decades that followed.

All three of the features Jones selected as definitive are directly related to his use of psychoanalytic theory to interpret the nightmare. It seems likely, therefore, that the definition was arrived at more on theoretical than empirical grounds. Because Jones saw all dreams as expressions of unconscious content and all fear in dreams as relating to unconscious sexual conflicts, the distinction between waking and sleeping nightmares must have seemed of secondary importance to him. The omission of wakefulness from his criteria, however, did more than miss a distinction later documented in sleep laboratories. Inclusion of the extremely varied contents of bad dreams prevented a clear view of the striking patterns running through the Old Hag, as documented above. It also discounted a basic criterion of the folk traditions, which he attempted to explain. The supernatural traditions based on this experience do not include ordinary REM dreams as primary categories of supernatural attack. They refer to experiences in which various empirical data suggest a genuine waking experience. According to folk criteria, much of Jones's case material was comprised

17. R. Macnish, *The Philosophy of Sleep* (New York: Appleton, 1834).
18. Jones, *On the Nightmare*, p. 18.
19. Ibid., p. 26.

of "false positives." By overlooking this fact, Jones placed himself squarely in a tradition of scholarship that would heartily
agree with his statement that "difficulty in distinguishing
dreams from the experiences of waking life is naturally greater
in less tutored minds, such as those of children and savages."[20]

This conclusion seems especially unfortunate because in his
recognition of waking nightmares he had a potential connection between the nightmare and supernatural tradition that
does not require such an affront both to good sense and to the
dignity of "the folk" (or whatever one wishes to label those
holding beliefs different from one's own). His monograph has
had a strong and lasting influence, especially on the subject of
nightmare-culture connections, and his failure to see the implications of this distinction is therefore of considerable historical
importance.

In Jones's chapter on incubus and incubation in his section
entitled "The Connections between the Nightmare and Certain Medieval Superstitions," he elaborates his psychological
source hypothesis. Here he accepted an apparently very old
medical tradition of identifying some concepts of the nightmare with some concepts of the incubus and gave this connection a modern basis in psychoanalytic theory. Jones's use of the
term "medieval" was loose at best. Much of his concern is with
the witch hunts that occurred during the Renaissance and into
the seventeenth century, and he does show some awareness
that the beliefs he is considering existed long before medieval
times and still persist.[21] We are left to suspect that the word
"medieval," like the word "superstition," was intended primarily to indicate his distaste for the beliefs.

In addition to its relationship to the history of current
medical and psychological terminology, Jones's treatment of
the incubus raises some points of theoretical interest in connection with language. Jones, in effect, equates the nightmare
and the incubus, raising the question of whether what is at
issue is language or the phenomena to which the language refers. The words themselves and their cognates may have been

20. Ibid., p. 60.
21. Ibid., pp. 237–39.

used as synonyms by all or some of those who knew them, and such definitions may or may not accurately reflect relationships between the phenomena. Or, the words may have been understood as significantly different in meaning, even if they in fact referred to a single thing. The words may be either identical or analogous, and so may the experiences to which they refer. It is for this reason that so far I have asserted only that the Old Hag and the nightmare are closely related rather than that they are identical. Jones's emphasis on unconscious meanings tended to blur these distinctions. He thought that people meant the same thing by both terms, whether they knew it or not, and that both the terrifying and the erotic experiences were the same whether or not their content was similar. Jones's usage illustrates one of the dangers of the concept of unconscious meaning: it can cause distinct things to blur and blend into one another. If hypotheses about latent significance are not scrupulously submitted to empirical testing it becomes impossible to say, as the popular story about Freud has it, "when a cigar is only a cigar."

The word "incubus" is derived from the Latin *incubare,* meaning to lie down on. The word "succubus" is derived from the Latin *succubare,* to lie under. In Latin and then in English the words referred respectively to male and female demons believed to have sexual intercourse with humans. Because Jones interprets the nightmare as a symptom of pathologically repressed sexuality, he identifies the incubus as the same experience with a more manifest sexual content. The same assumptions about the nature of all dreams and the "meaning" of all fear in dreams that led him to discount the difference between sleeping nightmares and waking nightmares led him to discount the phenomenological differences between purely terrifying accounts and erotic accounts. This dogmatic insistence that latent sexuality is involved in all frightening dreams has been criticized by many recent writers.[22]

The presence of overt sexual content as a frequent fea-

22. John E. Mack, *Nightmares and Human Conflict,* Sentry ed. (Boston: Houghton Mifflin Co., 1974), p. 3; J. A. Hadfield, *Dreams and Nightmares* (Baltimore: Penguin Books, 1971), p. 177.

ture of the nightmare proper is also highly debatable. I have encountered a few explicit sexual details in Old Hag accounts, but these are rare and are not typically major components of a given experience. Some overtly sexual accounts have appeared in the course of my investigation, but these differed from the Old Hag in that they have lacked the paralysis feature and, in several cases, fear. These probably constitute either a distinct subtype of the experience or a different phenomenon altogether. Some of the instances Jones viewed as manifesting sexual content probably were in fact REM dreams, and erotic dreams, with or without orgasm, are a well-known phenomenon. It is possible that there are also erotic experiences of this kind that subjectively appear to occur in a waking state. Such events do not seem to have been reported in the literature, but this may be a result of the typically broad connotations of the word "nightmare," after Jones. At any rate, it would be a mistake automatically to assume that no more realistic experience lies behind the widespread incubus traditions. To do so would invite a repetition of the errors and confusion that have characterized writings about the Old Hag variety of experience.

From ancient times, it seems to have been recognized that at least two different kinds of experience were involved in traditions of supernatural contact related to sleep. Some terms for these experiences have been used only in a restricted sense, referring either to sexual encounters or to terrifying attacks with restraint and pressure. Others were used in a more general way and could cover either or both kinds of experience. In addition to the Latin "incubus," for example, there were the Greek words *Ephialtes* ("leaper"), *Pnigalion* ("throttler"), and the Latin *Inuus* ("one who sits on").[23] The reference to pressure as a primary feature is especially clear in Pliny's use of *suppressio nocturna* for the nightmare.[24]

---

23. Wilhelm Heinrich Roscher, "Ephialtes: A Pathological-Mythological Treatise on the Nightmare in Classical Antiquity," in *Pan and the Nightmare*, trans. A. V. O'Brien, Dunquin Series 4 (Zurich: Spring Publications, 1972), pp. 45–57.

24. D. P. Thompson, *Cassell's New Latin Dictionary: Latin-English, English-Latin* (New York: Funk and Wagnalls Co., 1960), p. 772.

The precise distinctions that were made in the classical world between voluptuous sleep-related experiences and attacks of the Old Hag type are difficult to determine. The distinction in Europe during the time of the witch hunts, the period with which Jones is primarily concerned, is clearer. Jones himself documents this distinction while simultaneously arguing that it is superficial and unimportant. He quotes, for example, the following passage concerning the incubus from the *Daemonologie* (1597) of King James I of England (the two speakers are fictitious characters who are made to argue the pros and cons of the reality of witchcraft).

> *Philomates:* Is it not the thing which we call the Mare, which takes folkes sleeping in their beds, a kinde of these spirits, whereof ye are speaking?
>
> *Epistemon:* No, that is but a natural sickness, which the Mediciners have given that name of *Incubus* unto, ab *incubando*, because it . . . makes us think that there were some unnatural burden or spirit, lying upon us, and holding us down.[25]

Jones uses this passage to support his contention that just when people were beginning to emancipate themselves from the belief in hallucinated beings in connection with erotic dreams and retaining the belief only in connection with nightmares, a theological elaboration of the incubus concept reanimated the ancient belief that the partner in a sexual dream was an actual being.[26] A more reasonable interpretation is that even though popular tradition included two relatively distinct categories, academic writers had already begun to confuse them by the application of a popular term for one category to the official explanation of the other.

A major medieval school of thought held that some or all nocturnal sexual encounters with "supernaturals" were in fact dreams.[27] Some of the debate about witchcraft focused on

---

25. Jones, *On the Nightmare*, p. 90.
26. Ibid., p. 89.
27. Ibid.; see, for example, Jones's reference to Gervase of Tilbury (A.D. 1214) for both opinions held simultaneously; and footnote 1 above for the Church's use of the dream explanation for witchcraft.

whether submission to an incubus was sufficient evidence that a woman was a witch. Those who held the dream explanation exclusively argued that this was an imaginary experience and could not constitute evidence. The incubus question was a part of the larger debate on whether witchcraft genuinely involved preternatural acts and powers or whether its primary crime was heresy. The issue was officially settled in favor of the preternatural theory by 1486, when Heinrich Kramer and Jakob Sprenger published *Malleus Maleficarum (The Hammer of Witches)*, a detailed manual used extensively during the witch hunts. In the section headed "Here follows the Way whereby Witches copulate with those Devils known as Incubi,"[28] the authors made it abundantly clear that they were exclusively concerned with overtly sexual experiences and that they considered such experiences to be diabolical.

Segments of both popular and academic society, then, were familiar with at least three types of nocturnal experience: a variety of dreams, sexual encounters with "supernaturals" sometimes called incubus or succubus depending on gender, and attacks of the Old Hag type without any obvious sexuality. Opinion differed concerning the cause and the objective reality of the latter two, as it currently does in Newfoundland in connection with the Old Hag. The word "incubus" was sometimes extended to include the Old Hag type of experience, especially among physicians, probably on the basis of the feeling of pressure often associated with the attacks. In general usage, the word kept its strong sexual connotations. The word "nightmare" and its cognates tended to retain a more limited meaning involving paralysis and pressure.

Because of his assumption that the two types of experience are identical at an unconscious level, Jones overlooked the possible significance of phenomenological differences and omitted information about the contents of the incubus experience. The presence of sexual connotations was sufficient information from his perspective. By his excessive reliance on theory with

28. Heinrich Kramer and James Sprenger, *The Malleus Maleficarum*, trans. with introduction, bibliography, and notes by Montague Summers (New York: Dover Publications, 1971), p. 109.

little concern for empirical confirmation, Jones encouraged that confusion between the study of words and the study of experience discussed above. An example of the effect of this confusion on later scholarship may be seen in Rossell Robbins's article on nightmare in which he quotes Jones extensively. He says that "although both the mare and incubus demons are projections of repressed sexual desires, for convenience of treatment the two complementary conceptions are distinguished: with the mare-demon, terror predominates; but with the incubus-demon, the main element (although mingled with dread) is pleasure."[29] He then provides portions of nine accounts of various experiences, only two of which are firsthand. Three of these actually contain the word "nightmare," and in these there are no sexual references; three have no name attached and are very suggestive of sex; one uses the name Lamia and contains specific sexual material; and one actually uses the word "incubus."

In all of this discussion, and throughout this book, three distinct kinds of subject matter are at issue: traditions and the language associated with them, experiences, and theoretical explanations. Any serious effort to study traditions or experiences requires careful description with attention to both consistency and variation. The establishment of a correspondence between a tradition(s) and an experience(s) must be approached cautiously, and perfect correspondence will rarely if ever be found. Theoretical explanations should be made only on the basis of thorough descriptions of what is to be explained, or one may accidentally create much of what is being accounted for. For this reason, in the first three chapters of this book I have tried to separate a tradition and a type of experience to better understand their relationship. This is also the reason why I have not yet attempted a theoretical explanation. Jones, however, was so certain of his theory and had so little regard for the traditions he considered that the distinction between the theoretical and the empirical all but disappeared. In his work, one can hardly distinguish the experiences themselves, when they are presented at all, from their interpreta-

29. Rossell Robbins, *The Encyclopedia of Witchcraft and Demonology* (London: Bookplan for Paul Hamlyn, 1959), p. 356.

tions. The lack of scientific precision attributed to popular thought is found here in academic disguise. Considering the breadth of his scholarship and the quantity of information he assembled, it is truly regrettable that Jones did not untangle more of what he found. But perhaps this failure is understandable given his theory-laden approach and the lack of objective knowledge about sleep at the time he wrote.

I have considered Jones at great length for two reasons: first, because he dealt more extensively with the nightmare in a restricted sense and its connections with culture than any other twentieth-century author, and second, because he has had a great and lasting influence on those who have written on both subjects since. Now we shall turn our attention to some of those more recent authors.

In 1935 Hulsey Cason, in *The Nightmare Dream*, identified nightmares with ordinary bad dreams. This connection is not surprising because technical distinctions based on measurable differences between dreams and other sleep-related phenomena were not yet available. Nonetheless, each time this assumption was made in print it became more difficult for subsequent researchers to consider alternative possibilities. In his first sentence, Cason cites Jones on both the history of knowledge about the nightmare and Jones's three cardinal features (dread, oppression or weight at the chest, and helpless paralysis). He notes, as Jones had, that the nightmare may occur during sleep or during the hypnagogic state and supplies additional citations to support the existence of the hypnagogic variation. He also gives the following capsule description: "Many persons at all times and in all parts of the world have seen shadowy dark-robed figures, have had a sense of something heavy in the air, and have felt that a presence was reaching long dim hands after them."[30] This broad description fails to mention paralysis or consciousness of one's real surroundings; although it does have some resemblance to the Old Hag type of experience. It is the closest that Cason's study comes to describing that experience.

In his brief introduction, Cason states that because of

30. Hulsey Cason, *The Nightmare Dream*, Psychological Monographs 46, no. 5, whole no. 209 (Princeton: Psychological Review Co., 1935), p. 1.

Jones's monograph, "it will not be necessary to review all of the available literature on nightmare (incubus) and night terror *(pavor nocturnus)."* ³¹ Had he carried out his own review, he might have discovered some of the problems of taxonomy and definition with which his subject of study was loaded. Worse still, he adds yet another distinct class of sleep-related phenomena to the meaning of the word "nightmare," even though Jones did not mention night terror by that name or its Latinesque medical label, *pavor nocturnus.* Cason thus includes in his study all of the phenomena set out at the beginning of this chapter—bad dreams, night terrors, and hypnagogic hallucinations with sleep paralysis—but calls them all by a single name and classes them all as "dreams."

Cason surveyed several hundred subjects including normal adults, normal and blind children, "feeble-minded" patients, and "insane patients." The subjects were interviewed individually using a detailed interview schedule that included such topics as education, average amounts of sleep, and sleep position. These topics were selected after "a careful study of the nightmare literature in medicine, physiology, psychiatry, and psychology." Unfortunately, the potential usefulness of this survey for answering specific questions was lost when Cason failed to heed Jones's warning about the danger of a wide definition of nightmare in questionnaire studies. At the beginning of each interview, the topic of study was described to the subjects as being "AN INVESTIGATION OF NIGHTMARES. A nightmare is a distressing or terrifying dream—and the following features are sometimes present: (1) Agonizing dread, (2) Sense of oppression or weight at the chest which alarmingly interferes with respiration, and (3) Conviction of helpless paralysis." ³²

Cason correctly states that this is "the definition proposed by Jones." ³³ The problem lies in the fact that as used it is not a definition. The definition is "distressing or terrifying dream," and here "distressing" broadens the meaning still fur-

31. Ibid., p. 3.
32. Ibid.
33. Ibid., p. 5.

ther to indicate all "bad" dreams, whether frightening or not. Jones's three features are added only as description. All questions then simply use the word "nightmare," as in, "How many times have you had a nightmare in the past month?" With this beginning, it is no surprise that his findings differed from those of Jones and other authors who had attempted to deal with specific phenomena. He disagrees "with G. S. Hall's statement that *pavor nocturnus* comes on in the beginning of the night." But Hall was right because *pavor nocturnus* properly defined is night terror; night terror is a stage 4 disorder; and stage 4 occurs primarily during the first third of the night. Cason's examples from later in the night were almost certainly REM dreams, which are common at that point in sleep. Cason also contradicted Jones's finding that nightmare is most likely when the sleeper is on his back, reporting that "the side was in general the most common sleeping position."[34] All of Cason's findings represent an average of responses for at least three different kinds of events, each of which occur and are accurately reported at very different rates. His results place him in the position of a man who is told that the camels at the zoo have humps; he then goes to the zoo and states, "I shall define camels, or elephants as they are sometimes called, as any animal found at the zoo, some of which are said to have humps." He would, of course, find that some "camels" have humps, and some have trunks, as claimed by those who call them elephants, but most have neither.

The information Cason gathered would have been very useful if connected with any single phenomenon. Some Old Hag experiences seem to have been reported, and the clues are intriguing. In analyzing the most frequent subjects, Cason says that "the most common kind of person mentioned . . . was the strange man."[35] He also states that trying to move but not being able to was frequently reported but does not say how often it was associated with the impression of wakefulness. He does describe the content of thirty-two "nightmares" that he considers representative. Of these, one (his case 5) may have

34. Ibid., pp. 4, 16, 19.
35. Ibid., p. 17.

been of the Old Hag type; although the information given is not sufficient to be certain, and one (his case 23) would fit Jones's definition of the nightmare but involves no awareness of real surroundings. The remainder all appear to be distressing REM dreams.

Almost twenty years after Cason's monograph, J. A. Hadfield published *Dreams and Nightmares,* a book that proved popular and remained in print for another twenty years. Although the title sounds more promising than Cason's, Hadfield repeated the basic error of combining all three phenomena under the single term "nightmare." He begins his discussion of nightmares with an acknowledgment that the matter of definition is a difficult one, commenting at different points about night terrors, bad dreams in general, and Jones's narrow definition. He assumes, however, that he is speaking of a single entity with a variety of possible characteristics and decides that he must accommodate all of those characteristics within a single conceptual category. His conclusion about definition is as follows: "We therefore suggest that the distinction between an anxiety dream and a nightmare is one of degree rather than kind, but *we shall use the term nightmare specifically of those anxiety dreams of such intensity that they completely overwhelm the personality* [Hadfield's emphasis]. . . . But we shall not keep too strictly to this description, since there are all degrees in between the anxiety dream and the nightmare."[36]

Hadfield follows Jones in connecting traditions of incubi, vampires, werewolves, and witches with the nightmare. But because his definition of the state is much more general, so are the connections he is able to suggest. Hadfield does make some progress by deciding that in nightmares "we cannot agree that the fear is always of sexuality, although it is commonly so."[37] Thus, after forty years Jones's insight into the problem of defining the nightmare had not had a measurable impact, but at least his purely sexual interpretation had been brought into some question. Hadfield is the last writer I shall consider who wrote before the discovery of REM sleep. It was not until much

36. Hadfield, *Dreams and Nightmares,* p. 178.
37. Ibid., p. 177.

later that the word "nightmare" was connected with a specific sleep stage based on laboratory observation.

In 1965 Henri Gastaut and Roger Broughton published "A Clinical and Polygraphic Study of Episodic Phenomena during Sleep" in which they considered many phenomena including dreams, night terrors, sleep paralysis, and hypnagogic hallucinations, along with such events as sleep talking, sleep walking, and nocturnal enuresis. They discussed sleep paralysis in connection with both falling asleep and awakening, noting that "understandable intense anxiety may occur until the bond is finally broken by movement," and suggested the possibility of concomitant hallucinations. They described "hypnagogic imagery" as a "discontinuous series" of images occurring as the subject's consciousness is progressively obscured by the passage into sleep proper and observed that these images are recalled only if the subject is awakened and asked about them. Both of these descriptions are accurate; although the description of hypnagogic hallucinations covers only the first of the two types of HH which I described earlier in this chapter. Gastaut and Broughton briefly discussed frightening dreams and noted that they rarely lead to spontaneous awakening. They said that this form of dream, even when leading to awakening, "is to be differentiated from the true nightmare or incubus."[38]

These authors' consideration of night terrors is of greatest importance here. They called these nightmare of adults (incubus) and night terror of children and stated that the two differ in only three ways aside from the age of the subject. The children's attacks are more common, involve more activity (more thrashing, attempts to walk or run, crying out), and are much less likely to be connected with psychiatric problems. They found that both adult and childhood attacks occur during slow wave sleep (stage 3/4), especially stage 4. For a full description of the behavioral features of this experience we must consider both the 1965 article and one published by

38. Henri Gastaut and Roger Broughton, "A Clinical and Polygraphic Study of Episodic Phenomena during Sleep," *Recent Advances in Biological Psychiatry* 7 (1965):198–221; quotations on pp. 210 and 198.

Broughton in *Science* in 1968 in which he gave additional details from his work with Gastaut and redefined some of their initial concepts. In this second article, Broughton gave the following descriptions of their observations of childhood and adult attacks respectively:

> The child abruptly sits up in bed and screams. He appears to be staring wide-eyed at some imaginary object; his face is covered with perspiration and his breathing is labored. Consoling stimuli have no effect. After the attack dream recall is rare and usually fragmentary.... The child has no recollection of the episode the following morning. . . .
>
> During an attack the adult suddenly cries out in his sleep and shows all the signs of intense anxiety: sweating, a fixed facial expression, dilated pupils, difficulty in breathing.[39]

In addition, Broughton notes that the characteristics of confused arousal are present: "(i) mental confusion and disorientation; (ii) automatic behavior; (iii) relative nonreactivity to external stimuli; (iv) poor response to efforts to provoke . . . full and lucid contact with the environment; (v) retrograde amnesia . . . (vi) only fragmentary recall of apparent dreams, or none at all."[40]

Broughton here has described the basic night terror as outlined at the beginning of this chapter, and most of these findings have since been replicated by other investigators. These characteristics, however, do not justify calling this "the true nightmare or incubus." The authors then quote Jones, note his three cardinal features, and report that in what fragmentary recall they have been able to elicit from their subjects they have found a sense of oppression, paralysis, and terror developing, in that order.[41] Subsequent studies, however, have not found either the oppression or the paralysis features. Charles Fisher et al., in three authoritative papers published

39. Roger J. Broughton, "Sleep Disorders: Disorders of Arousal?" *Science* 159 (1968):1071.

40. Ibid., p. 1073.

41. Gastaut and Broughton, "A Clinical and Polygraphic Study of Episodic Phenomena during Sleep," p. 213.

more recently, have quoted Jones's three cardinal features but stated that of those three, only fear was encountered in stage 4 night terrors observed in their laboratory, even though they made an intensive effort to elicit recall of psychological content in general and reported greater success in doing so than did Broughton and Gastaut.[42] It is not clear how Gastaut and Broughton derived the features of oppression and paralysis. Michel Hersen, in a review of nightmare literature in 1972, has suggested that their approach to interviewing their subjects involved accidental "experimenter suggestion" leading to a "combination of retrospective distortion and examiner contamination."[43]

If this is in fact the explanation, it was probably a result of the authors' efforts to reconcile their findings with Jones's description of the classic nightmare, which they recognized as distinct from ordinary dreams. Extreme terror and the difference from ordinary dream states constituted the similarities between the two; oppression, paralysis, and detailed descriptions of content made up the differences. To account for these differences, they hypothesized that content was retrospectively elaborated after the terrified awakening and was based on a combination of recalled sleep sensations and cultural input. After listing commentators on the nightmare from Caelius Aurelianus in antiquity to Jones, they state their hypothesis as follows:

> The authors, as well, agree that dreaming is not associated and that the oppression occurs first, followed by subjective paralysis, which in turn evolves into intense anxiety or terror. Although a structured dream is almost never described during the classical

42. Charles Fisher et al., "A Psychophysiological Study of Nightmares," *Journal of the American Psychoanalytic Association* 18 (1970):754; Charles Fisher et al., "A Psychophysiological Study of Nightmares and Night Terrors: Physiological Aspects of the Stage Four Night Terror," *Journal of Nervous and Mental Disease* 157 (1973):91; Charles Fisher et al., "A Psychophysiological Study of Nightmares and Night Terrors: Mental Content and Recall of Stage Four Night Terrors," *Journal of Nervous and Mental Disease* 158 (1974):187.

43. Michel Hersen, "Nightmare Behavior: A Review," *Psychological Bulletin* 78 (1972):39.

adult nightmare, one frequently encounters a thought or an idea that the subject uses to try to rationalize or justify these three major components of his attack. Thus, in the literature of the Middle Ages, one finds descriptions of a witch, a demon, or an old lady who comes at night to sit upon the sleeper's chest or to attack him. Today the thoughts most frequently met with are those of being in a tomb, in a dark cave, under a pile of rocks, and so forth.[44]

The source of the ideas of the tomb, dark cave, and so forth is unknown. They may be recollections of the basic experience of confused arousal during slow wave sleep, as Gastaut and Broughton have suggested. But they are no more compatible with the recall of a waking nightmare experience than is the REM dream content described above. The content Gastaut and Broughton ascribe to medieval cultural input, as Jones did, differs from their "modern content" in that it reflects events subjectively experienced in the sleeper's real surroundings, not in an imaginary setting such as a tomb. This difference, which these authors have attributed to the passage of time and accompanying cultural change, is in fact the contrast between two different experiences. This assertion is supported by a comparison of the features found in confused arousal from slow wave sleep, quoted from Broughton above, with the characteristics of "classic nightmare" descriptions and the Old Hag accounts given in Chapters 3 and 5 of this book. Lucidity, good orientation, awareness of surroundings, and complete recall are the rule in the latter; whereas their opposites typify the confused arousal state. Such a mistake is understandable given the history of the word "nightmare" and the general lack of knowledge concerning the Old Hag experience. Gastaut and Broughton included the following comment in their discussion of the NT "nightmare": "It is possible, however, that sometimes hypnagogic or dream activity may culminate in a true nightmare. But most terrifying dreams, with or without awakening, do not reach this intensity."[45] If they had been fortunate

---

44. Gastaut and Broughton, "A Clinical and Polygraphic Study of Episodic Phenomena during Sleep," pp. 213–14.

45. Ibid., p. 215.

enough to observe and record an experience of the Old Hag type in their sleep laboratory, they would have realized the extent to which the hypnagogic event differs from the NT. One of the drawbacks of laboratory study on any subject is that it is much less likely than field study to provide interpretable data on phenomena that are unfamiliar at the outset.

In his *Science* article, Broughton further linked NTs and the folk meaning of the word "nightmare" by reproducing Henry Fuseli's (1781) painting "The Nightmare"[46] as an illustration of the rationalization he believed accompanied NTs from antiquity through the eighteenth century. (This is the painting that is reproduced on the jacket of this book.) The 1782 version of the same painting had been used by Jones for the frontispiece of his monograph. The painting is a much better representation of the Old Hag experience (limp paralysis, supine position, pressure, frightening intruder in the sleeper's real surroundings) than of a night terror (hypermotility, little or no visual content, lack of contact with real surroundings). Both of these articles on episodic sleep-related phenomena also include brief descriptions of the etymologies of incubus, nightmares, and the French *cauchemar*.[47]

These two articles are major contributions to the sleep literature. Broughton's article in *Science* has had special impact because it focuses on three related phenomena (enuresis, somnambulism, and night terrors) and articulates the concept of "disorders of arousal" in connection with slow wave sleep. But the articles have added to the confusion of terms by using "nightmare" and "incubus" for adult night terrors and by providing a theoretical explanation relating physiology, psychology, and culture to discount the distinctive features necessary for a recognition of the waking nightmare or Old Hag as a distinct phenomenon. Furthermore, this new explanation reversed the implications of Jones's explanation (psychological source) and bolstered the cultural source notion on the basis

46. Broughton, "Sleep Disorders," p. 1072.
47. Gastaut and Broughton, "A Clinical and Polygraphic Study of Episodic Phenomena during Sleep," p. 218; Broughton, "Sleep Disorders," p. 1071.

of a great deal of psychological and physiological information but very little cultural data.

In 1970 John E. Mack, a psychiatrist, published *Nightmares and Human Conflict*. The book has been well received, widely quoted, and remained in print in paperback through 1980. Mack's work is an extensive review of the literature relating to all aspects of nightmare studies, but he does little to untangle the confusion caused by the very broad and shifting meanings of "nightmare" and related words. Recognizing the lack of consensus, he begins his first chapter by stating that "since the term is used so variously, my preference in defining *nightmare* is toward inclusiveness." He then briefly considers several definitions, including those of Jones and Hadfield, and joins the latter in finding Jones's list of features too restrictive. He concludes, "I would define the nightmare as an anxiety dream in which fear is of such intense degree as to be experienced as overwhelming by the dreamer and to force at least partial awakening."[48]

Using this broad definition, Mack follows Jones in considering connections between the nightmare and culture. As it did in Hadfield's case a general definition leads Mack to general connections. This vagueness does make Mack's brief assessment of the relationship more reasonable than was Jones's dogmatic insistence on concealed sexuality. Nonetheless, Mack ultimately supports the notion that nightmare traditions illustrate man's supposed difficulty in distinguishing dreams from objective reality. He says that this distinction has been possible "only in the past century, and especially since the work of Freud and Jones."[49] It is unfortunate that he was not more cautious in attributing this basic confusion to the great bulk of humanity, because he, too, was aware of the basic concept of a frightening, sleep-related experience occurring in a waking state. In his chapter on nightmares and the new biology of dreaming he discusses the existence of REM dreams in which the dreamer has difficulty moving and the intriguing correlation of this phenomenon with general motor inhibition during

48. Mack, *Nightmares and Human Conflict*, pp. 1–2.
49. Ibid., p. 11.

stage REM. He then considers the sleep paralysis of narcoleptics and the possibility that this state "may represent the perceptual component of the D [i.e., dream] state occurring in the presence of motor inhibition, but without the other physiological features of sleep, that is, dreaming while partially awake."[50] We may observe that if a person dreams while awake he should not be criticized for denying that he was asleep during the experience, but Mack did not develop this implication.

In 1972 Michel Hersen published "Nightmare Behavior: A Review" in *Psychological Bulletin.* This paper is of interest here primarily because it crystallizes and adds new references in support of Gastaut and Broughton's idea that nightmare content has changed as cultural input has altered. Hersen states that "thematic material elicited from reports of nightmare sufferers has altered markedly over the centuries."[51] His references for what he takes to be the older themes in "nightmare dreams" are Jones, Gastaut and Broughton, and Jerome M. Schneck.[52] For modern content he cites Cason, Hadfield, Gastaut and Broughton, and an article specifically dealing with the contents of nightmare reports by Marvin Feldman and Edward Hyman.[53] Schneck's article to which Hersen refers is a brief discussion of Fuseli's painting "The Nightmare"[54] which Schneck connects with sleep paralysis as distinguished from both NTs and nightmares. I shall return to Schneck's work in reviewing studies of sleep paralysis. Hersen, however, does not deal with sleep paralysis as such and lumps material relating to it together with REM anxiety dreams and adult night terrors under the single term "nightmare."

Hersen provides a good critical summary of problems involved in the use of self-reports. He concludes that the weaknesses of past attempts to analyze the contents of "night-

50. Ibid., p. 194.

51. Hersen, "Nightmare Behavior," p. 39.

52. Jerome M. Schneck, "Henry Fuseli, Nightmare and Sleep Paralysis," *Journal of the American Medical Association* 207 (1969):725–26.

53. Marvin J. Feldman and Edward Hyman, "Content Analysis of Nightmare Reports," *Psychophysiology* 5 (1968):221.

54. Schneck, "Henry Fuseli, Nightmare and Sleep Paralysis," pp. 725–26.

mares" should be redressed by efforts "to categorize thematic material gathered from nightmare reports, occurring in Stage 2 sleep, Stage 4 sleep, and the REM stage, in order to permit quantitative comparisons."[55] Such a conclusion must be regarded with extreme caution because of the problems created by the use of such categories as "oppression" to include "weight at the chest" or "helplessness" to include paralysis. At least for the Old Hag or waking nightmare, a very clear and precise description is needed, and categorization tends to blur the necessary distinctions. Quantification will no doubt be useful at some point, but it can scarcely proceed successfully from the current state of knowledge.

The most careful recent attempt to bring order out of the chaotic tangle of meanings surrounding the word "nightmare" is that published by Fisher and his associates in 1973. Recognizing that terminology constituted a major obstacle in the field, they proposed a four-part classification: stage 4 night terrors, REM nightmares, stage 2 anxious arousal, and hypnagogic nightmare. They recognized the popular usage that is an important factor in all surveys by noting that REM nightmares "are frequently characterized by subjects as nightmares."[56] Fisher's four classes include as distinct entities the events I described early in this chapter, combining SP and HH to yield "hypnagogic nightmare," and add stage 2 arousals (which appear to be more closely related to NTs than to the Old Hag experience).

Given their clear recognition of the differences among these categories, it is unfortunate that Fisher and his colleagues did not turn their attention to what they called the hypnagogic nightmare and did not comment on the implications of their precise classification for discussions of the nightmare-culture connection. Their interest was strongly focused on NTs and REM nightmares, however, and their work on these topics has been extremely productive.

I shall close my consideration of the development of "nightmare" and related words by looking at some of the ways

55. Hersen, "Nightmare Behavior," pp. 36, 46.
56. Fisher et al., "A Psychophysiological Study of Nightmares and Night Terrors: Physiological Aspects of the Stage Four Night Terror," p. 80.

they have been used recently. These examples are not presented as major developments in nightmare research, although some of them do make contributions. They are instead provided to illustrate the current state of the literature with regard to terminology.

The 1977 edition of *Modern Clinical Psychiatry* includes nightmares and night terrors in the chapter entitled "Special Symptoms." Facing the first page of this chapter is a reproduction of the 1781 version of Fuseli's "The Nightmare." In the half page devoted to the two types of events the author uses "incubus" as a synonym for "nightmare" and applies both terms to children as well as adults. He describes it as a REM phenomenon that culminates in crying out and awakening in an acute anxiety reaction. He states that the subject may "complain of tightness or heaviness in the chest,"[57] which he attributes to hyperventilation. For night terror the author gives the synonym *pavor nocturnus* and a description differing from the above only by a greater tendency to motor activity and the presence of confusion. He classes this as a NREM event.

Thus the nightmare is presented as a special kind of REM dream as in Hadfield and Mack, but labeled with the paired terms used by Gastaut and Broughton to refer to adult night terrors. In addition, there is an echo of Jones's "oppression or weight at the chest" from the "classic nightmare."[58]

In 1978 John M. Taub and associates published a study comparing the contents of recently experienced nightmares to the contents of confabulated nightmare accounts created by another group of subjects. They begin by quoting Fisher et al.'s four-part classification of anxious arousals, but then immediately refer to the NT as a "type of nightmare," and this general, inclusive use of the term continues through the article. For the subjects of the study, nightmare was defined as "a frightening dream that awakened them."[59]

The findings of this investigation are important in that

57. Lawrence C. Kolb, *Modern Clinical Psychiatry*, new ed. (Philadelphia: W. B. Saunders Co., 1977), pp. 719–20.

58. Ibid., p. 720, describes this feature in connection with SP and HH.

59. John M. Taub et al., "Nightmare Dreams and Nightmare Confabulations," *Comprehensive Psychiatry* 19 (1978):285–91; quotation on p. 286.

they note the characteristics of experiences recognized by subjects as frightening dreams. Some of these might include Old Hag experiences as well as REM anxiety dreams, although the Old Hag experiences are probably too infrequent to have had much effect on this study, which collected one nightmare from each of forty-two subjects. In the discussion of their results, Taub and his associates recap the notion of the historical evolution of nightmare contents, citing Hersen, Gastaut and Broughton, Jones, and others, and then propose that their own "results extend findings on the nightmare phenomenon beyond the hypothetical realm into a more intricate and a wider array of content variables than reported in any previous study."[60] That is probably true, but this array of content cannot be compared to the content of distinct events such as Jones's nightmare or Gastaut and Broughton's "nightmare (incubus)."

In 1979 Bernard D. Beitman and Albert S. Carlin published "Night Terrors Treated with Imipramine," a case report, including a good description of the patient's attacks, in the *American Journal of Psychiatry*. The authors begin with an effort to distinguish night terrors from nightmares—a further illustration of the continued confusion created by the alternate combination and redivision of the two terms in the literature. They state, "The more common nightmare is characterized by less intense anxiety, lower levels of autonomic discharge, *greater motility,* and *more vocalization*" (my emphasis).[61] In fact, the first two are characteristics of nightmare; whereas the second pair are hallmarks of the night terror.

In addition, several current editions of professionally used medical dictionaries employ entries for "incubus," "nightmare," and "night terror" that are typified by:

Dorland's Medical Dictionary (1974)
  Incubus: 1. a nightmare. 2. a heavy mental burden.
  Nightmare: a terrifying dream; called also *oneirodynia*.
  Night terror: (no entry)[62]

---

60. Ibid., p. 289.
61. Bernard D. Beitman and Albert S. Carlin, "Night Terrors Treated with Imipramine," *American Journal of Psychiatry* 136 (1979):1087–88.
62. *Dorland's Illustrated Medical Dictionary*, 25th ed. (Philadelphia: W. B. Saunders Co., 1974).

Taber's Cyclopedic Medical Dictionary (1977)
Incubus: 1. a burden. 2. a nightmare.
Nightmare: A bad dream accompanied by great fear and a feel-
    ing of suffocation. Once believed to be caused by a
    female monster or spirit that sat upon the dreamer.
Night terrors: Form of nightmare in children causing them to
    awaken in terror, screaming.[63]

In these definitions, the general run of REM anxiety dreams, stage 4 night terrors, and alleged premodern belief intermingle freely but with no hint of paralysis, wakefulness, or even sexuality.

Finally, L. B. Raschka in "The Incubus Syndrome: A Vari-ant of Erotomania," states: "The term 'incubus syndrome' is proposed to describe patients suffering from the delusion that they have been sexually approached at night by an unseen lover."[64] The author gives two case histories of schizophrenic patients with such a delusion. In neither case is any hallucina-tion connected with the alleged sexual assaults, nor is there any recollection of the events that the patients believe have taken place while they were soundly asleep. No awakenings, anxious or otherwise, are described. Such delusions among psychotics seem to have practically no connection with any of the phe-nomena considered above except for the presence of an erotic element. Of the twenty-nine references that follow Raschka's paper, only one of the works cited above is included: Robbins's *The Encyclopedia of Witchcraft and Demonology.*

NARCOLEPSY, HYPNAGOGIC HALLUCINATION, AND SLEEP PARALYSIS

Although from the time they were first described in the nine-teenth century both HH and SP[65] have been known to occur

63. *Taber's Cyclopedic Medical Dictionary*, 12th ed. (Philadelphia: F. A. Davis Co., 1977).
64. L. B. Raschka, "The Incubus Syndrome: A Variant of Erotomania," *Canadian Journal of Psychiatry* 24 (1979):552.
65. HH and SP have not been subject to the terminological confusion documented above; therefore I summarize here only the major findings of this field and touch on the points of contact between this material and the nightmare literature.

idiopathically, since the 1920s they have been consistently associated with narcolepsy, which is "a syndrome consisting of
excessive daytime sleepiness and abnormal manifestations of
REM sleep. The latter include frequent sleep-onset REMs periods, which may be subjectively appreciated as hypnagogic
hallucinations, and the dissociated REM sleep inhibitory processes, cataplexy and sleep paralysis."[66]

Cataplexy differs from SP in that it occurs during daytime
activities, often following the eruption of expressions of strong
emotions such as laughter. It may be either partial (a brief
weakness) or complete. Like SP it may be ended by stimulating
the patient. HH and SP are thought to occur separately or together in about one-half of the narcoleptic population. Narcolepsy itself is estimated to occur in from 0.02 to 0.07 percent
of the general population.[67]

Hypnagogic Hallucinations

A useful study of HH in normal subjects was published by
Gerald Vogel, David Foulkes, and Harry Trosman in the *Archives of General Psychiatry* in 1966. Their most important finding
for our purposes is that in the course of 216 planned awakenings (6 per subject night, 4 nights per subject, 9 subjects) they
received "no reports of hallucinations without loss of control
and loss of awareness of surroundings."[68] They recognize, of
course, that this finding does not mean that HH cannot occur
while the subject is still oriented, but it does suggest that prior
loss of contact with surroundings is much more common. For
these awakenings, the investigators considered stage 1 and the
period of wakefulness immediately preceding it as the hypnagogic period and found HH to be distributed throughout this

66. Sleep Disorders Classification Committee, "Diagnostic Classification of Sleep and Arousal Disorders," p. 72.

67. Constantin R. Soldatos, Anthony Kales, and Roger Cadieux,
"Narcolepsy: Evaluation and Treatment," *Journal of Psychedelic Drugs* 10
(1978):319.

68. Gerald Vogel, David Foulkes, and Harry Trosman, "Ego Functions
and Dreaming during Sleep Onset," in *Altered States of Consciousness: A Book
of Readings,* ed. Charles Tart (New York: John Wiley & Sons, 1969; reprinted
from *Archives of General Psychiatry* 14 [1966]:238–48), p. 84.

range. They received HH reports from 75 percent of awakenings before stage 1 and contrasted all retrieved HHs to REM dreams by stating that HHs "were usually shorter, had less effect, and were more discontinuous; that is more like a succession of slides than like a movie."[69] This description, taken together with the consistent loss of contact with real surroundings before HH, demonstrates that these "normal" HHs are unlike the Old Hag experience. This is the same conclusion suggested by Gastaut and Broughton's description of HH given above.

The HHs of narcolpetics, by contrast, are generally said to "occur more frequently and they are more vivid, emotionally charged and usually unpleasant,"[70] a description that resembles the Old Hag experience; although it seems highly unlikely that all Old Hag subjects could be narcoleptics. Michel Ribstein's recent excellent summary of HHs in narcolepsy reinforces this appearance of similarity. In his clinical description, for example, he includes what he calls "psychic hallucinations." These, he says, "may often take the form of an impression that someone is present: 'I feel someone prowling; I can neither see nor hear him, but I do know that he is there' "—for all practical purposes, a case of the "sensation of presence" as in the Old Hag. The following examples of cenesthesic reactions are just as striking: "I am lying in bed and I rise in my room; I am reassured, since I know it is not true, and I am awfully worried to be so high above my bed and I am afraid of falling down"; and "I rise high up in the sky. I perceive something supernatural which attracts me and wants to divide my body from my mind." Other examples, however, that seem much less like the Old Hag include "landscapes or scenery" and "an orchestra playing a symphony." Ribstein also notes that the narcoleptic may be either indifferent to the HH, viewing it like "a short movie," or very much involved. Some hallucinations that involve the patient seem to take place in the subject's actual surroundings; whereas others are set in other locations as in REM dreams. The engaging experiences set in

69. Ibid., p. 77.
70. Soldatos et al., "Narcolepsy," p. 320.

the real surroundings are most like the Old Hag. In these cases, Ribstein gives such examples as the following: " 'Hallucinations are precise. I believe them although I question them, and in spite of this doubt, I go and check my door or look in the stairs,' " and the use of such preventives as prayer and drinking water from Lourdes.[71] Again, the similarity to Old Hag accounts is inescapable. In narcoleptics HHs are usually explained as being a result of stage 1 REM, a finding that is considered to be evidence of narcolepsy when it occurs within ten minutes of sleep onset.[72] Some hallucinations similarly suggestive of the Old Hag have been reported in connection with narcoleptic cataplexy attacks.[73]

Sleep Paralysis

The following description is taken from the thorough review of SP in narcoleptics by Yasuo Hishikawa in 1976: "Sleep paralysis may be described as a brief episode characterized by the inability to perform voluntary movements either on falling asleep (hypnagogic or predormital sleep paralysis) or on awakening (hypnopompic or postdormital sleep paralysis). It usually occurs when the patient is lying on a bed. . . . Occasionally sleep paralysis is accompanied or just preceded by vivid and terrifying hallucinations." Hishikawa also notes that the subject "is fully aware of his condition and can recall it completely afterwards."[74] He adds that the struggling person may at times make faint noises and that if neither the struggle nor an external stimulus (such as being

71. Michel Ribstein, "Hypnagogic Hallucinations," in *Narcolepsy: Proceedings of the First International Symposium on Narcolepsy,* Advances in Sleep Research, vol. 3, eds. Christian Guilleminault, William C. Dement, and Pierre Passouant (New York: Spectrum Publications, 1976), pp. 146–61.

72. Sleep Disorders Classification Committee, "Diagnostic Classification of Sleep and Arousal Disorders," p. 72.

73. See, for example, Johanna van den Hoed, Edgar A. Lucas, and William C. Dement, "Hallucinatory Experiences during Cataplexy in Patients with Narcolepsy," *American Journal of Psychiatry* 136 (1979):1211.

74. Yasuo Hishikawa, "Sleep Paralysis," in *Narcolepsy: Proceedings of the First International Symposium on Narcolepsy,* Advances in Sleep Research, vol. 3, ed. Christian Guilleminault, William C. Dement, and Pierre Passouant (New York: Spectrum Publications, 1976), pp. 97, 98.

touched) terminates the episode it will end spontaneously, usually within ten minutes or less.

The ability accurately to perceive the environment during SP was reported by Hishikawa and Z. Kaneko in 1965 as the result of an experiment in which they flashed a bright light on narcoleptic patients during various states of wakefulness and sleep and then examined both EEG and behavioral responses to this stimulus. They found that the patients perceived and recalled all of the flashes that occurred during SP (taking place in sleep-onset REM), but perceived and recalled either less or nothing at all during other stages of sleep and drowsiness, including stage 1 without SP.[75] These results were partially replicated and extended by H. Nan'no et al. in 1970 using an auditory stimulus (calling the subject's name repeatedly).[76] This evidence of lucidity and awareness of real surroundings corresponds to my Old Hag data but differs in that some narcolepsy references describe the SP subject as being unable "even to open his eyes."[77] There are two possible reasons for the dissimilarities: either some Old Hag victims believe their eyes to be open when in fact they are not, or narcoleptics are more frequently unable to open their eyes during SP than are normal people. Both may in fact be correct, but the question cannot be settled on the basis of current information.

The Role of REM

As with HHs, SP has been shown to be connected with the intrusion of REM into the sleep-onset period, a time at which it does not normally occur. REM physiology is known to consist of two components, both arising in the reticular formation in the brain stem. These are distinguishable from one another by EEG and have been connected with specific structures within

75. Yasuo Hishikawa and Z. Kaneko, "Electroencephalographic Study of Narcolepsy," *Electroencephalography and Clinical Neurophysiology* 18 (1965): 249–59, cited in Hishikawa, "Sleep Paralysis," p. 98.

76. H. Nan'no et al., "A Neurophysiological Study of Sleep Paralysis in Narcoleptic Patients," *Electroencephalography and Clinical Neurophysiology* 28 (1970):382–90, cited and discussed in Hishikawa, "Sleep Paralysis," pp. 111–12.

77. See, for example, Hishikawa, "Sleep Paralysis," p. 98.

the reticular formation. One component is connected with dreaming; the other is responsible for the inhibition of muscle tone during REM. This separation of function has been demonstrated in laboratory animals by the selective destruction of those structures associated with muscle inhibition. The result in cats has been "unrealistic" but coordinated activity during sleep; that is, they appear to dream and carry out the actions contained in those dreams.[78] It is, obviously, the dream-related component of REM which is thought to account for HH during sleep-onset REM and the inhibitory component used to explain SP.

HH with SP and the Old Hag

Both the objective and subjective elements of the description of SP fit very well with the Old Hag experience. When those HHs described above as involving the subject and taking place in his real surroundings are added, the correspondence seems to be perfect, at least phenomenologically. The laboratory findings in the cases of narcoleptics with HH and SP even hold the promise of physiological insight into the Old Hag phenomenon. This leaves us with four primary questions to consider about the relationship of HH and SP to the Old Hag.

1. *What is the relationship of the Old Hag to the HHs of normal subjects?*[79] On the basis of the information in the sleep literature and the Old Hag research discussed above, we may hypothesize that there are in fact three varieties of HH. The first type in normal subjects was described by Vogel and his colleagues. These HHs may occur at any time from the beginning of

78. For a recent example see Michel Jouvet, "What Does a Cat Dream About?" *Trends in Neurosciences* 2 (1979):280–82.

79. One point to consider, although I do not have enough information for an extensive discussion, concerns the posture of the victim. I have been told by those working with narcoleptics that there is no apparent connection between the supine position and SP or HH in these patients, nor is any connection mentioned in the literature. If the attacks occur in narcoleptics without regard to posture, whereas about 90 percent of first attacks in normals take place in the supine position, this difference may be an important clue to the mechanisms involved. In normals the supine position (probably interacting with other factors) may somehow mimic the effects of the lesion responsible for the attacks in narcoleptics.

drowsiness all the way through stage 1, and they are experienced in the absence of REM. Their content may vary depending on when in the sleep-onset period they occur, but they are consistently shorter, have less effect, and are more discontinuous than normal REM dreams. The second type may also take place at any time during sleep onset, but they occur in the presence of REM. These are more like normal REM dreams than are non-REM HHs.

The third type of HH is a special case of this second type in which sleep-onset REM occurs before the "progressive obscuring of consciousness"[80] and "loss of awareness of surroundings"[81] that is part of the natural process of falling asleep, or for some reason the intrusion of REM interrupts this process and returns the subject to that level of conscious awareness normally associated with wakefulness. This latter seems to be the case when SP occurs other than at the beginning of sleep onset, something occasionally reported by both narcoleptics and Old Hag victims but considered to be relatively uncommon. This coincidence of conscious awareness and REM inhibition constitutes the paralysis of SP, as has been observed by many researchers. The relationship between SP and "depth" of sleep is further supported by the finding that awareness of surroundings (and therefore SP) is inversely related to the length of time between sleep onset and the beginning of REM. The crucial period of time has been reported to be "several minutes."[82]

If this classification is accurate, comparisons between "the HH of normals" and "the HH of narcolpetics" have been misleading. If the Old Hag is in fact a REM HH in the presence of SP, then it appears that a substantial number of normals have them too, and in normals they have the same characteristics as in narcoleptics. They are merely less common among normals. At the same time, there is every reason to expect that

80. Gastaut and Broughton, "A Clinical and Polygraphic Study of Episodic Phenomena during Sleep," p. 198.

81. Vogel et al., "Ego Functions and Dreaming during Sleep Onset," p. 84.

82. Hishikawa, "Sleep Paralysis," p. 111.

the non-REM (i.e., normal) HHs also occur among narcoleptics. In other words, the described differences are those between two different phenomena: the HHs most frequently experienced by normals (non-REM HH) and those most frequently *reported* by narcoleptics (REM HH). The distinction between experience and reporting is made because non-REM HHs tend to be forgotten and do not constitute an annoyance that would lead to symptom reporting. The REM HHs are annoying and are likely to be reported by anyone diagnosed as having a sleep disorder, but this is not necessarily an indication that they occur with an absolute frequency greater than that of non-REM HH, even among narcoleptics.

2. *At what rate do HH and SP co-occur?* This question has two sides. Whenever REM HHs occur after the loss of consciousness of the sleeper's surroundings, SP will not be subjectively experienced any more than it is during ordinary REM dreams. Without awareness of one's body, the inhibition of motor impulses cannot be directly perceived. There remains, however, the possibility that the indirect perception of this inhibition may be connected with "dreams" of paralysis or difficult movement. This possibility has been raised occasionally over a long period of time as, for example, when Havelock Ellis described it in his *World of Dreams* in 1922.[83] If this is the case, at least some such dreams may be hypnagogic or hypnopompic REM hallucinations rather than normal dreams. Nonetheless, SP narrowly defined must be expected only when conscious awareness is present. So much for HH without SP.

How frequently does SP occur without HH? The reports reviewed by Hishikawa suggest that 50 percent or more of subjects reporting SP also report HH.[84] Documentation is better for narcoleptics than for normals, and it is not clear how frequently this coincidence in individuals is connected with coincidence in specific episodes. To appreciate fully the difficulty of answering this question, we must recall the variety of forms of HHs that have been described. Ribstein's "psychic halluci-

83. Havelock Ellis, *The World of Dreams* (Boston: Houghton Mifflin Co., 1922; reprint Detroit: Gale Research Co., 1976), pp. 98–104.

84. Hishikawa, "Sleep Paralysis," p. 99.

nations" would be easy to miss simply because they contain no recognizable sensory component. If careful questioning were not performed, they might well be classed as "delusions" rather than hallucinations. I base this statement, and my own conclusion that these are not merely delusions, on the interview material I have obtained on the "sensation of presence," of which numerous examples are given in Chapters 3 and 5. These sensations have the character of perceptions rather than inferences, despite the lack of identifiable sensory components. Recognizing the difficulty of identification, the question of the frequency with which SP occurs without HH must be considered unanswered, but HHs of some sort are probably present more often than is generally recognized or reported.

The narcolepsy literature has not provided any comparative analyses that I know of on the apparent difference in content between REM HHs alone and those that occur with SP, but those descriptions of content that are available suggest that HHs with SP are most likely to correspond to the Old Hag experience. In the course of my Old Hag interviews, I have occasionally received accounts of some sense of restricted motion without a clear impression of wakefulness. These were generally excluded as false positives on the basis of the wakefulness criterion. The more clouded the consciousness in these accounts, the more varied the contents were, including the imagined surroundings. This would seem to suggest that HHs with and without SP represent segments of a continuum that varies in level of awareness (or, to put it the other way, depth of sleep). If this is the case, it is particularly interesting that the more lucid and clearly conscious the subject is, the more his experience seems to conform to a single pattern.

3. *What are the relative frequencies of these experiences among normals and narcoleptics?* I have already noted that about half of all narcoleptics experience HH and/or SP. Given the uncertainty concerning the rate at which the two states co-occur, it is difficult to estimate accurately what fraction of all narcoleptics experience the two together. The figure may well be about 25 percent.

Most of the authors who have reported cases of idiopathic SP have noted that it probably is much more common than realized. Hishikawa agrees with this assessment and notes that "it seems likely that sleep paralysis in otherwise normal persons seldom bothers them enough to make them seek medical treatment."[85] Judging from Old Hag accounts, even when a person is greatly bothered he may still be reluctant to report such bizarre experiences in the absence of other symptoms having a more obviously medical appearance.

One of the few surveys of normal subjects which has looked for SP and HHs in normal subjects was described in an article published by G. Browne Goode in 1962. Goode's sample totaled 359 subjects in four different groups. Of this total, 4.7 percent (17 individuals) responded positively to his paralysis question. His HH (he used the term "sleep hallucination") question dealt with "very vivid and realistic 'dreams' upon falling asleep or awaking from sleep. (Exclude the ordinary dreams of sleep.)"[86] This question received a positive response of 70, or 55.5 percent. In assessing these results, my own paralysis findings and the problems involved in the distinction made by many respondents between "paralysis," being "afraid to move," and so forth would suggest that the 4.7 percent is low and that the 55.5 percent includes some episodes that might be called SP if they were accompanied by a full description of phenomenological details.

Goode's sample contained a large majority of medical (231) and nursing (53) students, which is useful for comparison since much of my own recent data have come from medical students, as noted in Chapter 3. The only other survey of the subject in normals, that I am familiar with, was carried out exclusively with medical students and was reported by Henry C. Everett in 1963. Everett found that eight students out of fifty-two who returned his questionnaire had experienced at least one episode of sleep paralysis. This constituted 15.4 percent, or about the same rate of positive responses that I have found with my "standard" approach, that is, without extra reassurance or definition. Everett notes, "If the

85. Ibid.

86. G. Browne Goode, "Sleep Paralysis," *Archives of Neurology* 6 (1962): 229.

15.4 percent figure is incorrect, it probably errs on the small side. False positive replies were ruled out by follow-up interviews with those answering 'Yes' to symptoms of sleep paralysis." Goode did not use such a procedure. Several of Everett's positive respondents expressed hesitancy in admitting to the symptoms, one stating that he planned to answer "No" until he saw that a friend was answering "Yes." Of the seven interviewed (one had not signed his name and could not be followed up), all said that they had never heard of the experience in others before seeing the questionnaire. Most of the features reported were similar to those I have obtained in interviews, including the "feeling of being separated from the rest of my body" and "a tingling sensation."[87]

The *Diagnostic Classification of Sleep and Arousal Disorders* published in 1979 lists "Familial Sleep Paralysis" to cover SP without narcolepsy. This entry states that in some families the disorder has been found to affect several generations and continues: "Surveys of normal individuals have identified sleep paralysis in 3–6 percent of respondents, but this figure is far too high."[88] Undiagnosed narcolepsy and other disorders are suggested as variables that might have confounded the surveys and led to an excessively high estimate. My own findings and those reported by Everett suggest just the opposite. Follow-up interviews have indicated more false negatives than false positives.[89]

One possible mechanism for the occurrence of SP with REM HH in non-narcoleptics is suggested by the observation that normal subjects experience sleep-onset REM periods dur-

87. Henry C. Everett, "Sleep Paralysis in Medical Students," *Journal of Nervous and Mental Disease* 136 (1963):285–86.

88. Sleep Disorders Classification Committee, "Diagnostic Classification of Sleep and Arousal Disorders," p. 110.

89. A part of this apparent discrepancy is probably attributable to variations in criteria for the definition of a non-narcoleptic sleep paralysis syndrome, particularly regarding the number of attacks reported. This point is raised by William Dement in the discussion section following Hishikawa's article "Sleep Paralysis" in *Narcolepsy*, p. 123. He states that he has found an incidence of at least one SP attack as high as 40 to 50 percent in a sample of more than three thousand undergraduate students.

ing daytime naps and at nocturnal sleep onset following sleep deprivation.[90] This fits well with the observation that the Old Hag is experienced disproportionately during naps or at times of fatigue. The Old Hag data suggest that not all such episodes occur under these conditions, but they may partially account for the greater than expected rate among non-narcoleptics.

Although the rates of occurrence of SP and REM HH cannot be fixed with certainty, two points seem clear. First, the difference in rates between narcoleptics and normals is much less than had been thought; and second, the overall rate in the total population is much higher than generally recognized.

4. *What pathological implications may this experience have, especially when found in normals?* Because this is so often a concern of those who experience them, the possibility must be considered that SP and REM HH in non-narcoleptics might be pathological. Many early writers raised the possibility that SP might be connected with epilepsy.[91] In the course of my interviewing, I have encountered two subjects who feared this possibility. One of them had reported an Old Hag attack to a physician while at college. The physician told him that it "might be epilepsy" and that when he returned home he should have complete neurological testing. He feared the effects that such a diagnosis would have and therefore never again mentioned the attacks, which continued to occur once a year or so. When I interviewed him, he had considered himself a "hidden epileptic" for eight years. During that time, he had assumed that he should not marry and was concerned about whether it was safe for him to drive a car, even though he had never had an episode that was not connected with sleep. A remarkably similar case is given by Louis J. West,[92] who describes a surgeon who had considered himself an epileptic on the basis of SP (he was ignorant of the literature on the subject). He had never revealed

90. Hishikawa, "Sleep Paralysis," p. 115.
91. The same connection was made in Case 3 above from Newfoundland.
92. Louis Jolyon West, "Dissociative Reaction," in *Comprehensive Textbook of Psychiatry,* ed. Alfred Freedman and Harold Kaplan (Baltimore: Williams & Wilkins, 1966), p. 896.

his suspicions for fear of losing his career and had been treating himself with a combination of anticonvulsive drugs with dextroamphetamines to remain alert. West says that when the surgeon first learned by chance of the existence of idiopathic SP, he was reduced to tears. Subsequent EEG studies demonstrated that he in fact did not have epilepsy.

The existence of such cases demonstrates that not everyone in the medical community is aware of the existence of idiopathic SP and that this ignorance can have unfortunate consequences. In addition, failure of non-narcoleptics to present with SP as a complaint is not entirely the result of lack of concern! Fortunately, it is now known, as reported by Hishikawa, that there is no EEG evidence to support any connection with epilepsy. The association is apparently an error stemming from certain clinical similarities between the two.[93]

Several other medical authors have suggested that SP is a neurotic symptom. In 1965 Stephen B. Payn presented the case of a woman whose SP he considered to be "an extreme form of inhibition, representing a compromise between fulfillment of her sexual and hostile impulses and a defense against them."[94] Jerome Schneck has reported several cases in which he suggested a connection between the paralysis and sexual conflict.[95] In addition to the theoretical foundation which psychoanalysis provides for identifying paralysis with conflict, the specific features of many SP attacks with REM HH have encouraged the connection in exactly the same way that Jones connected the incubus with the nightmare. For instance, Schneck described the following features in a case published in the *Journal of the American Medical Association* in 1960: "On falling asleep or awakening, she would find herself completely paralyzed. She would feel . . . someone climbing onto her bed and on top of her. (I have encountered this impression in other

93. Hishikawa, "Sleep Paralysis," p. 101.

94. Stephen B. Payn, "A Psychoanalytic Approach to Sleep Paralysis: Review and Report of a Case," *Journal of Nervous and Mental Disease* 140 (1965): 432.

95. See, for example, Jerome M. Schneck, "Sleep Paralysis," *American Journal of Psychiatry* 108 (1952):923.

patients with sleep paralysis.) The pressure of this weight on her would be great, yet no one could be seen."[96]

There are at least two basic objections to the interpretation of these attacks as neurotic symptoms. First, they are extremely consistent in their content, as has already been discussed and documented. This consistency seems incompatible with the variety of psychodynamic etiologies advanced to account for it. This point stands out especially when we consider the way that psychoanalysis interprets the content of normal REM dreams. In those interpretations, the individual differences, which are tremendous in REM dream content, are argued as representing the specifics of a given case. In typical attacks of SP with REM HH, the striking interindividual similarities would have to be reconciled.

The second objection is that the entire experience seems to be too common, as well as too consistently patterned, to be pathognomic. Any condition afflicting 15 percent or more of the general population, but remaining largely undiagnosed, must hopefully not be too serious. Of course, neither of these objections removes the possibility that when this experience does occur in a psychiatrically ill individual the phenomenology, which may even be somehow "obligatory," could be used to "express" or "work out" conflicts and so forth. This possibility was considered, for example, by Payn.[97]

Whatever the case may be for such secondary psychodynamic significance, it seems that only a lack of awareness of the surprisingly high rate of occurrence and consistency of contents has allowed this state to be described as being of pathological significance. The strongest genuine connection between this state and any disorder is that with narcolep-

96. Jerome M. Schneck, "Sleep Paralysis without Narcolepsy or Cataplexy: Report of a Case," *Journal of the American Medical Association* 173 (1960): 1129.

97. Payn, "A Psychoanalytic Approach to Sleep Paralysis," pp. 427–33. For an attempt to connect HH without narcolepsy with psychopathology in a psychiatric in-patient population and to differentiate these HHs from those occurring in normals, see Carrick McDonald, "A Clinical Study of Hypnagogic Hallucinations," *British Journal of Psychiatry* 118 (1971):543–47.

sy, and even there the significance may be of greater theoretical than diagnostic importance.

INTEGRATION: THE NIGHTMARE AND THE OLD HAG MEET SLEEP PARALYSIS

Bringing all of the material just reviewed to bear on the Old Hag leads to the following conclusions about terminology:

1. The Old Hag corresponds to the old meaning of "nightmare," but all academic literature on the nightmare, including Jones's work, has moved farther and farther from dealing directly with that limited entity.
2. Sleep paralysis with hypnagogic hallucinations (which should be understood to imply the sensations of wakefulness and accurate perception of real surroundings) includes the Old Hag.
3. The term "incubus" in popular usage means an explicitly erotic experience and is distinct from Old Hag accounts as gathered in the present study, but that meaning has been so muddied by interpretations concerning unconscious meanings and by varied applications through the centuries that the word no longer has any single, clear referent in the literature.
4. "Night terror" clearly refers to a well-documented stage 4 phenomenon that is distinct from the Old Hag despite some connections suggested in recent literature.

A striking feature of the two bodies of literature concerning the nightmare and sleep paralysis is their isolation from one another. Rarely does a major article attempt to integrate the information and theories of both sets of writings. An outstanding exception is Sim Liddon's paper "Sleep Paralysis and Hypnagogic Hallucination: Their Relationship to the Nightmare," published in 1967 in the *Archives of General Psychiatry*. Liddon takes Jones as his basic authority on the nightmare and uses that word in its limited sense and suggests the possible connection with SP. He does accept the idea that *pavor nocturnus* is "a condition closely allied to the nightmare,"[98] an understandable conclusion both because of the constant confusion surrounding the two terms and because he wrote before Broughton's *Science* article called widespread attention to the stage 4 origin of night terrors.

Even though he appreciated the basic connection Liddon did not have access to enough clear and careful descriptions of content, especially modern ones, to fully appreciate the implications of this connection for the culture-nightmare nexus. He notes the "convincing sense of reality" in SP and suggests that it may have played a major role in the development of "superstitious belief." But he follows the lead of many other writers in saying that the basic experiences were "embellished" in a manner "consistent with the culture at the time."[99] If he had been familiar with the details of more modern accounts, I think he would have found that the embellishment has been less than most have assumed and that the acceptance of the experiences as real is by no means absent even among many sophisticated modern victims. Such recent accounts and data about their frequency and distribution might also have led him to be more critical of some of the psychodynamic interpretations he reviewed. Nonetheless, Liddon's article remains the best one yet written on these connections. It has not, however, had a great impact. Mack, for example, cites Liddon on the changes in the meaning of the word "nightmare" over the past hundred years but does not use the article to sharpen his own excessively inclusive definition.[100]

Schneck's brief article "Henry Fuseli, Nightmare and Sleep Paralysis" is another careful analysis that has had less impact than it warrants. Although brief, Schneck's essay outlines the major differences among SP with HH, REM nightmares, and night terrors. The differences are illustrated using the Fuseli painting that must be familiar to many readers by now be-

---

98. Sim C. Liddon, "Sleep Paralysis and Hypnagogic Hallucinations: Their Relationship to the Nightmare," *Archives of General Psychiatry* 17 (1967):91.

99. Ibid., pp. 93–94, 88.

100. Mack, *Nightmares and Human Conflict*, p. 2.

cause it has been reproduced in so many books and articles containing a section dealing with nightmares, regardless of the definition in use.[101] Still, as noted above with Hersen's citation of Schneck's article in connection with what Hersen took to be old-fashioned nightmare content, the implications of these distinctions have not been readily picked up.

I take the connections between the two streams of literature to be basically as follows:

1. The phenomena of SP with REM HH have been treated as varieties of ordinary bad dreams from Jones to the present by many who have written about the nightmare. They are not. They are distinct in content and physiology.

2. Subjects' reports of SP with REM HH have been considered *post hoc* elaborations of the experience of night terror. They are not. This distinction is even greater than that which separates these phenomena from ordinary REM dreams.

3. The contents of SP with REM HH have not been well described in the SP literature, where subjective data have been of relatively little interest. The connection of SP with nightmare in the old sense has been obscured as a result.

4. Attempts to provide *post hoc* explanations of the contents of both modern and historical Old Hag accounts (i.e., SP with REM HH and nightmare in the old sense), often very superficial, have greatly contributed to the confusion of both literatures.

This last point deserves special attention. All of the cultural and social forces that have mitigated against open discussion of the Old Hag experience in its isolated form have allowed it to wander through the sleep literature as a confounding "false positive." If its contents, frequency, and distribution were as well known in twentieth-century academia as they are in rural Newfoundland, much of the confusion in the nightmare literature would not have occurred. It is the

101. Schneck, "Henry Fuseli, Nightmare and Sleep Paralysis."

existence of an experience with stable contents which is widespread, dramatic, realistic, and bizarre—but practically unknown—that has been largely responsible for the difficulty. The situation is one in which folk observation is ahead of scientific observation. Without sleep laboratories and without polygraphs, folk tradition has apparently maintained an awareness of the distinction between REM intrusions into wakefulness and REM occurring in its proper place. Tradition has not said what REM is, but that would be explanation, not observation. Confusion between observation and explanation by scholars is one reason why students of sleep from before Jones to some of the most recent writers have not seriously considered the possibility that the folk observations could be basically accurate: that the victims are awake and that they do hear and see and feel odd-sounding things. The observations are rejected because they are often accompanied by, and sometimes seem intrinsically to suggest, explanations that are hard for most researchers to accept (witchcraft, demons, and so forth). But even the most preposterous explanation should not prevent us from seriously considering an observation repeatedly made by large numbers of our fellow humans, whatever their education. It was just such a rejection of untutored observation that delayed for so long the "scientific" discovery of giant squid, gorillas, meteors, and any number of other wild and wonderful (but apparently unlikely) facts of this world. In those cases, *post hoc* scientific rationalization was used to explain how people came to believe in such things. Seasoned fishermen were said to mistake floating trees with large root systems for huge animals attacking their boats; farmers were said to have overlooked large iron-bearing rocks in the midst of their fields until they were pointed out by lightning; and in this case, "children and savages" were said to have difficulty knowing when they were awake and when they were asleep.

This rejection of unauthorized observation, however, speaks only to the confounding of the nightmare literature and perhaps to a slowing of progress in the study of idiopathic sleep paralysis. It does not account for the continued separation of the two literatures. There are probably many reasons for this separation. One that has struck me is the fact that students of the nightmare have shown a fascination with subjective material; whereas the sleep paralysis literature has reflected a studied effort to avoid becoming involved with subjective information and to confine serious attention to objectively measurable events such as EEG and REMs. Many nightmare theorists (or dream theorists in general) have allowed their interpretive efforts to make the subjective content in which they were interested appear so malleable as to be almost without any form of its own. Jones's monograph provides many examples of such forcing. This approach has been at least partially responsible for the reluctance of the more objective investigators to broach the topic, because it appears to support all theories slightly but none well. This impression has been cast into doubt for the contents of SP with REM HH by the cases presented in Chapter 3 above. Such full accounts make it clear that there is in fact a pattern or perhaps several patterns. These patterns are visible and researchable; although they cannot be easily or superficially dealt with. A rush to make a system for encoding these contents into gross categories such as "helplessness," "aggression," "passivity," or what have you will create patterns rather than allowing those already present to serve as data. Still, I have no doubt that a cautious phenomenological analysis, constantly submitted to empirical verification, can lead to quantifiable units. If the rigor of the modern sleep researcher can be brought to bear on these contents with anything like the energy that has been expended on the physiology of sleep, progress should come quickly.

SUMMARY

This review has important implications for students of belief and psychology. The former must assume some of the responsibility for assuring that their data do not simply become cultural grist for the psychological mill.[102] These materials need

102. I have discussed this problem both in general and in connection with the Old Hag as sleep paralysis in the context of the history of contact between folklore studies and psychology in "Psychology, Psychoanalysis, and Folklore," *Southern Folklore Quarterly* 38 (1974):187–97.

to be carefully analyzed, not merely ground up. And that process must be rigorously empirical no matter how strong one's commitment to a particular theoretical orientation. On the other hand, psychologists interested in considering cultural materials and experience in all their complexity in real world settings must not make facile assumptions about cultural processes. Furthermore, a steadfast unwillingness to listen to subjective accounts does not constitute empirical rigor. It is good scientific practice to seek the simplest theory possible to account for a set of data, but that should not be accomplished by simplifying the data. This is one of the arguments for using whole texts as well as more easily quantified questionnaire results as data in this book.

This review has also illustrated some of the ways that social and cultural factors have conditioned the responses of sleep researchers to historical nightmare accounts. Among these factors the operation of language has been of great importance in alternately allowing and preventing the development of new knowledge. Part of the time when authors thought they were analyzing systematic observations they were in fact performing etymology. Part of the time when they thought they were discussing etymologies to lend historical interest to their papers they were manipulating observations that constituted potentially useful data. On the other hand, the use of a neologism permitted sleep paralysis research to escape many of the obstacles which the careless use of a folk term brought to nightmare research.

If this is what the Old Hag has told us about the psychological literature, what have psychologists told us about the Old Hag? There seem to be five major points:

1. The Old Hag experience probably occurs when REM phenomena intrude into wakefulness.
2. Narcoleptics who experience the Old Hag may be likely to do so more frequently than other victims, and those rare individuals who have reported experiencing the Old Hag in the midst of physical activities may be narcoleptics having cataplexy attacks.

3. Night terrors may well have been included by observers (since the sleepers themselves are generally amnestic for the episodes) in the traditional picture of the Old Hag, constituting a kind of false positive in the cultural record.

4. Confused accounts with limited similarity to "classic Old Hag accounts" may in fact be closely related, constituting REM intrusion into partially obscured consciousness. The Newfoundland second meaning for Old Hag involving certain kinds of dreams, for example, may refer to REM HH without SP.

5. Finally, the nightmare literature has raised the possibility that the Old Hag may have a special subcategory of explicitly sexual experiences, or she may have a less frightening cousin who is no more widely recognized in modern culture than the Old Hag herself. This will all depend on how close to the mark Ernest Jones was.

These conclusions allow reasonable give and take between science and tradition. No favors are being granted that are not also returned. Where does this leave our analysis of the Old Hag? Can we say that sleep research has "explained" the Old Hag? No, we cannot. We cannot because what has been gained has been a description of physiological events that seem to account for the production of the state, that is, paralysis in wakefulness, preceding or following sleep, during which a complex and frightening experience may take place. The specific contents of the experience, however, have not been explained. They seem if anything more odd than they did before. If they are related to ordinary dreams by the presence of REM physiology, why is their content so consistently the same without apparent regard for culture?

In an excellent article on connections between hallucinations in general and dreams, from a neurological perspective, William Dement and his associates stated the following about content:

> We have completely ignored one large and important area of the overall problem. Our understanding of hallucinations and

dreams will be complete only when we can account for specific details, that is, when we know exactly why one particular dream or hallucinatory episode is experienced in preference to all other possibilities. *Post hoc* deductions about psychological determinants of specific dream content may be rejected out of hand. The only excuse for the massive literature in this realm is a semantic confusion in which "meaning" and "causality" are equated.[103]

Dement was speaking of the content of individual experiences. When the same proposition is applied to a particular kind of content repeated in the experiences of many independent subjects, both the need and the potential importance of such an accounting are greatly multiplied. Perhaps, then, the most important aid the Old Hag can offer psychology at the moment is a new class of observations and a new problem.[104]

103. William Dement et al., "Hallucinations and Dreaming," in *Perception and Its Disorders: Proceedings of the Association, December 6 & 7, 1968,* Association for Research in Nervous and Mental Disease Research Publications, vol. 48 (Baltimore: Williams & Wilkins Co., 1970), p. 353.

104. The nature of this problem may lead those interested in Jungian psychology to question my failure to discuss here the theory of the collective unconscious. One reason for the omission is that the only two Jungian essays I have found that touch on the classic nightmare have suffered from the same lack of access to a thorough and accurate description of the experience as have those of Freudian writers. These two are James Hillman, "An Essay on Pan," in *Pan and the Nightmare,* trans. A. V. O'Brien, Dunquin Series 4 (Zurich: Spring Publications, 1972), pp. i–lxiii; and Jolande Jacobi, "Dream Demons," in F. J. Sheed, ed., *Soundings in Satanism* (New York: Sheed & Ward, 1972), pp. 36–45. The other reason is that the theory of the collective unconscious has not generally been held to provide a sole and sufficient source for such detailed and complex psychological products as the Old Hag.

5

The Old Hag and Culture

  The literature reviewed in the preceding chapter represents the efforts of one segment of American culture (i.e., the academic community) to assimilate the occasional dramatic report of what Newfoundlanders know as the Old Hag to existing knowledge. Given the general lack of information about the nature and frequency of the attacks, it is not surprising that these efforts went in so many conflicting directions.

  Analogous efforts must be expected when Old Hag attacks occur in the presence of traditions of the supernatural which lack beliefs tightly focused on these attacks. In some cases interpretations are likely to be ad hoc; in others the attacks actually form a stable subcategory within a larger stream of tradition. Now that I have devoted substantial space and effort to a description of the phenomenology, distribution, and frequency of the Old Hag and the elucidation of what it is not, attention can be turned to traditional settings of the attacks.

  What follows is intended to be suggestive of the possibilities and is not exhaustive. It is also intended to demonstrate that the examination of the Old Hag in its various cultural contexts requires as much caution in the analysis of experience and establishment of identities as did the first stages of this investigation. If an experience is missing some of the primary features, it cannot be identified as an Old Hag attack, although in written accounts such omissions cannot definitely rule out the identification. If this is not kept in mind, the painstakingly discovered Old Hag experience can disappear among a welter of loose associations as surely as facile symbolic interpretations often overwhelm the very texts they are used to explicate.

I have divided the examples given in this chapter into groups on the basis of the traditional category with which they seem most closely related. The first category, "hauntings," is the most general and includes the longest single text. I do not consider hauntings to be more closely connected with the Old Hag attack than the other categories, but space will permit only one extensive example, and one of my most interesting ones happened to belong in that section. Similar extensive examples exist for other categories but will have to await future publications. Similarly, a complete concordance of the features presented in this chapter and in the accounts already considered and a full discussion of the points raised by these narratives are beyond the scope of this book. A lack of comment, though, does not suggest a lack of importance. These accounts are rich in their implications and their suggestions for future research. Nor am I suggesting that the Old Hag attacks are a "key" to the complete explanation of any tradition. Whenever a single theory or method is advanced as providing the complete explanation of a complex body of cultural or psychological data, we should be very skeptical. I have no aspirations toward the erection of such a monolith using the Old Hag as a foundation sacrifice. I also caution others who find these data as exciting as I do to resist the temptation to use them in that way.

HAUNTINGS

I use "haunting" here to refer generally to the association of a place with spectral beings. These may or may not be ghosts, and the word "ghost" has different meanings for different people. I shall begin this section with a fairly simple account from print.[1]

1. "The Lineback Ghost," in Paul G. Brewster et al., eds., *Games and Rhymes; Beliefs and Customs; Riddles; Proverbs; Speech, Tales and Legends,* Frank C. Brown Collection of North Carolina Folklore, vol. 1 (Durham, N.C.: Duke University Press, 1952), pp. 672–73.

Case 19

"The Lineback Ghost"

This narrative deals with the haunting of a storehouse which was said to have been connected with the murder of a man and his wife at the time of the revolutionary war. It was collected in 1940 from a seventy-eight-year-old informant who claimed personal experience with the ghost. The story concerns a ghostly man and a ghostly dog seen in and around the storehouse, loud noises there at night, and the violent shaking of the storehouse at night. The various elements are combined into a three-page narrative, but I quote only the section that seems most suggestive of the Old Hag.

> Well, I have a friend . . . and he heard of the ghost being so rapid there, so he came on purpose several miles to sleep in the house to see if he could hear anything. And behold, it got on him that night and like to smothered him to death in the bed. He said when it got off it went like newspapers being torn up and went right down through the head of the bed.
>
> Well, my little experience there in sleeping: I was there by myself one night. I hadn't gone to sleep yet, but something crawled up on me just after I had gone to bed and commenced pressing down and I gave a main kick and kicked it off the lower end of the bed.

This text clearly illustrates the basic problems of identifying Old Hag attacks in narratives collected in the conventional manner. The account, very properly, is allowed to unfold spontaneously with as much or as little detail as the narrator elects to provide. This basic text is not subsequently amplified by questions about exactly what sensations were present or requests to clarify ambiguous descriptive elements because such texts are conceived of by many collectors as literature rather than as documentation of events that actually took place. Thus most of them are inadequate for positive identification of any specific subjective event, including the Old Hag.

In the present case, for example, the portion quoted bears an unmistakable resemblance to Old Hag attacks. Of the four primary features, two—impression of wakefulness and realistic perception of actual environment—are apparently present. A third—fear—seems a reasonable inference. But the fourth—

paralysis—is uncertain. We may infer that the informant's being nearly smothered in bed indicates restraint, and it is possible that the "main kick" in the second part came with the breaking of the paralysis. The presence of pressure (see Cases 4, 6, 10, 13, 14, and 15 above) and suffocation (see Case 10)—both well-documented secondary features—reinforces the suggestion of an Old Hag attack. Nonetheless, the information is inadequate to make a positive identification. The presence of these features in a narrative that includes traditional haunting themes and motifs unconnected with the Old Hag makes the need for a stronger case that much more pressing.

The following account provides an example of the ideal haunting narrative in all of the respects just discussed. Because the account raises serious questions, the way I obtained it is of interest.

Case 20

In the spring of 1975 I spent a week at Western Kentucky University as a guest of the Folklore Department at the invitation of Lynwood Montell, the chairman. Knowing that I was interested in belief in general, Lyn suggested that I might enjoy hearing a tape he had made the preceding November. It was an account of the events taking place in an allegedly haunted house as told to him by two of the three young women who currently lived in the house. They had sought advice and help at the university and around Bowling Green because the haunting was rendering the house uninhabitable. Because Lyn's interest in belief legends was well known, someone had suggested they pay him a visit, and they did, thus giving him an opportunity to obtain a detailed description of what had happened in the house.

I was astonished to find that the tape contained several complete Old Hag attack descriptions that had been experienced by several people. It also contained a great variety of other elements traditionally connected with hauntings. By itself Lyn's tape would have been a useful find. But I also had the great good fortune of being able to locate one of the two young women he had already interviewed as well as the one he had not and to interview them myself.[2] I gave them no indication of what part of their story was of greatest interest to me, simply asking them to go back over the entire series of events in detail, with a special emphasis on the recollections of the one with whom Lyn had not spoken. The result was an opportunity to compare the two interviews point by point, and I was surprised to find that there were no substantial differences as a result of either time or the addition of a third point of view. At the time I had one article on the Old Hag in press, but nothing about my research had appeared in print, and I had not yet spoken on it in Bowling Green, so there was no way that the three young women could have fabricated the Old Hag-like parts of the account.

The two interviews together comprise seventy-five pages of transcript and so must be presented in a condensed form. I have combined materials from both interviews (always indicating the source) into one narrative, connecting direct quotations with summaries and comments. Although this is a less than ideal method, a complete variorum of the two full texts, together with necessary comments, would require a separate monograph. I have not changed the order in which the events took place, and all sections given in the informants' own words are directly and accurately quoted. As in the cases given above, any omission of words that occurs in the midst of quoted materials is indicated with ellipses.

This complicated narrative is not presented in its entirety to argue any specific connection between the Old Hag elements and the great variety of other described features. Rather it is presented in this manner to indicate the complex cultural and experiential context in which the Old Hag phenomenon is sometimes embedded. The full explication of all features of this context is beyond the scope of the present book.

I shall call the three women Carol, Ruth, and Joan. All three were in their early twenties at the time of the interview. Carol

2. I am indebted to Michael Stoner, then a graduate student in folklore at Western Kentucky, for making his apartment and tape recorder available for the interview on very short notice.

had completed two years of college and then left school; the other two had graduated from Western Kentucky University. All three had been raised in Kentucky, although Joan had also spent some time in other parts of the country.

The house in which they experienced the problems recounted here is of the "hall and parlor type," estimated to be about one hundred years old. One-half of the house is of log construction, and this half, where Carol's and Joan's bedrooms were located, was said to be the part where most of the events took place. The women were friends of two couples who had lived in the house previously at different times. They had heard rumors that one of these people, the woman who immediately preceded them, had been involved in witchcraft. At one point they seriously considered this as a possible cause of their difficulties, though they eventually discarded that hypothesis.

Soon after they moved into the house on July 15, 1974, all three developed gastrointestinal symptoms, chiefly nausea and diarrhea. Their malady was tentatively diagnosed as hepatitis and blamed on contaminated well water. They stressed that the diagnosis was not certain and said that the symptoms had disappeared about two months after they moved into the house, which would have been roughly two months before their interview by Lyn Montell. Montell also asked them about drug use in connection with their experiences in the house, and they insisted that although they drank alcoholic beverages and occasionally smoked marijuana, the experiences recounted were not temporally connected with marijuana use, nor was there a consistent connection with alcohol.

Following introductory background questions, Montell asked Carol and Ruth what had been the first significant event at the house.

CAROL: I guess the first would be your dream.

RUTH: OK. Yeah. We'd lived there about two weeks——

MONTELL: This is the first thing, now, that happened after the water episode (i.e., the "hepatitis")?

RUTH: Right. And none——Like, all of this——I don't know how much it relates, but we've just put all of this together. All the strange happenings. (This was) two weeks after we moved in. Everyone was gone. It was in the afternoon. I was lying down on this couch and I was having this dream. And it was a very paranoid dream! It was just——You know, like I was really struggling in this dream, to get out of it. And I woke up, and I was awake and I was lying on the couch. And I could see the door. And I was looking at the door trying to get out! Trying to get to the door! Trying to leave and get out of this—— whatever I was in. But *something* wouldn't let me! I couldn't get out. I couldn't move at *all!* And finally, about the time they came in—Joan and Carol, and Jerry, this friend of ours—came in and came over and I just started crying. I was so *glad* that they had come and gotten me out of it!

If they hadn't come, I don't know what would have happened, you know. Because I was just lying there *paralyzed.* You know, like, that could have been just a dream. I don't know, but that was the first happening that was very strange.

MONTELL: . . . (Speaking to Carol.) So what happened after you all came home?

CAROL: OK. Well, Ruth just became really hysterical, you know. Crying, "I'm so glad you all came." She was just frantic and wouldn't even tell us about the dream, it was so intense at that time. So we just, you know, didn't even think a whole lot about it. Just thought it was a bad dream.

Five months later, when I interviewed Carol and Joan, this event was still fresh in their minds, and I was able to elicit additional comments about it.

CAROL: (There was that time) in the living room when Ruth had that dream. Which was the first thing that happened and we didn't really even know whether to relate that to the total experience or not.

HUFFORD: Could you tell me about that dream?

CAROL: Joan and I walked into the house and Ruth's in the living room, um, asleep. And we awaken her when we go in, and she starts crying and bawling, "Oh, my God! I'm so glad you all woke me up! I've been trying to wake up and get out of this room for so long, and I haven't been able to." And she said she kept having this recurring dream. She'd wake up. She'd realize where she was. She'd see the doorway. And she'd try to get up off the couch and leave the room, and wouldn't be able to. She'd fall back to sleep, and have the same dream. Like this happened several times.

JOAN: Yeah.

CAROL: And finally when we walked in she was able to move.

JOAN: Well, it was really a hot day, too, and she said she was just freezing.

CAROL: Uh-huh.

JOAN: She was just really cold.

HUFFORD: So this was during daylight hours?

JOAN: Yeah. Yeah. About 3:30 or 4 o'clock in the afternoon.

CAROL: Yeah.

JOAN: We got back and she'd been having this dream for awhile.

HUFFORD: . . . What was it she dreamed when she went back to sleep?

CAROL: She was dating this guy at the time, and it was a dream about his parents. Like they were——It was a persecution-type dream where she was trying to flee from them for some reason ——the details are kind of vague. But, you know, like she couldn't get away from them. And then she'd wake up and try to leave the room and couldn't move.

JOAN: It was a real paranoid dream. Everybody was persecuting her. Nobody was on her side. Just all these horrible——What did she say? A few——Did she say wolfish looking faces? Everybody was like horribly distorted. Nobody looked——Everybody was really cruel looking. It was just a real paranoid dream!

As we continued to discuss Ruth's experience, Carol and Joan expressed the impression that she had been lying on her back and stated that "it obsessed her for about three days after that. Like she was just——That's all she could think of for about three days." Although such elements as the feeling of coldness could not be checked in Ruth's absence, some can be accepted, such as Carol's estimate that Ruth was found around four o'clock in the afternoon. The account is credible because the elements that repeat Ruth's own account are faithfully recounted, including the uncertainty about the connection between this and the other events in the house.

Following her telling of this episode to Montell, Carol went on to a different set of observations.

CAROL: So the next thing that happened is that we had this old refrigerator that we had bought, and it was a really dreary, drab refrigerator. A real old one. So we decided one day to paint it. And just, you know, anybody that came into the house that wanted to add a little saying or draw a picture on the refrigerator, they were welcome to do it. And so we had some really nice collections of things on there. And, like, one night we went to bed. And there was this——I forget what it was that was written down on there.

RUTH: What was written on there was "It is the right——the right of people to throw off such a government." It was written in water color, real big on the side.

CAROL: On the top.

RUTH: Oh, yeah.

CAROL: And it was smeared the next day. And there was——like a couple of days later something else——The paint was completely dried. But we'd wake up in the morning and something else would be smeared off. Or just half of it, you know, wiped off completely. And——

RUTH: This first time it happened there was no way anyone was in that house to do it. . . . Like no one did it and it was smeared off completely. And someone did it on purpose, you know. It wasn't like the dog licked the refrigerator, which we thought of, you know. But——

MONTELL: Then, what did you think of at this time?

RUTH: We had already thought of the possibility of a ghost before that. Like when Joan and I——Joan and I first mentioned it, I think. Did something happen before that? It seemed like we had heard some noises, because I remember the first thing I thought of when I found out about the refrigerator being smeared was that it was a ghost. We were thinking at this time, you know, that there was a ghost.

CAROL: I know. I remember that for about a month you and Joan were hearing all these things. And I would never be there. Just hearing about them through you all. I'd never experienced anything at all.

RUTH: Well, that was the first thing that occurred to me when I found out about the refrigerator being smeared. That it was the ghost. Because we had before that heard noises, and Joan and I, sort of jokingly, you know, said, "Well," you know, "we have a ghost in our house. How nice."

When I interviewed Carol and Joan, this lighthearted early attitude was clearly described, along with its eventual disappearance.

JOAN: It's silly to be afraid. I don't like the feeling and I don't want to be a——you know, a little sissy girl. I'm just not into that.

CAROL: It was like something that we all three were intent on *not* submitting to. Like, "We can overcome this," you know. "We are not going to tuck our tails and run."

JOAN: "We're going to be friendly with you. We can all live in this house together" (laughter) you know.

CAROL: Sure. There's room for——you know, "Bring a friend." (More laughter.)

HUFFORD: But you eventually decided that was wrong?

JOAN: Oh, *definitely!* Definitely!

The following segment is from Montell's interview.

CAROL: So periodically Ruth and Joan were the only ones that were hearing these things at this time. They would hear, like, voices, and footsteps on the stairs going up into my room. And noises in my room. That's usually where it seemed to hang out.

RUTH: But it wasn't happening when you were there——when Carol was there. It would always be when she was gone. There for a time you were going home a lot, and staying home for a couple of days at your parents' house. And Joan and I would hear noises on the stairs and all these things in her room.

MONTELL: What kinds of noises?

RUTH: Thumpings. Footsteps on the stairs was the main thing. The bed, like shaking, when nobody would even be in the room.

CAROL: Tell him about——

MONTELL: The upstairs bed?

RUTH: Right. Right. In Carol's room.

CAROL: And one night, like, I was in bed reading. And I heard——I was just reading and all of a sudden I heard my name called. I hear "Carol" (in a loud whisper) in a sort of whisper. But a real *insistent* type tone of voice. And I——It really scared me because I immediately thought of my mother. And I thought, "Maybe Mother needs me." You know, like maybe she's sick or something. So the next day I called my mother, to see if she was all right. And she said, "Yeah. Everything's fine." You know, nothing going on. And so I didn't explain anything, you know, because I didn't think she'd comprehend too well. But Ruth, I think, heard her name called a couple of times. I heard mine called maybe five or six times altogether. And you said your's was a woman's voice?

RUTH: I don't know. When mine was called I'm really not sure what it was. I was lying on the couch reading in the afternoon. And I heard this "Ruth," you know. This type thing. Called my name about twice. A couple of times. But I can't really say that it was a male or a female's voice. I'm not sure.

MONTELL: Real low?

CAROL: Yeah.

RUTH: It was like "Ruth!" (In a loud, clipped whisper.)

CAROL: It was real fast.

MONTELL: It seemed like the same type of voice, then, with each of you?

CAROL: Yeah. I think it was.

MONTELL: And neither of you were asleep?

CAROL: No. I was wide awake reading.

RUTH: I was reading also, when it happened to me.

MONTELL: And what did each of you do? I don't think you told about that. Did you respond to the voice?

CAROL: Oh, *no way.*

RUTH: I didn't say a thing.

CAROL: It didn't even frighten me. Like I say, I immediately thought it was my mother, you know. Like it was some kind of communication between my mother and I. I didn't even consider any kind of force or anything in the house. I just thought, you know, somebody needed me.

RUTH: Yeah. It didn't frighten me at all either. I didn't even tell anyone about it for a couple of days. . . .
(Later on) one night I was there by myself. And this was before anybody was really upset about it. All these things had occurred but, you know, like I wasn't scared at all to stay by myself. I was out there and everyone was gone away somewhere——home or something. And I woke up. I guess it was about three in the morning. I woke up to this INSANE racket in Carol's room. I mean, it was *so loud!* It was the loudest thing that's ever happened in the house. It sounded like someone was just picking her iron bed up and *throwing* it on the floor. And picking it up——Just throwing it all around! And I woke up and immediately thought, "Well," you know, "that's the ghost. But it's over in Carol's room. It's not going to bother me," you know. And it didn't frighten me that much. And I told them about it the next day.

CAROL: You were always a bit hesitant to tell me these things because they were always going on in my room.

RUTH: Yeah. We didn't think it was going to happen to us. We thought it was going to stay over in Carol's room. We'd just let it stay there. . . . We were real reluctant (to tell her) because Carol did express that she was frightened that it was only in her room. So a lot of the things we wouldn't tell her. And then it ended up after that and all these other things, we ended up telling you everything that happened.

CAROL: Yeah.

RUTH: Everything that went on.

CAROL: And the next thing was you and Joan's experience.

RUTH: OK. One night Joan and I——I guess it was about 7:30 ——we were sitting there watching TV. And it was a real stormy, rainy night. And——OK, you know how the house is laid out. We were sitting in the living room. And at the time the front door——We didn't use the front door. It wasn't on hinges. It was just laying up against the doorway. And we heard this knock on the door. This prominent loud knock. And we thought, "Well, that's weird." Because any friend of ours would not come to that door, they know, you know, that we don't use that door.

CAROL: Plus, the house is on a hill and you can see any car that comes.

RUTH: Yeah. The lights would shine. There were no cars. Nothing. You know, no cars at all around. And you've got a very long driveway. No one would walk all the way up there just to pull a prank, I'm sure. Anyway, we heard the knock on the door. Joan and I looked at each other, and immediately we sort of panicked. You know, and Joan said, "Come in," and no one answered, and we heard it again. And at that time we both just sort of freaked out. So I ran into the kitchen. We turned out all the lights. Ran into the kitchen. I got a knife and Joan got an ax. And we were really panic-stricken. And we were standing in the kitchen looking in through the——through the living room trying to see into the hallway. And we heard the door open. The front door open, I guess.

MONTELL: It would be the central hall door?

RUTH: Yeah, right. But it couldn't have opened because it wasn't on hinges.

MONTELL: You just heard the sound?

RUTH: We just heard the sound of the door opening. So, you know, we waited and we heard footsteps in the hallway, and we weren't going to wait around any longer to find out who it was, or what it was! So we just went out the back door with our ax and knife in hand, and ran around behind the building. And it was pouring down rain, and we walked all the way down the driveway in the mud and rain and lightning and everything and went to a neighbor's house, and called some friends. And some friends came out, and picked us up. And we all went up to the house with these two guys. We all went up to the house, and we made them go through every room. And there was nothing there. There was nothing strange about the house at all. And we didn't spend the night there that night. And that was *the* beginning of, you know, the panic, I think. That night.

When I interviewed Carol and Joan, they stressed that they did not accept this fear without resistance.

JOAN: You start thinking, "Well, what really did you expect to happen when you heard this banging on the door?" And it wasn't like——You start feeling like, "Well, am I just scared to live out here in the country by ourselves?" But we had lived out in the country for years, you know. It just wasn't that big a deal. That's what people always say, "Poor little girls, out in the country by themselves, scared to death," you know. Without a car.

CAROL: Every little creak, and——

JOAN: But it wasn't like that! I mean, this was *BAM! BAM! BAM! BAM!* On the front door. And you can hear a car coming, you know, five minutes before it gets there.

After Ruth had described this episode, Lyn asked the two women whether they believed in ghosts. Ruth replied, "Oh, I know there are." Carol said, "I've experienced them before. Oh, twice before." Lyn then asked Carol to recount those two experiences. The first involved a noisy and frightening encounter when she was in the eighth grade and she and her boyfriend were parking at night on the property of a man who had recently committed suicide. Because this event is not directly connected with either the Old Hag or their experiences in the house, I shall not give the details here. Her other experience is directly relevant.

CAROL: OK. I went with a friend to visit some friends of his——I didn't know the people that we were visiting, Frank and Rose Smith. They lived on this 1000 acre farm that had seven houses on it. And two of the houses were identical. And all their friends lived in these seven houses. So it was a little community. And so we arrived at their house at about nine o'clock at night and they showed us through the house. And it was a really fine old house. And we sat downstairs and talked for awhile, and I said, like you know, "I'm really tired from the trip. Do you mind if I go to bed?" And they said, "No. There's two bedrooms upstairs. Take your pick." So I go marching upstairs. The stairway opens up into this little hallway-type room. And they had like a stereo and some rocking chairs sitting around in it. So I went in this one bedroom. And I was in there in bed. I was lying on my side facing the doorway. The light was out in the room, but it was on in the hallway. And the door opened. The door knob jiggled and I just thought it was the wind from the windows because there was windows all along one side of the wall opposite the door. And I just thought it was wind, and didn't think anything about it. And then the door opened. And instead of looking at the door I was looking at the light, that was on the other wall from the hallway outside, the light that was reflected. And I didn't see anyone come in. But then I looked back at the doorway and there was this bright shimmering——substance, you know. Like, this very vaporous looking thing. And as soon as I saw it, I was just *stiff*. And I couldn't move. I was just s-s-scared stiff. Paralyzed! And it just sort of floats over to the foot of the bed. And I heard this "hhhhhhhh-hhhhhhhh" heavy breathing, and I thought, "Oh, my God!" And I'm rationalizing, I'm saying, "It's a dog! It's a dog! It's me! It's *me* breathing!" And so I held my breath and the breathing continued. And then it abruptly stopped. And whatever it was came around to the side of the bed and walked behind my back. And I'm straining my eyes trying to see it, but I can't move my head, because I knew as soon as I did I was just going to be this close to it, and I couldn't stand the thought. Well, I just——I couldn't move!

MONTELL: What age were you then?

CAROL: I was, I was about 19, 18, I guess.

MONTELL: It was that recently.

CAROL: Yeah. It was when I was in college here at Western. And so, I started to tingle. Like my spine, all up and down my back was just *intensely* tingling. But that's the only part of my body that was. And I started getting flashes of a knife, and I thought, "My God, I'm going to be stabbed in the back with a knife." And

I was so scared I couldn't scream. I couldn't get up and leave the room. I was just——paralyzed! And then I felt pressure on the bed. The bed went down and I was just——I just freaked. But still, you know, I was motionless and speechless. And then the pressure moved and came back up, and whatever it was came back to the foot of the bed. Just hovered there for awhile. Went over to the door. The door closed behind it. And then the rocking chair in the hallway started rocking. But as soon as the bedroom door closed I was just exhausted and limp. And I knew there was a ghost outside the room in a rocking chair rocking, but I wasn't scared at all. It's like the presence had left, and I just——I didn't feel bad at all. And so the next morning I went——I woke up early and I went downstairs, and Rose was up and I said, "Rose! Do you have any of the history of this house?" And she just turned around real quickly, and she says, "Did you feel something?" And I said, *"Damn right* I felt something!" I said, "There's a ghost up there." She says, "Yeah. We know. We didn't want to tell you because we didn't want to unnecessarily frighten you." I said, *"God!"* You know, "You should have prepared me!"

Montell: Now who all lived there?

Carol: Frank and Rose and their little girl who's maybe two years old. And they said that, like, they'd be there during the day, and the record player would start playing upstairs. Or they'd hear the rocking chair rocking. So they asked the landlord about the history of the house. And he said fifteen years before, two men had lived there, were friends. And one of them had killed the other. He didn't know the reason. Well anyway this guy had killed the other one and stuffed his body in the closet, this little-bitty square closet that goes into the wall, upstairs in the hallway. And they didn't find the body until four years later. I asked them, I said, "How was he killed?" And they said, "I don't know." And I said, "Find out." I said, "I'll bet you anything he was stabbed in the back with a knife!" I said, "Because I really, the whole time this was going on I——I felt like this ghost or whatever it was, was trying to tell me, 'This is what happened to me.'" And so I ran into them two months later, at this diner, and I said, "Hey, Frank, did you find out how that guy was killed?" He said, "Yeah. He was stabbed in the back with a knife." And it just blew me away!

That's the first time I ever really realized I'd come in contact with a ghost. But again, you know, I thought it was a ghost and it touched me.

MONTELL: The sensation that you felt that night. I guess it was at night. Was it the same sort of sensation that you felt out here, or not?

CAROL: Yes. Except this was all centralized, located in my back. The rest of it, has been like all over my body.

Returning to the chronology of events in the house, Carol and Ruth described an evening watercoloring session with friends during which one of their guests painted what they called a "demon." Carol said that it was "a horrible looking picture," but that they hung it on the wall along with the others done that evening. That night Carol had a frightening dream in which this demon chased her through a huge building. Though neither the painting nor the dream appears related to the other events recounted, it is evident that at this point all three were unsure as to which happenings in the house were part of the "haunting" and which were mundane. Given their mounting fear, such a reaction is understandable.

Shortly after the painting incident, their search for someone who could help them render their home less exciting led them to a fellow student who was reputed to be "really heavy into the occult." Ruth said that this student, Jack, "was really interested. He was real eager to help. I think he was *too* eager." Although Carol considered him to be a "phony," they invited him to the house. Jack decided that Carol was a witch and was somehow involved in the etiology of the haunting. He administered an ESP test to the women. He went into what they considered a fake trance and claimed contact with miscellaneous spirits. He attempted to force the spirits in the house to materialize. Finally, he left an amulet and asked to be invited back to hold a seance. He was firmly told that they did not want a seance, and they have not spoken with him since.

Following Jack's disappointing effort at assistance, Carol had a terrifying experience which she described in detail. Several features are similar to those in the attack she experienced in Frank and Rose's house.

CAROL: I was in bed. Again it was three o'clock in the morning. I know exactly that it was three o'clock because after it was all over I ran downstairs and I checked the clock, and it was three in the morning. And——OK, so Ruth, Joan and I had all gone to bed about one o'clock, and I had read for awhile. So I had been asleep for maybe an hour and a half, and I was awakened by this laughter. Like "A-ha-ha-ha-ha" (high-pitched). This real hysterical, cackling laughter. And I was real dazed or sleepy and I thought, "What are Joan and Ruth doing?" I mean, I knew they had gone to sleep when I did. And I just couldn't imagine why they were down there making that insane laughter. And then I——It was like a matter of about four seconds. I hear this rustling on the stairs. It wasn't really footsteps, but it was just a noise out there. And then I smelled this really foul odor. And I'm still dazed and confused and I'm thinking a dog——One of the dogs has come and gone to the bathroom in my room. And then my bed starts rocking sideways making this insane racket, and I'm still rationalizing, you know. I thought, "Well, it's the dog," you know, "And he's up on the bed scratching fleas. And that's what's causing it." And then I was touched on the neck and in the shoulder area, right in here. And from that point outward I just tingled all over. And again I couldn't move and I couldn't scream. Until I finally thought the word *"No!"* And as soon as I thought, "No!" I thought, "I can't fight this." And then it went away. So then I turned on the light. And I checked and there were no dogs in my room. They were hardwood floors at the time, and we had no rugs down. So a dog or any person you would have heard walking. And there was no dogs, no indication that a dog had gone to the bathroom in my room. So I jump up and I started screaming, "Joan! Joan!" And I ran downstairs into her room and I said, "Joan!" She said, "What is it, Carol? What is it?" I says, "Did you hear that laughter?" And I was shaking all over! And she said, "No, what laughter? I didn't hear any laughter, Carol." She says, "But I was awakened by this noise in your room. It sounded like somebody was throwing your bed around." And I said, "They were! They were!"

MONTELL: You heard this, then?

RUTH: No. *I* didn't.

MONTELL: OK. Joan heard.

CAROL: Joan heard it. I awakened her. Joan's room is right below mine.

In my interview five months later, Joan agreed that she had heard the noise. She had just remarked, "There were so many times we heard noises, voices——"

JOAN: There was the night you heard . . . the voices of two women laughing upstairs. . . . I had awakened because I heard the thumping upstairs. . . . I had been awake for a little while and I was really surprised just to hear you, "Joan!" You know, running down the stairs.

CAROL: . . . I remember looking at the clock, and this was after I'd sat on your bed and said, you know, like, "Wow! Did you hear the laughter?" And you said, "No. But it sounded like somebody was throwing your bed around." And I was saying, "Yeah! Somebody was!"

As soon as Carol had compared notes with Joan, she woke Ruth and the three of them spent the rest of the night in Joan's room, as described from Lyn's interview.

CAROL: We all slept together that night. The rest of the night.

RUTH: In Joan's room.

CAROL: And at dawn we thought we heard noises up in my room.

MONTELL: All three of you heard the noises then?

RUTH: Yeah. We slept in the same, in Joan's bed that night.

CAROL: We finished the night out in Joan's room.

MONTELL: Where did you hear the noises coming from, though?

CAROL: Upstairs in my room. . . . And then right at dawn we heard footsteps coming down my stairs. And the front door, the wooden door, didn't open, but we heard footsteps on the front porch. And then the screen door slammed. And that was right at dawn.

That night the three recalled the rumors that the woman who had occupied the house immediately before them was a witch, and they began to wonder if she might be involved in what was happening. Subsequently, both Joan and Ruth questioned the woman, and Carol spoke with her boyfriend. Joan thought the response she received was rude and perhaps suspicious, although Ruth later found the woman reasonable. Eventually, they decided that they had "pretty much ruled that out completely," meaning this woman's alleged activities as a witch.

The next crucial event to all three was an experience of Joan's, which Carol and Ruth described briefly for Lyn. I was able to get the full details from Joan.

JOAN: The last night I spent in the house it happened to me, although it wasn't the first time it had happened. I just——I'll take this one night because it was the most intense. And I was just at the point in my head that I wasn't going to be driven out of my house by this ghost.

CAROL: Joan, you were being real brave about it. Joan was still sleeping by herself. And Ruth and I were sleeping together at this point.

JOAN: And I was determined. You know, I'd stay out there at night by myself, if nobody——Because without a car it was real inconvenient and a drag to go into town sharing a car, and having to stay in town all night waiting for somebody to give you a ride back home. So I was just going to stay there. And I just didn't, you know, I didn't want to be driven out of my home. So the last night I was there I had gone to bed, and Ruth and Carol had been out. They had been working in town and had come home later. And I had gone to bed before them. And I heard them come in and go upstairs. I guess they were, you know, they were sleeping up there. They'd gone to sleep, and they'd left the light on. They slept in the same bed with the light on at this point.

Well, I woke up, I guess, about three or four in the morning, and it was to a bad dream. I just felt——I just woke for no reason. I don't know——I'd woken up at twelve, and I went to sleep when they——when you got home.

CAROL: And you'd been sick for two days.

JOAN: I'd been sick.

CAROL: That's when you had that virus. Remember, you were having really bad stomach cramps, and diarrhea and nausea.

JOAN: Yeah. Yep. Anyway, I woke up at four o'clock in the morning, and I'd been having——I was sort of conscious of having——of being——It wasn't like waking up. It was like being in—— Like watching a TV screen through your——although your eyes are closed——and just watching——It wasn't like a dream, really. It was like you were, you were made to watch these things going on before you. You were just a watcher, you know. It wasn't even like a dream. And you weren't participating, so much. I was like seeing mass murders. Now I kind of put the tag on of Germany, or like Hitler mass murdering the Jews. And I was just——Like I was watching a TV documentary or something, of all these horrible killings. And then I started, "No," I said. "No." Like, "Leave me alone." I was trying to say, "Well, this is just a bad dream," you know. "Just get away. Just leave me alone. If this is just in my head——Is this in my head, or is somebody doing this *to* me? Or some*thing* doing this to me?" So I was trying to reject it. Just eject it out of mind, but I couldn't. And then it started getting heavier. It was like, then I started seeing these axes *flashing* through the air! And I saw myself, like it was urging me to do something *evil*. It was like a power——

I was just frozen. I was just *stiff*. I could not move! I don't think my eyes were open either. That's one thing. My eyes were not open.

CAROL: Didn't you say that like you were sick, and when you woke up you were aware of the discomfort you were feeling. And didn't you say that *it* entered your body and all the pain went away?

JOAN: Right. Yeah. I did.

CAROL: She felt *good*.

JOAN: Right. Right. It was like there was a *tingling* sensation that just——that you realize is not, you know, coming from within your body, or something. It is *in* your body, but you know it's not originating there. Because I had been sick a couple of days. And I just felt, you know, like I'd been crampy and had a lot of diarrhea and shit. And then I just felt *good!* And I was just lying there and all of this stuff starts going on in my mind. And I just

——think——well, *"I can't move!"* I tried to get up. My first thought was to get up and turn the light on. I could not do it. And I don't think my eyes were open——I'm sure they weren't. And then I opened my eyes, and I just said, "Get away." I said it out loud. I finally was able to say, *"Get out!* Leave me alone!" I said it out loud.

And I got up and Samson was in the room. And——that's my dog——and then I thought, "Well, it's gone." You know, "I've done this. I've gone through this before. I've told it to leave and it's left before, so I can go back to sleep now and things will be all right." So I tried to go back to sleep. Well, within fifteen minutes I could feel it again. And it was——I felt like it was *urging* me to do something I didn't want to do. And I started thinking, "Well, am I going crazy?" Or, you know, "Is this real or am I making it up? Am I doing this to myself?"

CAROL: At this point we were all doubting our sanity.

JOAN: "Or is something else doing it *to* me?" Really! I was just, you know, "Joan, what are you going to do?" You know. "This is crazy! You've got to overcome this! Is this you doing it? Or——It *must* be!" Like I was just going nuts. I was just thinking, "God, now am I really this far gone to be seeing these things in my head?" And, you know, wanting to do evil to somebody else. Not *wanting,* but just fighting it. They wanted me to——I saw myself in this——The second time I woke up, before this dream that I was having——or not dream, it was like a picture show in front of me——I was watching myself *murder Ruth and Carol!*

CAROL: With an ax!

JOAN: With an ax.

CAROL: She was chopping us up!

JOAN: Right.

CAROL: Didn't you say at one point you got halfway out of bed, or halfway sitting up and it entered you again and forced you back?

JOAN: Well, it was like I had just gotten it together to get up, and I just——I was just——I *couldn't do it!* I couldn't move.

HUFFORD: Did you get to sleep after the first experience, and you woke up to this again?

JOAN: No. I was just settling down. Trying to get my shit together. And it just came back. OK. And then the second time——I don't know why! I just don't know why. It was just like, "Well, I'm not getting out of bed again. It's gone. I'm *not* getting out of bed! What *am* I going to do?" you know. So I just went——I just laid back down after fighting it off the *second* time. Well, the *third* time it was just *too much!* I just couldn't handle it! I just jumped out of bed, ran up the stairs as fast as I could, and got in there and the light was on and I thought, "Oh, great," you know, "I won't have to——" I said, "Carol! Ruth!" You know, they were just out. They were just out. They'd been drinking. They were just out. So, I thought, "Well, I'll just sleep in the other bed there. I'm all right." You know. "There's two other people in the room. The light's on. I'm fine." You know. "I'll get under the covers and I'll just lie here."

"Well, I start——I lie down and I start hearing this "Joooa-aann." Just my name being called out. And I'm just going "Oh," you know, "No. Not now. This can't be happening to me now." So I was just lying there and it wouldn't quit and I thought, "This has *got* to be in my head. This has just——This isn't really——" you know. It just sounded like a far away——It was a man's voice, just kind of "Jooaan. Jooaan." Just from a distance. Just calling. It was just unceasing. It went on for——I'd say anywhere from half an hour to an hour and a half. I don't know how long. But until it was dawn. Until the light broke. It was probably about——It might have been two hours.

CAROL: It was moaning, too.

JOAN: Well, that was like after. While my name was being called, I thought, you know, "What am I going to *do?!*" And every now and then I'd say "Carol! Ruth! Wake up!" But I couldn't get out of bed. I was——I just *couldn't* move. I *wouldn't* move. It didn't even cross my mind to get out of that bed and, you know, run away or do anything. I was just, like, listening. Just sweating it out.

CAROL: . . . I remember when it happened you said, "And I felt that the presence was in the doorway, but either I *couldn't* look, or I wasn't inclined to look."

JOAN: Oh, no! No. I was looking. What was happening was—— OK. I started hearing my name called, and then I heard these steps. Footsteps coming up the steps to the bedroom. And I thought, "Well, Skip—who's sleeping in Ruth's room—is freaked out. He's scared about something too, and he's coming up to sleep in the room with us too." You know. He had, I guess he had just come over there to sleep because he'd just moved out of his house. And I thought, "Well, it's Skip." But I was——

The light's on in the room. It's not dark at all. It's bright. And I heard the footsteps coming up, and I heard this heavy breathing like somebody was chugging up those stairs, you know. You know, having a bit of difficulty maybe. And then I hear this *moaning*. And like a *presence* in the doorway, and a moaning. Just, "Ooohhh." Just like——Oh, *classic* moan! And I just——I just went, "Oh. Oh, noooo way!" But I *couldn't move,* you know. I was looking at the doorway. My head was kind of turned . . . I was just *there!* I didn't even want to move. That's what they asked me afterwards.

HUFFORD: But you didn't see anything?

JOAN: No. Nothing.

HUFFORD: What was it that they asked you afterwards?

JOAN: They said, "Well why didn't you just *make* us get up?" And I just said, "Well, you know, there was no explanation for it. I guess I could have gone over and just said, 'Get up! Get up!' but I just couldn't do it." I just didn't——It just wasn't in my mind to do it. I just, you know, went through this thing. You know, this——I was *supposed* to go through it or something. I don't know. I have no explanation for it.

But it was, you know, the whole night was just one of horror. I mean, I just——just to know that you didn't have control over what was going on in your own mind. It really freaked me out. And that was the last night I spent in the house, too.

HUFFORD: How did that end, then? . . .

JOAN: . . . Time passed. I just lay there and, you know, the noises stopped. The moaning stopped. The voices were still——The voice calling my name was still there. But I just, you know, I just stayed there until——

HUFFORD: Awake?

JOAN: Yeah! I was *awake!* I didn't go to sleep, believe me! I was just, just kind of staring, I guess. Just petrified. And all these weird things going on. Thinking I'm crazy, you know, "Am I crazy? Would I really have tried to kill Carol and Ruth?" You know. "What would have happened if I hadn't gotten out of that room?" (Then) . . . I kind of thought, "Well, maybe I'm not as insane as I could be," because I was thinking pretty rationally about being insane. (Laughter.) You know, it was really weird! It was really weird.

There followed a brief discussion in which Joan indicated that her dog never showed any signs of being upset during these events. I then asked her to go back over the sensations involved in the attacks in her own bed.

HUFFORD: Going back downstairs. When, after the first time you got up and felt everything was all right and you lay back down. You felt it coming over you, you said. Describe the sensation as exactly as you can.

JOAN: Well, at first I just kind of sensed something there. I don't know how to explain that.

HUFFORD: In the room?

JOAN: Right. Just a presence or just a——

CAROL: You could feel it.

JOAN: And then physically it's like a tingling through your shoulders. And then kind of a heaviness, maybe. Or a pressure. A heaviness in your chest and it kind of just spreads down through your body until you just can't move. Well, or like you just don't *think* about moving really, at first. It's not like you're really concentrating on, "Well, I've gotta get out of this thing," you know. "I can't let this happen," right away. Because it feels *good.* It's not a bad feeling.

CAROL: It's a real pleasant sensation.

JOAN: It's not a bad feeling at all. Until you start thinking—— well——

HUFFORD: Here I'm stuck.

JOAN: A tingling. Well, I don't know how to say——How do you describe "tingle?"

HUFFORD: Is there any sensation you've ever had that's similar to this?

(SOMEONE ELSE IN THE ROOM): Like when your leg's waking up from being asleep?

CAROL: No. It's not like that at all. That's more of an irritation type.

JOAN: Yeah. This is a very pleasant like, rippling——

CAROL: Very sensual[3]—— (Laughs.)

HUFFORD: Rippling?

JOAN: Yeah.

HUFFORD: Through the surface of your skin?

JOAN: No, more inwardly.

CAROL: Inward.

JOAN: It's like in—in your body.

CAROL: It's like your nerve ends are just all being stimulated by some real pleasant—vibration or something. And it's a real pleasant sensation.

JOAN: It is.

HUFFORD: Vibration. Joan, do you think of vibration in connection with it too?

JOAN: It depends. Well——

CAROL: Well, people use that in a real general sense now.

JOAN: Yeah. It depends on what you mean by a vibration, but I don't know——You know, I wouldn't really think of it as that.

---

3. In Case 18 above and in the final section of this chapter I have presented some evidence that suggests a possible connection between this "tingling" and "out-of-body experiences." The comments here about the initial pleasantness and even "sensuality" of the feeling may also indicate a link to those overtly sexual experiences, "incubus" and "succubus." In considering this possibility, however, we should keep in mind the full range of the tingling phenomenon—including very unpleasant sensations at times—and look for further evidence. Simply assigning the unpleasantness to repressed sexual conflict, an obvious temptation, will not suffice.

HUFFORD: It didn't seem like a motion or anything?

JOAN: No. No. It was more like, just——a presence——I don't know how you can——A vibration and a presence could be the same thing, but——

HUFFORD: Well, when you said that you sensed a presence there, I asked, "In the room?" And you said, "Yes." Did you mean in yourself?

JOAN: No, it was in——It was physically away from me in the room. Like maybe five feet away from me in the room.

HUFFORD: But you didn't see it?

JOAN: No. No. I didn't even think of looking for something to see. No.

HUFFORD: You knew it was there but you didn't think of looking at it?

JOAN: Right. Because at this point I was pretty much used to it. Let's put it that way. I knew——not *that* used to it though!

HUFFORD: Have you any idea why you think it was five feet away?

JOAN: Well, because my bed is——the foot of my bed is maybe six feet and from there my head is——you know——it seemed like maybe at the foot of my bed. Like in the room and the room wasn't that big.

HUFFORD: So you had a sensation of its location without seeing it?

JOAN: Yes.

HUFFORD: Did you have any sensation of anything else about it? Its appearance or size or motion?

JOAN: No.

HUFFORD: Or intent?

JOAN: The *intent*, maybe. I felt like it was trying to control me. It was trying——After, you know, after I thought about it for awhile—all night long—I realized that I had to get away. That I wasn't strong enough to overpower it. That it——it wanted to overcome my will. That it was intent on either doing something to make me—I don't know—freak out mentally——Or it wanted me to do something evil physically. And by that time it just seemed——I don't know. I think it takes awhile to——whatever this force is—I just call it the force because I have no theories about it——But whatever it is it takes its time to *know* you, and know the people in the house, and just everybody's little routines.

CAROL: Yeah.

JOAN: And their personalities and their strong points *and* their weaknesses. And kind of get to know everybody before anything happens.

HUFFORD: Oh, by the way, how were you lying? On your side?

JOAN: On my back.

HUFFORD: . . . Can you think of any other experiences you've ever had that approximate (this one)?

JOAN: Any other time besides——Yeah. In a house that Judy and Betty and I——Well, we had just moved out there. I was in the house by myself and I was sleeping. I had gone to bed and I was expecting other people to come home that night. And I thought I heard somebody come home, close the door, and walk in the house. And I thought somebody had come home, but no-body——I called out somebody's name and nobody was there, so I went back to sleep. And I was having these real weird dreams. And I had——I started——When I had kind of gone back into a sleep I started having this tingling sensation, and just a freezing, you know. Like just total paralysis. Total paralysis. And I just couldn't move. I broke out in a sweat at this point. I remember breaking out in a sweat. And just kind of staring, like rigidly, for about an hour or so, until I was just so exhausted from the tension of it that I just kind of fell asleep. And I don't ——It was just a weird thing. I just——This was the first experience I ever had with anything like that.

HUFFORD: How old were you?

JOAN: Twenty-one.

HUFFORD: Same tingling?

JOAN: Yeah. The same sensation totally.

In Lyn Montell's interview, after a brief description of Joan's experience, Ruth and Carol moved their focus back in time to touch on several events that preceded Joan's final departure from the house.

RUTH: We were getting real upset about it. I mean scared to stay there. I would not sleep by myself ever. You know, we would get really frightened. And one night after work I went down to a bar in town. And I was sitting there just with some friends. And this couple at the table next to us kept looking at me. And kept staring at me, and smiling and giving me good vibes, you know, and I kept looking over at them, you know. There's something. . . . We're communicating somehow. So I went over and sat down and introduced myself, and she said——the girl, there was a girl and a guy——She said, "I don't know why," she says, "I feel something really weird from you. Like I know you're really upset about something. And you know, I'm just wondering if it has anything to do with witchcraft or anything like this?" And I said, "Wow, I can't believe you said that!" I'd never seen her before. She's not from Bowling Green. She's from Louisville. She was just visiting here for the weekend. Her and her boyfriend are down here. And I went, "I can't believe you said that," you know. And I proceeded to tell her about our house and everything. And she said, "I knew something was troubling you, you know, and I could just *feel* it. And you sitting over there I could feel something was wrong." And at the time it really was bothering me because we were going to have to go home that night. And I was scared to go home. I was real scared to go home. And she told me that her father was a warlock. And that he had left her family when she was pretty young, maybe 10 years old or so. He left her family because of the fact that he was a warlock, and he didn't want to involve his family in it. You know, black magic, or whatever it was he was into. And she said, you know, "I myself am not into it a whole lot, but I am receptive to it." Because of him, I guess. And she knew something was wrong. And we talked about it for awhile. And she told me to look her up when I was in Louisville. But it blew me away that someone who didn't even know me could feel the vibes. Could feel that something was present. That something was wrong. So that night I went to pick up Carol, and Carol and I were going to stay there by ourselves that night. So we went to the house, and coming up the driveway we saw the porch light was on and several of the lights in the house were on, that we had not left on. Especially the porch light, I'm sure was off when we left. So we go around and we parked in back of the house. We go inside the house. And by the time we get in the house, the porch light has been turned *off*. And you know——

CAROL: So we said, "Come on dogs," and we grabbed the dogs and we left.

RUTH: We left. And went to a friend's house.

In both interviews the women then described frightening events ranging from loud bangings in the night and hearing their names being called to what they regarded as unintentional thought transference among themselves and others who stayed at the house. Then they told of their recourse to a Roman Catholic priest in Bowling Green. Although none of the three was Catholic, or an adherent of any organized religion, they had accepted a suggestion that a priest might be able to help. In describing this encounter, Carol said, "At first we could tell he was real skeptical and hesitant to believe us. Thought maybe it was just in our heads. And after we talked to him he said, 'I'd be glad to come out and bless the house, and bless you all.' " While in Bowling Green, I was able to contact this priest and discuss the case with him at some length. He said that he had in fact been skeptical at first, but that their account included details that rang true and that he did not think they would be likely to know about. He did not specify these details. He did bless the house, but the frightening events continued, as described from Montell's interview.

CAROL: (After the blessing) we didn't stay there because the car was broken down. For four nights we didn't stay there. I was completely convinced that everything was all right. It was gone. Nothing was going to happen. He had left this crucifix hanging in our house. And he also left some holy water and a blessed candle. And that night that we went out there we couldn't find the holy water anywhere. But the crucifix was still there, and the candle was still there.

And I went up to my room. I had been asleep. I had read for awhile and then turned out the light, gone to sleep. And the cat, Ruth's cat, came and jumped on my bed, and started curling up around my neck. So I had to throw the cat off the bed about ten times. So I was wide awake, and I was just trying to get back to sleep when *it* touched me again and I couldn't move! I was freaked out totally and then finally it went away and I just yelled "RUTH!" And so Ruth was with a friend and they came over, running over to my room. And I told them what had happened, and I said, "You all are sleeping here with me!"

And so I got on the couch and they got in the bed. And Bill (Ruth's friend) had this dream.

Because Carol's description of Bill's experience is more complete in my interview, I shall now switch to that transcript.

CAROL: (He) said that he did this, had these dreams——he called them dreams——like during his childhood repeatedly. You know, like recurring dreams. And he said they were always frightening experiences. And so it was several years——like he's twenty-three or twenty-four now. He said for like about seventeen years or fifteen years, he hadn't had this dream. And this night . . . he said he had that recurring dream. And he said he woke up and he couldn't move, and he was just lying there thinking, "I'm never going to come to this house again! These girls are foolish for staying here!" And so, he and Ruth got up that morning at about six o'clock, after Bill said finally, after he laid there for so long, he finally managed to move. And everything was all right, and he woke Ruth up. They got up and went downstairs, and he said a couple hours later——I was sleeping on the couch in my room——he hears this *moaning* coming from my room, and he says, he runs up the stairs thinking, "Ah! Carol needs me. She's in trouble!" He said he walked in the room and I'm just snoring, you know, like sound asleep. And Bill just said, "You all are crazy! You're crazy for living here. Get out!"

HUFFORD: So he had, in the past, fifteen or sixteen years before, experienced this where he would wake up from dreams and be unable to move? And it happened to him again there?

CAROL: Yes. And it happened to him in the house. And he thought that the house was, like, the cause.

Joan's final encounter and departure from the house had taken place shortly before Lyn's interview, and Carol and Ruth left soon after that interview. In the spring of 1975 Joan and Carol told me that all three of them felt much better since they had left the house. They also mentioned in both interviews that while they lived there they had been "at each other's throats" much of the time and that their close friendship had been endangered. Since they have left the house, however, they were once again as close as ever. Although I have not recounted all of the events covered in the transcripts of the two interviews, and the two interviews together did not include everything that had happened at the house, the above is sufficient to give an idea of the context in which the paralysis attacks took place.

In reaction to information about Old Hag attacks, especially such striking narratives as the one just given, I have found a consistent tendency for scholars to focus on ultimate explanations of the phenomena. Those with either a parapsychological or a supernaturalist perspective argue that such evidence supports their contention that current physical knowledge is inadequate to explain all observable phenomena. Others either explain each piece of evidence separately, using a combination of psychological, social, and physiological explanations, or insist that a further elaboration of current theories will render the entire mass of data congruent with their world view in ways that are not yet evident. Because my study is still in the early stages of data gathering, it is necessary to retain a cautious viewpoint and to avoid drawing conclusions until more is known. So far, it is possible to support a hypothesis about the role—or lack thereof—of culture in the production of one class of personal experience frequently interpreted by the subject as supernatural. The more obvious ways of explaining away this class of experience can be rejected, and it can be tentatively associated with a particular state of consciousness. Any further leap to final explanations would still be premature.

Taking this cautious approach, several observations can be made about the material given above. First, there was apparently no opportunity for contamination, intentional or otherwise, of these accounts by my own work because it was not yet in print. Montell's interview occurred months before my first visit to Western Kentucky, and my own interview was done before I had spoken on the subject there. When interviewing the women, I did not indicate which portions of the "haunting" were of greatest interest to me, and I gathered extensive material on all aspects. All of the Old Hag–paralysis accounts given in both interviews were provided spontaneously. The great detail on these points and the other happenings at the house were a result of the interview method employed. Montell treated Carol and Ruth as observers rather than as storytellers, asking questions about both their observations and their interpretations that are often omitted in the collection of "folk tales." I obviously did the same, but Montell's use of this approach is to be commended because he did not have the specific motivation that I did. Clearly, if we wish to know more about the nature and role of personal experience in traditional accounts of the supernatural this is the most effective way to conduct interviews.

All three of the young women were prepared to consider a supernatural explanation, and they easily located others who appeared knowledgeable on the subject. As I have noted above, supernatural belief traditions are more generally distributed in North American culture than has generally been acknowledged, and interviews such as this one support that contention. However, more lengthy inquiry into the bases and modes of thought involved in these belief contexts is needed. Although there is no indication that Carol, Ruth, and Joan were personally involved in, for example, modern Gardnerian witchcraft or spiritualism, they knew something about the subjects. Some of this knowledge came from the popular press and movies and some from oral tradition. Their knowledge was sufficient to allow them critically to evaluate the advice and help they received, as illustrated by their response to the efforts of Jack, the student "medium."

The most intriguing aspect of this case from the perspective of the present study is the number of paralysis attacks reported to have taken place at the house. Five episodes seem identifiable as Old Hag attacks: Ruth's experience in the afternoon in the living room, which begins the story; Carol's episode that included the sounds of laughter, the foul smell, and the bed-banging; Joan's repeated attacks the night before she left, which theoretically could be separated into at least two discrete parts, one downstairs and one upstairs; Carol's second described attack in the house following which she called Ruth and Bill into her room; and Bill's subsequent attack. Each of these also includes references to similar attacks that are not described in detail but are said to have happened in the house. Two additional attacks—one described by Carol and one by Joan—had happened before they rented the house, and they believed these were identical to the ones they experienced during the haunting. And Bill stated, as reported by Ruth and Carol, that he had a personal history of such attacks, but that none had occurred for over ten years before the night he spent at their house.

This evidence presents two separate clusters to be explained. First, two of the three women who reported the haunting had experienced an attack in a completely different setting a few years before, and a friend who spent the night at the house had also had a previous attack. Once the level of fear became intense, the total number of people who spent nights in the house appears to have reached ten or more. Given the 15 to 25 percent distribution figure arrived at earlier in this book, it is not surprising that of these, at least three had had previous Old Hag attacks. In terms of the impact of the Old Hag on traditional narratives, it is clear that the accounts of these prior experiences were elicited by the context and that such additional experience may be expected to form a part of lengthy discussions of hauntings.

Much more startling is the clustering of so many apparent Old Hag attacks in a single location over a few months' time and involving several people. If all of the attacks had involved a single person, they would have been following one of the well-established patterns of distribution. I have encountered numerous subjects who have had repeated attacks over a period of weeks or months, after which they ceased spontaneously. Here five or more attacks—probably at least three times that many—occurred within about 120 nights and involved four people. My data are not sufficient to allow a strong statement about the number of attacks per night of sleep in the general population. A reasonable calculation based on the information given in the first few chapters of this book and the estimates given in the sleep literature, however, will make this density of attacks appear enormously high. By themselves, these attacks suggest an environmental variable capable of greatly increasing the likelihood of Old Hag attacks. Such possibilities as the contaminated water and subsequent illnesses come to mind, but getting from such a factor to the production of the attacks is not an easy theoretical task.

With the exception of Bill's attack, on which there is incomplete information because he was not interviewed, these accounts are rich in secondary features: footsteps, prior dream recall, complex tingling sensations, directly perceived "presences," difficulty in expressing the experience of immobility, unpleasant odor. I shall not here discuss each feature and attempt to connect it with those considered previously. Interested readers may do so by using the index of features at the end of this book. Nevertheless, the presence of so many documented secondary features is reassuring that the phenomenon is indeed the Old Hag.

Finally, in addition to paralysis episodes, these attacks are associated with many of the events traditionally reported in connection with hauntings: furniture being moved; ghostly footsteps; people's names being called; the unhinged door being heard to open and close; strange smells; and still others not given in the above text. Potential explanations will doubtless occur to those who have an urgent need for them. They range from hysteria and suggestion[4] attendant upon a sleep paralysis epidemic of unknown etiology to the predictable behavior of ghosts. It is important to observe that these elements occur together in this account and determine whether the same pattern is repeated in other cases.

---

4. Several studies have been published concerning apparent epidemics of hysteria, including both delusions and hallucinations. See, for example, D. M. Johnson, "The 'Phantom Anaesthetist' of Matoon: A Field Study of Mass Hysteria," *Journal of Abnormal and Social Psychology* 40 (1945):175–86; and Alan C. Kerckhoff and Kurt W. Back, *The June Bug: A Study of Hysterical Contagion* (New York: Appleton-Century-Crofts, 1968). Even though the possibility of hysterical contagion seems established, the present case does not involve just any set of shared bizarre experiences but the Old Hag specifically. Hysterical contagion may prove to be a useful concept in the explanation of such apparently shared events, but by itself it does not account for the most challenging data.

Case 21

The informant in this case had heard from a mutual acquaintance that I had done research on sleep-related problems and came to ask me whether I could shed any light on the events she proceeded to relate. As did Case 20, this one occurred in 1975, and the informant said that she knew nothing specific about my work. She is a middle-aged Caucasian woman, well educated, with a full-time career in business. After she had sketched the details, I arranged for her to come to my office the following day so that I could tape record the account.

JANE: My niece was——Well it started when she was about age five. And she was having problems breathing, and it was attributed to nerves causing asthmatic attacks. That sort of thing. But the curious part of it was that the house that they lived in had very strange things happening in it. The man who had lived there before them had committed suicide. He shot himself in the garage of the home. They found guns buried in the gardens, hidden in the attic, that sort of thing. So he had evidently been contemplating this for a long period of time. His wife had, or his widow had remarried and moved away from there and that's when my sister and her husband moved into this home. Things would happen. I used to baby-sit for them quite a bit. Things would happen such as, you would hear footsteps. They had hardwood floors, and an open stairway. So if you would be sitting in their living room you could look on the open stairway. You would hear the footsteps, look on the steps, and you could actually see the steps move! Doors would open and close for absolutely no reason at all. The rocking chair would start rocking, that sort of thing. And the next thing that would happen would be, Ann would be screaming—that's my niece—would be screaming that she couldn't breathe. You'd run upstairs to her and she'd be sitting up straight in bed, staring straight ahead, and when you'd grab her, she'd start this screaming kind of thing. It didn't only happen when she was sleeping. It happened, it could happen to her when she was watching television. And, of course, this—the physician said—was all attributed to the asthma kind of thing. But if you would yell the man's name—who had committed suicide—his name was James. If you would say, "James, get out of here! Phyllis doesn't live here anymore," the doors would stop slamming, the rocking chair would stop rocking. That sort of thing. But there were many, many situations——they had called the family physician in, she had been given adrenalin. That sort of thing. And it was all attributed to the asthma. When they moved away from the home, there were no more problems. She was not screaming in the middle of the night. She was not having these severe asthma attacks. And at the present time the only time she has any kind of attack of asthma is when she is very, very upset. . . .

HUFFORD: Now, you said that she had one or two attacks while you were baby-sitting?

JANE: Right.

HUFFORD: Would you describe all of the details surrounding each of those?

JANE: Because she had asthma it was customary to go in and check on her several times a night after she had gone to bed. A lot of times I would walk into the room and she would be sitting up staring and I would grab her and then she would start screaming. Very tight in the chest, having a lot of problems. You know, breathing, that sort of thing. But we always, you know, checked on her. And, after she got awake, or when you touched her, then it was all right. But she always had this attack afterwards. But she was extremely frightened! Usually when you were baby-sitting and you heard noises it was always, it was always, "Go check Ann's room" kind of thing. But if you would yell, "James get out of here," then the walking sort of thing would stop.

HUFFORD: Well, now when we spoke before, you mentioned that one time you were sitting downstairs and you heard——the first thing that was involved here was that you heard footsteps somewhere. All right, could you run through that in sequence? Exactly what was it that happened?

JANE: That was——I was downstairs, and it was the, the stair steps moving, the walking up——and it was a long open hallway on the second floor of the home. You could hear the footsteps walking towards the bedroom, and when it went in Ann's room it was the screaming kind of a thing, just staring straight ahead, with the breathing kind of a thing. But you could follow the footsteps to her room. . . . I just kind of followed the sounds, and went to her room. It was when I went into the room that she started to scream. . . .

HUFFORD: Now you said that there were two times when something like that happened, and the second one was a little different?

JANE: That was when she was home from school at one time and she had a cold or something or other. And she was sitting on the couch——Or *lying* on the couch watching television. And I went in to check on her and see, you know, if her fever was up or anything like that. And when I went in she was——she scared the daylights out of me because I didn't think she was breathing. She was just staring straight ahead. I didn't know what had happened to her. And I kind of——on impulse grabbed her and shook her, in a kind of——way. And then it was the screaming, and she kept saying, "There's something sitting on my throat! I can't breathe!" Kind of a thing.

HUFFORD: Was she lying down or sitting up, or what position was she in when you found her just staring?

JANE: She was lying down.

HUFFORD: And that time you didn't hear any noises?

JANE: No. (And then another time) I was there. You could hear——This was the classic kind of occurrence. At the end of the open hallway there——like I said, it was an open stairway. And a long open hallway with the doors going into the bedroom. At the end of the hall was the door that went into the attic. *That* came down from the attic. The door opened and through the hallway——So it was almost like somebody was wandering around the house at any time. You never——it was no specific time when this would happen. . . .

If you'd start hearing the noises——My brother-in-law used to get very, very upset and start cussing at this noise kind of a thing. And just scream, "Now get the Hell out of here and leave us alone for awhile," kind of a thing. And it seemed like if he heard it first and started his yelling at whatever—you know—"You get out of here!" there wasn't an occurrence of this. . . .

Jane mentioned that immediately after being touched or shaken and brought out of an attack, her niece usually reached for her asthma medication. I then asked why she did not reach for it right away without waiting for someone to shake her.

JANE: She seemed to think that——She just felt like she couldn't move. She didn't really know——She couldn't explain what had happened to her. It was just something very heavy that she couldn't breathe. Something that scared the daylights out of her! . . . She always reached for the asthma medicine after she started screaming. Then she would reach for it. But if you walked into her room before she would scream, she'd just be sort of staring straight ahead.

HUFFORD: So, her eyes would be open?

JANE: Yeah. . . . She had a very panicky look. She's got very, very large dark eyes. And when she's frightened they seem like three times as large. And all I could see were her eyes staring, you know. Kind of straight ahead, very frightened.

Jane said that after the family left the house when her niece was about thirteen years old the nocturnal attacks ceased. She continued to have occasional asthma attacks, but these were less severe and they occurred under ordinary circumstances. In discussing the matter with her mother, she learned that her sister (the niece's mother) had been repeatedly awakened by similar attacks when she was a child. "She would wake up in the middle of the night, screaming that somebody was sitting on her chest, that she could not breathe." These attacks, though, were not accompanied by asthma, and the difficulty breathing ceased when the paralysis ended. While these were going on, she was treated both by medical specialists and by a powwow.[5] The family did not believe that any of the treatment helped, but the attacks finally remitted spontaneously.

In the case recounted by Jane, the clear presence of fear and immobility, together with the fact that the child's eyes were observed to be open, suggest an Old Hag attack. But there are not enough subjective details to verify the impression of wake-

---

5. A "powwow" is a folk healer who uses primarily magico-religious methods. Powwows have been popular and numerous for over a century in parts of Pennsylvania with a strong German cultural influence.

fulness and the realistic perception of the environment. Jane's niece may have been having attacks of *pavor nocturnus,* and certainly the emotional arousal that accompanies both that and the Old Hag attack could have triggered an asthma attack in one who is asthmatic. The lack of certainty about the features highlights the possibility that stage 4 night terrors (including the *pavor nocturnus* of juveniles) may be indistinguishable from the Old Hag in traditional accounts if the one who had the experience is not available for close questioning. On the other hand, the apparent ease of awakening and orienting the child resembles the Old Hag more than *pavor nocturnus.* [6]

Again, an apparent Old Hag attack is found in the company of traditional haunting motifs: chairs rocking by themselves, doors opening and closing, spectral footsteps, a history of violent death associated with the house, and the cessation of all these phenomena when the ghost is addressed by name and told to go away. These two accounts led me to search published collections of folk legends of haunting for evidence that this association is other than chance. Although most such texts suffer all of the descriptive deficiencies noted above, I did locate some clear descriptions of the Old Hag, although not all of them from firsthand. For example, in an article on the Bell Witch (a highly publicized nineteenth-century haunting that did not actually include anything obviously related to witchcraft per se) in the *Journal of American Folklore,* the attacks suffered by the daughter of the Bell family were described: "She would wake up in the middle of the night, screaming and crying that something cold and heavy had been sitting on her breast, sucking her breath and pressing the life out of her."[7] I have

6. Case 21 illustrates the difficulty of establishing a definite diagnosis retrospectively. The breathing difficulties could support a connection with *pavor nocturnus,* since sleep apnea episodes have been observed immediately before stage 4 night terror awakenings. Furthermore, sleep apnea is known to occur as a distinct syndrome. (For both points see the references in note 15, Chapter 3 above.) Although the picture Jane presents of her niece's attacks fits the Old Hag better than it does *pavor nocturnus* or sleep apnea syndrome, it is easy to see how it could be readily assimilated to one of these in the absence of a good description of the Old Hag.

7. Arthur Palmer Hudson and Peter Kyle McCarter, "The Bell Witch

not traced this reference to the older printed sources, in which such a search might be rewarded with further presumptive evidence of the Old Hag's involvement in this famous case.

Another example comes from a news story about a family's haunting in a small town in Ohio in October 1978. The story concerned local accounts of frightening and inexplicable events and the local residents' reactions to them. Some newspapers treated the story seriously, but others took the opportunity to poke fun. I have omitted all names on the assumption that at least some of the principals would not appreciate more exposure in print. One newspaper account includes the following description of the major phenomenon involved in the haunting. "Mrs. _____ described the incidents as 'a feeling of heaviness' beside her bed. 'Do you know the feeling when one of your children gets up in the middle of the night and comes in the room, and you wake up and see them standing there beside your bed? That's the same feeling, only it was so frightening that I couldn't turn over to see what was there. I felt paralyzed. I tried to speak and couldn't make a sound. It's the worst thing that's ever happened to me,' she reported."[8] According to a piece in the Toledo, Ohio, *Blade* for October 31, 1978, the same woman also mentioned feelings of pressure in connection with the experience: "She felt a strange 'heavy presence' bearing down on her legs, from ankles to knees as she was going to sleep."

These stories appeared in several different papers and do not seem to be a hoax. The Old Hag attacks, however, may have occurred as isolated incidents that were associated with unrelated local events after the attacks received publicity. The most important point about them is that again an account essentially presented as representing a haunting included Old Hag attacks as a central feature. We may conclude that the features of the Old Hag attack are such that they are easily assimilated to accounts of haunting and that such assimilation has in fact taken place repeatedly.

---

of Tennessee and Mississippi: A Folk Legend," *Journal of American Folklore* 47 (1934):51.

8. *Carey Progressor,* 18 October 1978.

WITCHCRAFT

Given the strong connections in Newfoundland between the Old Hag and traditions of witchcraft, it is not surprising that similar connections are found elsewhere, even without a clearly named and described traditional category for the paralysis attacks. A well-known feature of European and American witchcraft traditions is that witches are thought to ride. Popular representations often depict witches riding broomsticks. Folk tradition more often contains stories in which a witch is said to change a sleeping person into a horse, by means of a magic bridle, and ride the unfortunate victim outdoors through the night.[9] I have never found such an account in the field, and published ones are very rarely firsthand. The firsthand accounts typically focus on a less fantastic, though no less frightening, phenomenon. The following is an example from Pennsylvania.

Case 22

This black woman was thirty years old at the time of the interview. She was born in Pittsburgh, and her mother had been brought there from Alabama at a very early age. This woman was currently enrolled at an area college.

> FRANCES: This happened when I was younger and I must have been around nine, ten or eleven. I don't remember exactly how old. But I was laying in bed one night, and I know that I was awake, you know. I just——I know that I was awake. And beside my bed there's a door. And the door was white, painted white. And all of a sudden I saw this person coming out of the door walking towards me——And the person had on my mother's dress, and that was the favorite dress of my mother's. You know, that I liked on my mother. And the dress was brown and white and it had a yellow trim. You know, a sleeveless dress. I just re-

9. For two excellent articles on this and related beliefs and narrations see: Wayland D. Hand, "Witch-Riding and Other Demonic Assault in American Folk Legend," in *Probleme der Sagenforschung,* ed. Lutz Röhrich (Freiburg im Breisgau: Deutsche Forschungsgemeinschaft, 1973), pp. 165–76; Patricia K. Rickels, "Some Accounts of Witch Riding," in *Readings in American Folklore,* ed. Jan Harold Brunvand (New York: W. W. Norton & Co., 1979; reprinted from *Louisiana Folklore Miscellany* 2 [August 1961]:53–63).

member that dress so well! And the person just kept walking towards me, but I couldn't see a face. But I——you know——like, I didn't feel that it was my mother. You know, because I kind of felt afraid and I couldn't move, I remember that. . . . I couldn't move. I couldn't say anything. And the——It just kept coming towards me, kept walking towards me. And——I just had a—— you know, an eerie feeling. I was afraid, like, you know. But I couldn't move or say anything! And then, all of a sudden I just started to scream! You know, I could finally scream, and when I screamed my mother came into the room.

I asked Frances to elaborate on her inability to see the face and whether there was sufficient light in the room to identify her mother had she actually been there.

FRANCES: I think I would have been able to make out an outline. It was just a black nothing, you know——There wasn't any features or anything——was just a black nothing. . . .

HUFFORD: Could you hear anything while it was happening?

FRANCES: I don't remember anything like that. And my mother, you know, I told her about it. And she told me that it was a witch coming to ride me, because she believes in that stuff. I mean—— And my aunt does too, and she said, "It was probably a witch coming to ride you, and maybe because you were awake she wanted to look like your mother so that you wouldn't be afraid." Or something like that.

HUFFORD: And that's why the dress?

FRANCES: Yeah. Because, of course, my mother——I wouldn't let my mother wear that dress after that. (Laughs.) She had to discard that dress.

HUFFORD: Did she tell you anything to do to keep it from happening?

FRANCES: Yes. She told me that——to say, "Lord have mercy on me."

HUFFORD: Did you say that out loud or just to yourself?

FRANCES: Oh, I'd say it every night! (Laughs.) I didn't care. I said it about three times. . . .

HUFFORD: Had your mother ever told you anything about that kind of thing before? Did you know about witches riding people before that happened?

FRANCES: No. It wasn't something that——I guess my aunt and my mother had spoken about it. But *I* didn't know anything about it.

HUFFORD: How old were you at the time?

FRANCES: About nine or ten or eleven. Somewhere around in there where, you know, I *wasn't* that young that I didn't know, you know, whether I was awake or sleeping.

HUFFORD: Do you still feel that you were awake when it happened?

FRANCES: Yes. I know it. I just *know it!*

The rest of our conversation centered on a detail that I have encountered before, although not frequently. Frances believed that she watched the figure approach her at a normal pace for a long enough time for it to cover at least twenty feet, although the space between her bed and the far side of the hall was only four feet. The figure appeared small at first and became larger.

FRANCES: You know, like if you saw someone up the hall they look smaller, and as they walked toward you they get bigger. Well, that's the way it looked.

HUFFORD: Did you see it through the door, then? Down the hall?

FRANCES: No, because there's no hall there. It's a wall. . . . It was just walking——I don't know how to explain it to you.

HUFFORD: . . . Is it *as if* in that space there was more distance?

FRANCES: Right.

HUFFORD: And the person was coming from far away in that space?

FRANCES: Right. Right!

This seems to be one of the few instances when the victim's perceptions are not thoroughly integrated into the real environment. Because of the subject's difficulty in describing this feature, it must be watched for with special care. In some ways, the distorted perception of the image's size has more in common with "ordinary hallucinations" than do most of the features of the Old Hag. For this reason, it may represent an important clue, although many more such observations will be necessary before its importance can be assessed.

This account appears to be a basic Old Hag attack that occurred in the presence of family knowledge of the witch-riding tradition. As such, it does not pose all of the same problems that some of the haunting examples do, but it is illustrative of the ways in which the basic experience can be easily assimilated to witchcraft beliefs.

Two similar accounts from black tradition were reported by Richard Dorson in his *American Negro Folktales*. Here again the term "witch riding" was employed.

Case 23

Mr. Smith: Well, I had a witch or something ride me once. I don't know what the deuce it was. I heard it before day in the morning.

Mr. Dorson: A witch was riding you?

Mr. Smith: Yeah, I heard it when it come in the house. I was awake.

Mr. Dorson: Really?

Mr. Smith: It come up on the bed, and I could feel it when it pressed the bed—me and another fellow was in the bed together. And it got up on me, and I *couldn't say a word. I lay flat on my back,* and I commenced a-twisting this a-way, and a-whining in my sleep—"ennh, ennh, ennh"—and this boy ketched me. And I heard the thing when it hit the floor, 'bout like a big rat—bip—and out the door it went; you could hear it go on out. I said, "You better go, you devil you." (Laughter.) It was about four o'clock in the morning. That's true.

Mrs. Richardson: Mr. Smith, I know you ain't joking. Because listen, I laid down one day at twelve o'clock. My husband had went to carry the mule to the lot while I cooked dinner. I had some time; so I said, "Well, I'll take a little nap." I laid down, and begun to read one of those birthday almanacs, you know—I was interested in reading. It looked like a shadow come over my eyes, but I wasn't asleep. And I saw a woman come in the door. Both the doors were open—I lived in a little old two room house—and I was layin' cross the bed. And she walked in and stepped astraddle of me and she got on me, and she just started doing this a-way, "runh-runh-runh-runh." And she shook me till I said, "Well Lord, I know I'm going to die." Then I heard when she hit the floor—*vlop*. She got offa me and walked right out the door.

MR. SMITH: And I heard that thing just as natural.

MRS. RICHARDSON: And that was *twelve o'clock* in the day—didn't look like I went to sleep; I hadn't had time to go to sleep; she just overshadowed me.[10]

By no means, however, should it be thought that the witchcraft explanation for Old Hag attacks is limited in the United States to black tradition.

Case 24

This account was collected from the sister of a professional acquaintance. He heard her mention the attacks one day and, without giving her any indication of the nature of my research or any of my findings, he asked whether she would be willing to speak to me about her experiences. She agreed, and the interview began as follows. No preamble or introduction to the subject has been omitted from this transcript. The subject in this case is white, in her early twenties, and has had two years of college. She is employed full time in office work. She was born and raised in a small town in central Pennsylvania.

HUFFORD: Would you start by describing to me all of the experiences that you have had (of the kind that you mentioned to your brother yesterday)?

10. Richard M. Dorson, *American Negro Folktales* (Greenwich: Fawcett Publications, 1967), pp. 239–40. For a similar account collected from a black informant, see Charles Purdue, "I Swear to God It's the Truth If I Ever Told It!" *Keystone Folklore Quarterly* 14 (1969):10–11 ("John and the Nightmare").

LAURA: All the experiences I had. Well the first time I was at my girl friend's house and I——I had been sleeping. I went to bed early that night, and——I woke up but yet I couldn't move. I was paralyzed. But I was lying on my back and I could see everything that was in the room. I could see my girl friend sleeping on her bed and that's just the way it went for——not long. It wasn't long when all of a sudden a bright shiny light came into her bedroom. It was like right at her bedroom door——Just all of a sudden it was there! And I just saw it and I just started screaming. *Inside!* I could feel myself inside, screaming. And then all of a sudden I saw my girl friend get out of bed, I saw her come over and as soon as she touched me it was gone and I could move. And she said to me, "What are you doing?" And I just——I tried to explain it to her, but she couldn't understand it. I was *scared!* For the rest of the night I was *scared!*

But then the second time it happened I was here at home and my girl friend was staying with me. My parents had been away for a week, and I don't——I laid there and it was like I never fell asleep, but yet I went into like a state where I couldn't move again! And I saw everything else going on. The next thing I know, from about half way down the hallway—as far as I could see out in the hallway from my bedroom—I could see like this black shadow coming down the hallway. And as soon as it reached the doorway I started screaming inside again. And then my girl friend turned around, and before she woke me——I mean, you know, touched me, shaked me——I moved my hand and then it was gone again. Once again I was scared to death! So that's basically what happened.

HUFFORD: . . . How old were you and how long ago was it?

LAURA: The first one I must——I must have been about nineteen. Then the second one I was twenty, because they happened, I'd say, from like six, seven months between each other. One was in the fall and one was in the spring.

HUFFORD: . . . Why do you say you screamed "inside?"

LAURA: Well, it just seems like——I don't know how to explain it, but it seemed like for awhile, when I was screaming, like, like——my girl friend wasn't hearing it. And then all of a sudden——Because I was screaming for quite awhile before she even got up to come over, and then it just seemed like——How do you explain it?! Seemed like for awhile it was just going on inside of me, and then all of a sudden it came out!

Laura described her efforts to explain the experience to her girl friend, but in each case the friend simply said, "It was just a bad dream," and went back to sleep. She also described the odd perspective that Frances referred to in Case 22 above. This occurred in the second experience, and she stated that the dark shape appeared to move through about four feet of space in several minutes at a speed that should have required only several seconds. This observation invites comments on how slowly time seems to pass during unpleasant experiences, which may be a part of the explanation. When compared directly with descriptions of such alterations in the perceived pace of experience, however, these seem qualitatively different. They appear to have more in common with the perceptions that are reported in connection with altered states of consciousness. Unfortunately, the full illustration of this point from texts would consume too much space to pursue here.

After we had discussed the features of this experience in detail, I asked Laura what she had thought during the experience and whether she had been frightened from the beginning of it.

LAURA: Not really. No. In fact it didn't phase me until the light came. Then I was *scared!* And thoughts were running through my mind like, "What is this?! Is it the Devil? Is it God? What is this?!" I didn't know, and I was just scared. Scared!

HUFFORD: . . . Did you ever try to tell anyone else about the experience? Either experience?

LAURA: Just the one girl I worked with. She was the only one that really listened. And that was because it had happened to her.

HUFFORD: Could you tell me in all of the detail that you can recall, what it was that happened to her?

LAURA: Well, she said she had been sleeping and then she woke up but she couldn't move. And that she was aware of everything that was going on, and she just watched this black shadow walk by in her hallway, walk into her bedroom and sit on her chest. But she said then, when it was sitting there she could move. And she reached for her phone, because it was right by her bed. And she dialed a number——she said she didn't even know what number she dialed. It turned out to be her boy friend that she was dating at the time, and she told him it was hard to breathe. She couldn't breathe and that something was sitting on her chest! And all he kept saying was, "Gloria," he said, "turn on the light. You've got to turn on the light," he said. "Just turn on the light and everything will be all right. Turn on the light!" And she said it took forever for her to turn on the light. She had to reach for the light, but as soon as she did it was gone. And then right away her boy friend came over and everything. And she said that his one girl friend——He was originally from California and his girl friend out in California was into witchcraft and everything. And I don't know——for some reason it sticks in my mind that he was supposed to go back out, or she was supposed to come East——They were supposed to get married I think, or something, and she found out about Gloria.

The experience of Laura's friend, as described here, is unusual if it is in fact an Old Hag attack, and it contains elements that will require an intensive interview for explanation. More important here is its association with Laura's search for an explanation of her own experiences. Laura's two experiences are classic Old Hag attacks. Neither of the girl friends with whom she was sharing a room at the times of the incidents showed much interest or sympathy when she tried to describe what had happened. Subsequently, Laura mentioned the episodes to another friend who responded with an account of her own couched in terms of witchcraft. Such interaction was suggested in Chapter 2 to account for the association between firsthand experiences and knowledge of the tradition. The events connected with Frances's attack (Case 22) that led to the reinforcement and empirical support of the family's witchcraft traditions are also similar. Laura's friend's explanation may be related to modern, popular witchcraft rather than the folk stream of tradition that was Frances's family's reference point. For my purposes, this distinction is of secondary importance. The main point is that in a variety of cultural and social situations Old Hag attacks are readily assimilated to witchcraft beliefs.

Evidence that adherents of popular witchcraft traditions are familiar with the concept of this sort of attack is not hard to find. The following from a book published in 1970 entitled *Mastering Witchcraft* is an example:

> This process of "sending forth the fetch" is identical to that of present-day practices of astral, or etheric, projection. The fetch itself may be perceived with the inner vision of the victim or, on very rare occasions, with his physical eyes should he or the antagonist be in any way a "materializing medium." This is the basis for the legends of the werewolf and the vampire. . . .
>
> Because of the difficulty in accomplishing the projection, and the perils involved subsequent to materialization, sending forth the fetch is generally regarded as a work for the more advanced practitioner.[11]

This "projection" appears related to connections between the Old Hag and "out-of-body experiences" that will be discussed at the end of this chapter. This "how to" quote is reminiscent of Case 2, from Newfoundland, in which the dangers of hagging were mentioned. Although there are important differences between modern, popular witchcraft and the folk varieties, an examination of the phenomenology of experiences believed to be involved in witchcraft may suggest more common ground and historical connection than has previously seemed likely.

If current Old Hag attacks are often connected with witchcraft, we may reasonably ask whether the same may not have been true for witchcraft accounts when the belief in witches was more generally held. Three brief examples from the Salem witchcraft trials give an affirmative answer.

Case 25

These examples are taken from Cotton Mather's *On Witchcraft: Being the Wonders of the Invisible World,* first published in 1692. Early in Mather's account of the trial of Bridget Bishop

11. Paul Huson, *Mastering Witchcraft: A Practical Guide for Witches, Warlocks, and Covens* (New York: G. P. Putnam's Sons, 1970), p. 152.

he notes that it was alleged "that she had *Ridden* a Man" indicating that the phrase "witch riding" was well known at the time. He continues: "8. *Richard Coman* testifi'd, That eight Years ago, as he lay awake in his Bed, with a light burning in the Room, he was annoy'd with the Apparition of this *Bishop* and of two more that were strangers to him, who came and oppressed him so, that he could neither stir himself, nor wake anyone else, and that he was the night after, molested again in the like manner."[12]

According to Mather, some relatives subsequently offered to stay with Coman, and they, too, were "struck speechless, and unable to move hand or foot." "10. *John Louder* testifi'd, That upon some little Controversy with *Bishop* about her Fowls, going well to bed, he did awake in the Night by Moonlight, and did see the likeness of this Woman grievously oppressing him; in which miserable condition she held him, unable to help himself, till near Day."[13]

Bridget Bishop was not the only one accused of witch riding at Salem. Mather gives the following from the trial of Susanna Martin: "5. *Bernard Peache* testifi'd, That being in Bed, on the Lord's day Night, he heard a scrabbling at the Window, whereat he saw Susanna Martin come in, and jump down upon the floor. She took hold of this Deponent's Feet, and drawing his Body up into a Heap, she lay upon him near Two Hours; in all which time he could neither speak nor stir."[14]

The veracity of individual testimonies in the Salem material is questionable. The witch-riding tradition provided a model for either the fabrication of wholly fictitious accounts or bad dreams following the traditionally provided format, and the trials provided both a highly emotional atmosphere and an opportunity for settling grudges through false testimony. Different commentators have reached different conclusions about the role of these and other factors in the highly complex events

12. Cotton Mather, *On Witchcraft: Being the Wonders of the Invisible World* (Boston: n.p., 1692; reprint ed., *Cotton Mather on Witchcraft* [New York: Bell Publishing Co., n.d.]), pp. 106–9.

13. Ibid., p. 110.

14. Ibid., p. 115.

throughout the witchcraft persecutions in Europe and the New World. Clearly, however, any Old Hag attacks that did occur in such a setting would have been readily connected with the general beliefs about witchcraft and also with accusations and efforts to prevent future "ridings." The information developed so far on the Old Hag attack should be sufficient to allow reconsideration of certain aspects of the older witchcraft records.

Patricia Rickels published, in 1961, a small collection of witch-riding accounts from her own field work in Louisiana, where the attacks are also known to some as *Cauchemar*. She used the material from Bridget Bishop's trial in a novel and informative way. Of one of her *Cauchemar* informants, she reports, "I read her the account of one of Bridget Bishop's victims, written down in Salem, in 1693, and she approved it as 'Just right.' "[15] Although the terms and the exact nature of the explanations change, the attack itself remains easily recognizable—especially to a victim—as long as it is faithfully and fully set down.

DEMONS AND OTHER EVIL SUPERNATURAL AGENTS

Mormon tradition contains the best examples of demonic or "evil spirit" explanations of Old Hag attacks that I have so far located in English-speaking North America. The combination of a strong belief in the supernatural, which is, of course, shared with other religious groups, and a tradition of telling "faith-promoting" accounts of personal experience practically guarantees that Old Hag attacks will be discussed and readily accommodated. The following is an account I collected in Logan, Utah, in the summer of 1979.

Case 26

This woman, a middle-aged, white schoolteacher, came to me after a lecture to say that her husband had had the experience. I arranged to meet her the following day to tape record the story, and she said that in the meantime she would recheck the details.

15. Rickels, "Some Accounts of Witch Riding," p. 59.

SHARON: Well it was about in 1952, while he was in the Samoan Islands[16] in the small town of Tu Tu Illett. And he along with two other friends and a houseboy were sleeping in one of the native huts. And the native huts, of course, are always built up on legs, because of the damp weather. And then it is open with just poles holding up the floor, poles holding up the thatch roof. And it was one night just as they were ready to retire. He wasn't as sleepy as the rest, and so instead of going to bed, he laid down to read with his head at the bottom of the bed. Now while reading he fell asleep, and he said he was awakened by a scratching noise. And he thought it might be a rat, because rats are frequently known to dig under the floors or to run across the floor. But he became aware that it wasn't the same sound, the same kind of scratching, that he'd encountered hearing in other places. And then he said, as he looked out across the pine trees—which were all around the hut—there was a strange movement in them and a strange sound also. And there was a light which would come towards him and back off. And as he's laying there in a reclining position looking up he felt this heaviness upon him, and he couldn't move. And he said the more he wanted to move the more intensified became the light, and its movements and this scratching noise, and he wanted to yell out for someone but he *couldn't!* But evidently he was making some kind of a noise, but yet wasn't speaking. Because what intensified the experience even more was that he was awakened by the houseboy, who came towards him with his hand out to touch him and he could see this bright light in his eyes, which was no longer the light which he was experiencing in the trees, but the lantern. And he woke hysterically, and jumped and ran between his two other friends. And, well, what is even more fascinating about the story is, that he's telling the experience to other people and they said, "Oh, that wasn't too strange an experience," because they had heard it before from this particular hut. So therefore, they never slept there anymore, or had anything to do with that particular hut. But it is well remembered to this day as a very, very frightening experience. But he says—I was talking to him about it just last evening—and he said "You know I've never seen the light, or heard the noises, but often I'm still awakened in the night, with this feeling of not being able to move." And I said, "Well, you've never told me that." "Oh,"

16. He was engaged in Mormon missionary work.

he said, "Well, some people think it's weird——so I've never told you." So evidently he has had similar, but not as intensified, experiences.

Case 27

In the following narrative, sent to me by Jan Brunvand from a student collection, Satan is believed to be the attacker. The informant was a female student.

Dad was about twenty-five when he went to ——— to get an LDS ward settled there. He worked in a store and slept in a building which had four rooms in a row. All the others were empty.

It seemed like everything he tried went wrong. Everything was against him. He had just closed the store. He was never so discouraged in all his life. He walked to the place where he slept. It was warm and there were no windows so he left the door open for air. He went to bed, but he never even thought of going to sleep. He was so nervous.

Suddenly something pressed on his feet so hard it almost broke them off. It moved up his leg. It was such terrible pressure. All at once it snarled and fire shot from it. It was just like an animal, and he knew it was Satan trying to stop him from organizing a ward. Boy, he'd never had anything like this happen to him. Dad always said that the devil works on those who try to do something. Its eyes were this big (about the size of a fruit jar lid) around and like fire. Dad used his priesthood and rebuked it in the name of the Father. It jumped off the bed. He could hear feathers rustling. Dad got up and went to the neighbors.

Dad wouldn't ever tell us kids anything about it until Mama coaxed him one night.

In both the interpretation and the means used to end the attack, this case contains more distinctly Mormon elements than the previous one.

Case 28

This example uses less characteristically Mormon language, but carries the implication that demonic resistance to missionary activity lies behind the attack. A majority of the Mormon accounts that I have seen have come from the mis-

sion field. This preponderance is probably related to the perceived appropriateness of such a context for the experiences
and their consequently greater attractiveness for faith promo-
tion rather than to actual disproportionate occurrence on
missions. This point, however, is open to empirical investigation. The text was supplied by William Wilson from the Utah
State University Folklore Archive.[17] It had been collected by
a female student.

> My sister, a thoughtful, and spiritual girl, was serving a mission.
> After meeting with a family for several evenings, she felt that
> if she could only realize what doubts were bothering them which
> they seemed unable to express, she could facilitate their conver-
> sion. Consequently, she spent a long time that evening at prayer.
> She then climbed into bed and was nearly asleep——drowsing
> and dozing, when her heart leaped in fear. Someone had
> kneeled on the side of her bed causing it to depress and creak,
> and she was suddenly paralyzed so that she couldn't move nor
> call out. In a rush of fear she mentally called to her Heavenly
> Father to protect her and give her courage. The feeling went
> away as suddenly as it had come, and, after summoning her com-
> panion, the two sisters knelt in a prayer for thankfulness and
> they asked for continued help.

The inclusion of these three accounts should not be taken
to indicate that the Church of Jesus Christ of Latter-day Saints
is unique in providing a ready framework for the interpretation
of Old Hag attacks. The greater ease of access to Mormon accounts results from the homogeneity of the Mormon community and the strong social support that community provides for
the discussion of the supernatural. The Mormon situation is
analogous in some ways to the Newfoundland outport in which
a strong tradition about the Old Hag exists. In such a setting,
people speak more freely about their experiences. Some other
religious communities might provide similar encouragement.
Charismatic and Neo-Pentecostal groups, for example, which
emphasize the constant presence of the supernatural, would

17. I have omitted the collector's name here because, as in the previous case, to have given it would have identified the informant because of
the family connection. It was collected in Salt Lake City in 1967.

be good subjects for inquiries about traditional explanations of Old Hag attacks.

Case 29

The informant is a thirty-four-year-old black woman, who has had some college education but did not graduate. She is employed full time as a secretary. She was born and raised in Baltimore, Maryland. She did not identify the threat she felt, though she obviously considered it supernatural. Unlike the great majority of Old Hag attacks, this one was preceded by a ritual which the victim implies may have caused the experience.

Grace told me that several days before the attack she had a long and involved dream that seemed unusually clear but not particularly frightening. She mentioned this dream to an acquaintance who identifies herself as a "spiritualist" and who told her that she could learn the precise meaning of the dream in the following way.

> GRACE: She said first of all there must be absolute secrecy. Don't tell anyone that you're doing it. And she said, "Recite the Twenty-third Psalm, take a glass of water, take three swallows and put the glass under your bed."

Grace said she thought this was "ridiculous" and she "didn't think it was going to work. In fact I laughed at myself when I did it." A few days later, she set out to follow the "spiritualist's" instructions.

> GRACE: I took my three swallows of water. I turned out the light to go to sleep and I couldn't sleep. And we lived in an apartment that was well lit even with the lights out. We had a light out in back there. Right in back of my bedroom. And there was also a street light out in front. So that anytime you got up in the dark there was enough light to see, especially in the hall area, which was, you know, right off of the front room. And this particular night for some reason I remember the hall being very black, extremely black. I mean like all light had been shut out, and it felt like it was in a turmoil. There was a storm brewing in my hallway!

HUFFORD: You noticed this while you were lying there trying to get to sleep?

GRACE: Yeah and I know that it takes you awhile to get accustomed to the dark. Well maybe that's it, "Maybe tonight the street light is out and it's just taking me awhile to get adjusted." And I remember getting just a feeling of pure terror! The kind of terror that just keeps you so you *can't move!* I also remember thinking to myself, "Whatever is going on right now only has to do to me." I wasn't frightened for my child who was not where I could get to him without going through the hallway. And my husband was asleep next to me and I *knew* he wasn't going to wake up. I just knew he wasn't going to wake up, I could be completely wrong about it, I might have kicked him and he would have gotten up and said, "What's going on?" But somehow I just *felt* like he wouldn't wake up, so there was no sense in trying. And I watched this turmoil and you know, the fear was *real.* I mean I *knew* I wasn't asleep because I had barely turned out the light. And I knew this kind of fear was ridiculous because I was in my own house with my family around me, but it was there anyway. And the hall was just dark and I just felt something was there. And at the point where I was the most terrified I saw this glow at my bedroom door and then I saw my great-grandmother standing there and it was very vivid. It wasn't hazy! It wasn't a see-through type thing. It was like *solid.* I mean she was solid standing there and I recognized her right away. We were close and I remember what she looked like and all and I knew it was *her.* And when she died I was 4 and this happened in 1975. But 5 years ago I was 29 and I had never seen her or anything. I had often felt she was *close,* but I mean people tend to do that. You lose somebody you love, you want to think of them as being close. But she was *there.* She was *standing there,* and I remember the fear easing right away. The hallway got as light as it always was, with the way the light shone into our apartment and she didn't say anything. She didn't move towards me. She stood there until the hallway was light and I went on to sleep.

After giving this description, Grace said that she was certain that she was wide awake throughout the experience. She also said that she had never before heard of the dream interpretation ritual and that she had no intention of ever trying it again! In addition to the connection with the ritual, this case is noteworthy for its inclusion of a supernatural protector. Such protectors are, of course, mentioned frequently in supernatural traditions, although I have collected only a few other accounts of Old Hag attacks which contained such a clear protective presence.

Continuing to consider traditions of supernatural attackers through the subjective experience of the victim brings us to the vampire. As with most complex supernatural traditions, vampire attacks are surrounded by such a welter of associated events and interpretive statements that the Old Hag attack is not immediately obvious. Close examination, however, reveals clear examples even in Bram Stoker's literary creation, *Dracula*. As is usually the case, the attacks are most easily identified by a sudden paralysis in one who is lying down. The following case is a victim's description taken from *Dracula*.

Case 30

... when next I remember. There was in the room the same thin white mist that I had before noticed. . . . I felt the same vague terror which had come to me before and the same sense of some presence. . . . Then indeed, my heart sank within me: Beside the bed, as if he had stepped out of the mist—or rather as if the mist had turned into his figure, for it had entirely disappeared—stood a tall, thin man, all in black. I knew him at once from the description of the others. The waxen face; the high acquiline nose, on which the light fell in a thin white line; the parted red lips, with the sharp white teeth showing between; and the red eyes that I had seemed to see in the sunset on the windows of St. Mary's Church at Whitby. . . . For an instant my heart stood still, and I would have screamed out, only that I was paralyzed.[18]

It would be difficult, though perhaps not impossible, to learn where Stoker got his description of the attacks that recur throughout the novel. His source may have been the vampire tradition, with which he was apparently familiar, or he or someone he knew may have experienced an Old Hag attack. The role of the experience in "high culture" artistic creation consti-

18. Bram Stoker, *Dracula* (Garden City, N.Y.: Doubleday & Co., n.d.), p. 267.

tutes a field of inquiry potentially as interesting as the study of the Old Hag in the folk cultural context. From Fuseli's nightmare paintings to Guy de Maupassant's short story "The Horla" to such modern popular novels as *The Entity*,[19] there is a wealth of interesting puzzles to be solved. These include not only the role of the Old Hag or her traditions in the composition of such works but also the impact of these works on consumers of art and literature who recognize in them an experience which they may have always thought (or feared) was unique to themselves.

Bram Stoker's literary creation is not a completely faithful rendering of folk vampire traditions. It is reasonable, therefore, to ask whether those traditions also include the basic Old Hag attack. Predictably, the answer is that they do.

Case 31

This case is taken from Montague Summers's *The Vampire in Europe*. It is a part of a book published in 1653, which Summers says contains "probably the first histories to be recorded concerning Vampires by an English author since the Chroniclers of the twelfth century."[20] It concerns events that supposedly took place in Silesia in 1591. In this case, the vampire is said to be the revenant of a recent suicide.

> To the astonishment of the Inhabitants of the place, there appears a *Spectrum* in the exact shape and habit of the deceased. . . . Those that were asleep it terrified with horrible visions; those that were waking it would strike, pull or press, lying heavy upon them like an *Ephialtes:* so that there were perpetual complaints every morning of their last night's rest through the whole town. . . .
>
> For no sooner did the Sun hide his head, but this *Spectrum* would be sure to appear, so that every body was fain to look about him, and stand upon his guard, which was a sore trouble to those whom the Labours of the Day made more sensible of the want of rest in the night. For this terrible *Apparition* would

19. Frank De Felitta, *The Entity* (New York: Warner Books, 1978).

20. Montague Summers, *The Vampire in Europe* (New Hyde Park, N.Y.: University Books, 1961), p. 133.

sometimes stand by their bed-sides, sometimes cast itself upon the midst of their beds, would lie close to them, would miserably suffocate them, and would so strike and pinch them, that not only blue marks, but plain impressions of his fingers would be upon sundry parts of their bodies in the morning.[21]

The townspeople are said eventually to have obtained permission to dig up the body of the *"Spectrum,"* who was found with no evidence of putrefaction despite having "lain in the ground near eight months."[22] Failure to decay being widely held to indicate that the person involved has become a vampire, the people successfully dispatched the creature by cutting out his heart and burning it to ashes.

As do most traditional accounts, this one contains details that are not easily interpreted, but obviously the Old Hag attack has had an impact. Any Old Hag attacks spontaneously occurring during such a "disturbance" would be readily assimilated to the traditional view of what was taking place.

Case 32
Despite the impression given by popular fiction and dramatizations about vampires, these traditions are not restricted to Transylvania. They also occur in more modern settings. In the same book, Summers considers several accounts of vampirism reported by twentieth-century English investigators of the occult. The following is taken from a piece in the *Occult Review* which is quoted at length by Summers.

A miller at D——— had a healthy servant boy, who soon after entering his service began to fail. He acquired a ravenous appetite, but nevertheless grew daily more feeble and emaciated. Being interrogated, he at last confessed that a thing which he could not see, but which he could plainly feel, came to him every night about twelve o'clock and settled upon his chest, drawing all life out of him, so that he became paralised for the time being, and neither could move nor cry out. Thereupon the miller agreed to share the bed with the boy, and made him promise that he should give a certain sign when the vampire arrived. This

21. Ibid., pp. 134–35.
22. Ibid., p. 135.

was done, and when the signal was made the miller putting out his hands grasped an invisible but very tangible substance that rested upon the boy's chest. He described it as apparently elliptical in shape, and to the touch feeling like gelatine, properties which suggest an ectoplasmic formation. The thing writhed and fiercely struggled to escape, but he gripped it firmly and threw it on the fire. After that the boy recovered, and there was an end of these visits.[23]

It is impossible to know what signal was given by the lad who could neither move nor speak. Modern informants who have had frequent attacks of the Old Hag and who regularly sleep with someone have reported that they often ask their sleeping partner to listen for labored breathing and to shake them immediately when they hear it start.

When comparing the accounts of vampire attacks to other Old Hag attacks, the characteristic detail in the former of the draining of either blood or spiritual essence stands out sharply. When we view this traditional belief from the subjective perspective of the victim, it is hard to avoid a comparison with the fatigue generally reported by those who suffer a series of Old Hag attacks in close proximity to one another. In fact, in Case 31 above it is suggested that even those who avoided actual attack became fatigued by their efforts at constant vigilance. Although more evidence is needed, it is possible to hypothesize that the traditional belief about the sustenance the vampire gains from his victims is at least in part based on the observation of this increasing fatigue.

Although the phenomenology of Old Hag attacks at present includes a variety of tactile sensations, most of these refer to the victim being touched and therefore tell little about the physical feel of the perpetrator of the touching. Such a lack seems natural because of the victim's complete paralysis, which is the rule in these attacks. In this regard, the last case is informative for its description of the "gelatinous" thing the miller is said to have felt. There is a natural temptation to discard this observation on the grounds of a negative reaction to the interpretive notion of "ectoplasmic formations." However, similar

23. Ibid., pp. 163–64.

observations have come from traditions with completely different interpretive frameworks. For example, the following item
comes from the section on "hags" in *South Carolina Folk Tales,*
published in 1941 by the state's WPA Writers' Program.[24]
Here the word "hag" refers to a witchcraft tradition in which
the witch is said to travel to her victim invisibly by "slipping
out of her skin." This explanation for the witch's manner of
traveling about unseen is found in many different areas and,
to indulge briefly in speculation, may be a metaphorical allu-
sion to the "out-of-body" or "astral projection" ideas noted
elsewhere in this book.[25] The following description resembles
that attributed to the miller: "A person without skin is always
invisible. . . . But it is possible for you to feel them. Negroes
who claim that they have accidentally touched a hag at night,
say they never forget the horrible experience. The thing feels
like warm raw meat, and when punched, has the elastic quality
of rubber, it is averred."[26] The question remains of what connection can exist between an experience that seems uniformly
to involve paralysis and another that seems almost to require
movement. The connection in tradition, of course, does not
necessarily mean that there is a connection in actual experience. Like the other phenomenological features of the Old
Hag, the appearance of such descriptions in widely separated
traditions requires empirical investigation.

Case 33
Having considered malign entities with long folk histories,
I shall now present one example of an agent of the numinous
who is generally considered to be of very recent vintage: the
UFO creature. The UFO literature and related topics have al-
ways seemed to me to be worth consideration by folklorists and

24. Workers of the Writers' Program of the Works Projects Administration of South Carolina, comps., *South Carolina Folk Tales: Stories of Animals and
Supernatural Beings* (Columbia, S.C.: University of South Carolina, 1941).

25. In *The Vampire in Europe,* Summers remarked on the possibility of
this connection between the two traditions by calling attention to some of
the details from Salem witchcraft accounts (pp. 115–16).

26. Workers of the Writers' Program, South Carolina, *South Carolina
Folk Tales,* p. 47.

other students of belief. Scholars have made some forays into the area over the years,[27] but there has been little indication of sustained serious interest, even though some authors of UFO books provide material from field interviews. Although problems arise regarding the difference between the methods and canons of accuracy of journalism and those of academia (and the difference is not always as great or as complimentary to professional academics as we might wish), these books and articles are often well worth reading. Their interest lies both in what they tell us about the beliefs and experiences of those involved with UFOs and in their effects in shaping those beliefs.

John Keel's work is important in both regards. In a popular book, *Strange Creatures from Space and Time,* published in 1970, he included a chapter entitled "The Bedroom Invaders." He writes:

> In the past three years we have published two popular magazine articles on these bedroom invaders and we were amazed by the amount of mail those pieces drew. Many readers wrote to tell us, sometimes in absorbing detail, of their own experiences with this uncanny phenomenon. In most cases these experiences were not repetitive. They happened only once and were not accompanied by any other manifestations. In several cases the witnesses experienced total paralysis of the body. The witness awoke but was unable to move a muscle while the apparition was present.[28]

Keel notes the connection between the paralysis of these attacks and the paralysis often reported in UFO encounter narratives. Granting that this is not much to go on, he proposes the possibility that both experiences are "unreal visions," which are "not entirely subjective but . . . caused by some inexplicable outside influence."[29] He added to his own connection

27. From two different perspectives see, for example: Leon Festinger, Henry W. Riecken, and Stanley Schachter, *When Prophecy Fails* (Minneapolis: University of Minnesota Press, 1956); Jacques Vallee, *Passport to Magonia: From Folklore to Flying Saucers* (Chicago: Henry Regnery Co., 1969).

28. John A. Keel, *Strange Creatures from Time and Space* (Greenwich: Fawcett Publications, 1970), p. 189.

29. Ibid., p. 190.

of "bedroom invaders" with UFOs in another book published first in 1970 called *Why UFOs*. Here he described a series of strange phenomena experienced by himself and acquaintances subsequent to his decision to launch a "full-time UFO investigating effort in 1966." He ended a list of such occurrences with the following: "More than once I woke up in the middle of the night to find myself unable to move, with a huge dark apparition standing over me."[30] The Old Hag, then, can be as easily assimilated to UFO beliefs as it can to vampirism, witchcraft, or anxiety neurosis.

Case 34

So far this discussion has been limited to groups that, though differing from one another in significant cultural ways, nonetheless are representative of various aspects of modern North American culture. As the perceptive reader will already have guessed, these examples—both with and without cultural overlay—can be replicated over and over again in other populations. The present example is from the far North. In an article entitled "Eskimo Sleep Paralysis," Joseph Bloom and Richard Gelardin provide several examples and a discussion of Eskimo beliefs about the significance of the attacks. They summarize the attacks described to them:

> The syndrome occurs when an individual is going to sleep or waking up. It is characterized by an inability to move, an awareness of surroundings, a clear consciousness, and a feeling of great anxiety bordering upon panic. The person has no control over his body, may attempt to call out, but finds that he cannot utter a sound. The attacks may be accompanied by some prodromal warning: in the case cited the patient almost always experienced a buzzing sound prior to the attack and usually lasting through it. . . . Attacks usually ended spontaneously after a variable interval of time, but could also come when the person afflicted was touched by another person aware of his struggles.[31]

30. John A. Keel, *Why UFOS: Operation Trojan Horse* (New York: Manor Books, 1970), p. 255.

31. Joseph D. Bloom and Richard D. Gelardin, "Eskimo Sleep Paralysis," *Arctic* 29 (1976):22.

The authors found that of sixteen Eskimos asked about the attacks all knew of them and "some had experienced it." They report the words *augumangia* (in Inupik) and *ukomiarik* (in Yupik) as names for the experience. They state that traditional explanations of the attacks are supernatural and center on the belief that "when people are entering sleep, sleeping, or emerging from sleep, they are more susceptible to influences from the spirit world." Specific Eskimo explanations given include spirits in a "certain place [that] is haunted" and one patient who felt that "during an attack . . . she was not in her body, and that she was fighting to get back in. Apparently the paralysis relates to the body which has been left by its soul, and so is without the quality essential for life. There was the clear implication that if the state of paralysis continued it would result in death."[32]

This article again illustrates the disadvantages to scholarship occasioned by ignorance of the distribution of these phenomena. The authors state that "what is surprising is that sleep paralysis, which is described as a rare condition, seems from first report to be quite prevalent among Eskimos. The fact that the syndrome may be classified as a dissociative type of hysterical reaction may provide some clues to its seeming prevalence among the Eskimo population."[33]

Bloom and Gelardin class this experience as one "involving the non-empirical world" of the Eskimos. Given that the word "empirical" refers first and foremost to a reliance on observation and that the observations of the features of this attack as summarized and exemplified in this article show an excellent congruence with similar observations made elsewhere, the use of "non-empirical"[34] here seems a conceptual trap. The investigator in such cases may well disagree with victims about the ontological significance of the phenomena, but there rarely

32. Ibid., p. 23.
33. Ibid., p. 24.
34. Ibid., p. 21. Bloom and Gelardin patterned their use of the term "non-empirical" on that of Ernest Burch, Jr., in "The Nonempirical Environment of the Arctic Alaska Eskimos," *Southwestern Journal of Anthropology* 27 (1971):148–65. In that article the use of "empirical" to mean "true" rather than "based on observation" is fully illustrated along with the conceptual difficulties attendant on that use.

seems any empirical dissonance when firsthand accounts are employed. In fact, the existence of such experiences in stable form in different cultural settings, and their impact on local traditions, can only increase the appearance of empiricism in the development of supernatural beliefs.

Case 35

Another cross-cultural example comes from the Philippines.[35] For the location of this example, plus a large number of others which are beyond the scope of the present book, I am indebted to Wayland Hand.[36] According to folklorist Maximo Ramos, the *aswang* "is most usefully understood as a congeries of beliefs about five types of mythical beings identifiable with certain creatures of the European tradition: (1) the blood-sucking vampire, (2) the self-segmenting viscera sucker, (3) the man-eating weredog, (4) the vindictive or evil-eye witch, and (5) the carrion-eating ghoul."[37]

As has been true in all of the traditional categories already examined, with the possible exceptions of the Newfoundland and Eskimo traditions, the *aswang* does not resolve totally into Old Hag attacks. Other elements are present, and the Old Hag does not explain the entire mass of material. It is clear, though, that the Old Hag and the *aswang* often keep company. The following is an excellent example from the texts provided by Ramos.

35. For additional Filipino material see Chapter 2, note 3, concerning widespread knowledge of the role of the supine position in increasing the risk of attack.

36. Wayland D. Hand, professor emeritus and director of the Dictionary of American Popular Beliefs and Superstitions at University of California at Los Angeles has generously provided me with the opportunity to work directly with the extensive files of the Dictionary. He and his assistants also have sent me numerous references to relevant beliefs and narratives over the past several years. Although I have been able to use only a small fraction of these in this book, they have been invaluable in forming a clear picture of the relationship between the attacks and widespread traditions of supernatural assault.

37. Maximo D. Ramos, *The Aswang Syncrasy in Philippine Folklore*, Philippine Folklore Society Paper no. 3 (n.p.: Philippine Folklore Society, 1971), p. 2.

At about one o'clock, Aguas felt that somebody was staring at him. He opened his eyes and looked around. At the window he saw an old woman, the lower part of her body missing, staring at him, her greying hair standing up and with her lips open in a devilish grin. Her eyes were bloodshot and big.

He was so frightened that he tried to scream but nothing came out of his mouth. He tried to wake his companion up but he could not move. He tried to close his eyes but couldn't.

After a couple of minutes, the *aswang* flew away. Then Aguas told his friend his own experience. That night Aguas was not able to go to sleep and he just sat on his bed till morning.

At breakfast he was about to tell the owner of the house what happened but he was astonished at the portrait he saw in the dining room. It was the portrait of the landlord's mother and looked exactly like the *aswang* he had seen.

The landlord guessed what had happened to him that night and told him it was his mother and not to worry about her because she wouldn't disturb them any longer.

After breakfast Aguas went back to the city.[38]

Ramos received this account from a twenty-year-old male who had heard it from a friend of the principal character, Agua. The long beginning of the narrative, which I omitted, covered Aguas's insistence that he was too modern to believe in *aswang* and his friend's warning that the house in which they were to spend the night was known to be haunted by one.

OUT-OF-BODY EXPERIENCES

The material in this section constitutes a distinctly different perspective from what has been considered above in this chapter. Those categories are focused on what is believed to be the agent causing the attack. In this respect, they are conceptually similar to such psychological categories as "anxiety neurosis." This category, on the other hand, is defined in terms of process. It, too, has its psychological counterparts such as "hysterical dissociation."

There is a large body of popular, academic, and medical literature on this class of experience, and it represents at least

38. Ibid., p. 60.

as challenging and broad a topic of inquiry as does the Old Hag. References to out-of-body distortions of body image have been encountered in several of the accounts discussed in this book. The Eskimo example (Case 34) was especially graphic in this regard. All of the data that I have been able to gather indicate that the Old Hag is not in any direct sense simply an "ordinary" out-of-body experience. Numerous bits of evidence, however, suggest that at least some Old Hag attacks can lead into such experiences and may in fact comprise a state that is immediately antecedent to them. For the purposes of this book I can only adumbrate a small part of this evidence. An example follows.

Case 36

The subject of this interview was a twenty-year-old college student. She was from "New Jersey, near New York City" and said that she had "no real religious background." I identified her through a questionnaire survey which I carried out in central Pennsylvania in 1979, using basically the same technique described in connection with the Newfoundland survey. She was, therefore, initially a naive subject, and no potentially leading questions or comments preceded her first answers. She responded affirmatively to the question about awaking paralyzed and gave a description of the experience which tallied well with the basic Old Hag attack. She had not heard of it happening to anyone else. In this survey, I asked whether those who had had the experience could compare it to anything else. She answered by saying, "If I were to call it anything I'd probably call it an out-of-body experience." Because of this response, I arranged for a follow-up interview.

I asked her why she had given that analogy, and she responded as follows:

MADGE: The only reason why I would equate it with an out-of-body experience is because when it happened——I feel that I'm not only paralyzed but that I'm almost not in my body. . . . I feel as if I'm trying to rise back *into* my body. I don't feel as if I'm getting out when the paralysis experience happens. It's almost as if I'm coming *back*. And I have absolutely no awareness of

what's happened up *until* then, but I'm trying to regain or re-
cover from an experience.

It's almost as if I'm *underneath* the bed or something. The bed
is there, but I'm at least a foot lower than it.

About a week after this interview she contacted me and
said that she had had another experience since the interview
and thought that it might be of interest to me. The interview
from which the following extract is taken was done two weeks
after the first one.

MADGE: I'd gotten home pretty late on Friday night. The Friday
after Thanksgiving. And I was dead tired when I went to bed.
It was about 3 o'clock in the morning, and I have a room up on
the top floor of our house. So it was kind of cold. I just jumped
in bed and pulled up the covers. And I think I fell asleep in about
a second. And I don't know how long I was asleep, but it didn't
seem like too long. And I heard something, so, I thought it was
someone coming up the steps or something like that. Nothing
serious. But I was just curious as to what it was.

Well my sister was sleeping up in my room. I don't know why.
She just figured, I guess, that she'd wait up for me. So I thought
maybe she was getting up or something. So, I went to get up,
and I couldn't move——at all. And so I thought to myself, seeing
as we had talked about this the last time we talked, that there
was nothing too unique about this. So I shouldn't be worried
and I figured, "Well, I'll just let it go with what it's going to do."
Like I didn't try at all to move. And said to myself, "Gee, this
is——this is funny this is happening again," because it hadn't
happened for a couple of months. So I was just lying there and
I just thought to myself that I'd be really aware of what's happening so that I could try and figure out exactly for myself and for
you——because I wasn't too sure of some of the questions you
asked me the last time.

So this is about two seconds of time. I was sitting there and
woke up paralyzed, and I said, "All right, let's see what happens." And then before I know it—I guess I had a consenting
type of attitude to the whole thing—and I really felt that I rose
up out of my body and it was in like a very systematic way. My
head came *straight* up, and my feet kind of stayed where they
were at the foot of my bed until I was like almost standing

straight up. I guess almost in a board-like manner. There's nothing to it. And it was——it felt so fast to me that I had no control over what I was doing. I didn't really care to have control I was just——And I said to myself, "Now I know for Dr. Hufford that I was paralyzed first and then I (laughs) left." It was the first thing I said to myself when this is happening. So I was really aware where I was. And then all of a sudden I just started falling in space like doing "tumblesaults," but I wasn't moving forwards nor backwards, nor up and down. I was just like——going in a circular motion. . . . So it was kind of a unique feeling though because at one moment it would be scary and then I kind of felt like I was flying. (Laughs.) So, I was finally able to maintain an upright position. And I was about——say two or almost three feet off the ground. I could not touch the ground, I was trying to——As I was looking down at the ground I was concentrating on touching it, and I couldn't do that. So there was something that either pulled me or I just went on my own——But, my bed is up against a wall. Like we have one main wall that everything's on. The beds and dressers and everything. And right opposite in the room in sort of like a dormitory fashion—where part of the room goes out a little bit—there's a window and a window seat and everything. Well, it's just like I got *pulled* towards there. And I looked out the window and there was someone there, but it was a totally neutral person.

HUFFORD: Someone you know?

MADGE: No. No one I know. Totally neutral. I wasn't——I wasn't afraid of this person but this person wasn't friendly either. Like it wasn't scary. But this person was trying to get me to come through the window and this person had almost—— This person didn't care to convince me or coax me to come. Just had an attitude, "Well, if you come through the window you will follow me." That scared, that scared me pretty bad! Because I kind of felt like if I went through that window, "I'll lose contact with anything that is real to me!" Also because my bedroom is on the third story. (Laughs.) That took all this into account, and I was just like, "No! No!, I don't want to go!" I don't think I said anything, but I was just——I know I was shaking my head saying, "No!"

So I tried——From then on my whole goal was just to get back into bed and roll over. That's all I kept saying, "I just have to roll over! That's all I have to do!" So I went——When I traveled it was very fast! Like almost uncontrollable. I don't know, but faster than I could walk. But I was gliding the whole way. And I was always about three feet above the ground. So I got in between the two beds and there's like a little night table there and I reached out for my sister. She's a freshman in high school and she——I don't know why she was up there. She probably fell asleep reading or something. I don't know. So I was like, "Jane!" You know, "Help me!" I knew who she was. She never sleeps with me, but I knew that she was in the bed there and I kept reaching out for her and at one point I thought she touched my hand. And when she did I was able to pull down a little bit to the ground, but like all of a sudden her hand slipped off mine and I rose up! You know, about three or four feet in a second. It's like I felt like I'd flapped my wings and just took off again. So——And then I looked up and I could see this person outside of the window again . . . I was getting disoriented to this situation. I didn't know where I was looking. And this person was there kind of beckoning me to come through the window. And I wouldn't go!

So——I don't know. At the same time I was really thirsty, and my throat was just dry as could be. So I thought I had gotten into bed and rolled over. And so I said, "God, I'm so thirsty I can't believe it!" And I went to get up and right outside my room is a whole flight of steps, and they'll bring me to the rest of the house. And there's a bathroom right down there. So I thought, "I'll go down and get a drink." Except it's really critical that you grab hold of the banister or you fall down the whole flight of steps. (Laughter.) And I knew this so I got to the door and I was trying to find the banister and I could see it——and I was still like two or three feet above the ground! And I was trying *so hard* to touch the top step and I couldn't do it. And then I thought I heard someone at the bottom of the steps. Someone in my family and I just went down all the steps. I didn't go down *each* step. I just went down and I was able to touch——It was someone from my family and I was able to touch them. . . . And then I'm flying up again! I couldn't maintain that. And so I went back all the steps into my room and I don't know if I just gave up hope or I concentrated on getting into bed or what. But then I succeeded. And I was in the exact same position as how I fell asleep with my hands around the covers up at my neck because I was freezing cold and it was only about an hour and a half later. My throat was perfectly dry. I couldn't even swallow. My face was burning hot. I just felt like it was on fire.

Having finally terminated the experience, Madge got a glass of water and then spent the next half hour sitting up and going over the details in her mind. The clock indicated that about one and a half hours had passed since she had gone to bed at three o'clock. She then returned to sleep and passed the rest of the night uneventfully. She felt well the next morning, and there was no indication that her dryness of throat, sensation of coldness, and "burning hot" face had been connected with a fever or any other symptoms of illness. At the time of the interview she expressed the continued conviction that she had been awake during the experience and that it was, in fact, real in an objective sense. She also said that she did not enjoy it and, should it ever return, she would never again submit willingly to a continuation of the paralysis experience.

Madge's narrative raises more questions than can be considered here. Her experience, however, is not unique. Others I have interviewed have described full-blown out-of-body experiences following typical Old Hag attacks. Frequently, these have been cases involving the tingling or vibration mentioned in several of the cases given above, although Madge said that no such sensation was connected with her experience. Conversely, the popular literature concerning the cultivation of controlled out-of-body experiences includes numerous references to the inability to move, often combined with fear, as a not uncommon early feature of the process. For example, Robert Monroe, in one of the classics of this literature, states that one day when he lay down for a nap he saw a light which he at first mistook for daylight and then realized was not. This light, he said, touched him. "The effect when the beam struck my entire body was to cause it to shake violently or 'vibrate.' I was utterly powerless to move. It was as if I were being held in a vise."[39] During subsequent experiences, Monroe, like

39. Robert A. Monroe, *Journeys Out of the Body* (Garden City, N.Y.: Dou-

Madge, decided he would "stay with it and see what happened rather than fight my way out of it."[40] After repeated episodes, Monroe found full-blown out-of-body experiences to be the consistent sequellae to the paralysis experiences. Unlike Madge he decided that he enjoyed them.

At this point, a note of caution is necessary. Some readers may be considering whether they wish to elect to "go along with" a paralysis attack if they should have (another) one. I would advise strongly against it. Madge is not the only one who has reported having regretted her "openness" to the experience. I have spoken with people who have reported years of anguish, some of it involving symptomatology much like some of the features of psychosis, after having intentionally cultivated this experience. On the other hand, I have never encountered anyone who resisted the basic Old Hag experience who seemed injured by it even if it returned frequently. Emergency psychiatric treatment is at times sought by people whose presenting complaint is basically uncontrolled out-of-body sensations.[41]

The suggestion has been made that the typical fear response encountered in Old Hag attacks is the effect of a lack of "openness" to novel experiences, even implying that those who find the attacks frightening are opposed to fun and progress. Based on the interviews I have conducted and bearing in mind the populations with which I have worked, I am convinced that this interpretation is wrong, at least as applied to the Old Hag. The fear is a natural concomitant of most of the paralysis experiences.

Recognition of a connection between paralysis and out-of-body experiences is fairly old in the popular tradition. For example, in a classic book on the subject first published in

bleday & Co., Anchor Books 1971; reprint ed. Garden City: Anchor Press, Doubleday & Co., 1973), p. 22.

40. Ibid., p. 24.

41. See, for example, Raymond B. Kennedy, Jr., "Self-Induced Depersonalization Syndrome," *American Journal of Psychiatry* 133 (1976):1326–28; K. Davison, "Episodic Depersonalization: Observations on 7 Patients," *British Journal of Psychiatry* 110 (1964):505–13.

1951, *The Phenomena of Astral Projection* (a phrase that predates "out-of-body" experience), the paralysis is called "astral catalepsy."[42] The psychiatric literature also connects Old Hag–type and out-of-body experiences at a theoretical level by considering them both to be "dissociative" phenomena. Some traditions, most notably witchcraft belief, demonic possession beliefs, and the Eskimo traditions mentioned above, also suggest that the relationships between the two classes of experience require exploration. However, out-of-body traditions are far more varied in their contents and in the classes of experience into which they may be separated on phenomenological grounds than is the Old Hag. Although some of the directions for the exploration of this nexus can be indicated, and some of the methods employed in my investigation of the Old Hag should be useful in examining the out-of-body experience, a great deal of new work remains to be done on this subject.

42. Sylvan Muldoon and Hereward Carrington, *The Phenomena of Astral Projection* (New York: Samuel Weiser, 1969), p. 155.

Conclusion

On the basis of this study, I have drawn the following conclusions:

1. The phenomena associated with what I have been calling the Old Hag constitute an experience with a complex and stable pattern, which is recognizable and is distinct from other experiences.
2. This experience is found in a variety of cultural settings.
3. The pattern of the experience and its distribution appear independent of the presence of explicit cultural models.
4. The experience itself has played a significant, though not exclusive, role in the development of numerous traditions of supernatural assault.
5. Cultural factors heavily determine the ways in which the experience is described (or withheld) and interpreted.
6. The distribution of traditions about the experience, such as those involving the Old Hag or the Eskimo *augumangia*, has frequently been confounded with the distribution of the experience itself.
7. The frequency with which the experience occurs is surprisingly high, with those who have had at least one recognizable attack representing 15 percent or more of the general population.

245

8. The state in which this experience occurs is probably best described as sleep paralysis with a particular kind of hypnagogic hallucination.

9. Although there may be some connection between the etiology of this experience and narcolepsy, and although certain illnesses could be confused with the experience, the Old Hag experience itself does not indicate the presence of any serious pathology.

10. The contents of this experience cannot be satisfactorily explained on the basis of current knowledge.

Where do we go from here and what are some of the major implications of these conclusions for the study of belief? First, the experience needs a name so that it can be easily discussed. "Sleep paralysis with hypnagogic hallucinations" comes close. As discussed in Chapter 4, however, in current usage this term includes some experiences that are different from the Old Hag and omits many primary and secondary features of the Old Hag. Despite the theoretical importance of this connection, then, the term is too general. "Nightmare," if it could be restricted to its older meaning, would be an excellent name. Unfortunately, the additional connotations the word has picked up over the centuries are too firmly entrenched for it to be used. Of the other traditional names with which I am familiar, only the "Old Hag" and possibly the Eskimo words *augumangia* and *ukomiarik,* have a satisfactory balance between inclusiveness and exclusiveness. For these reasons, I have chosen to use "the Old Hag" as a convenient label, although, with the proviso that I tend to resist neologisms, I am open to suggestions of another term as long as it communicates accurately and does not carry a premature load of theory.

Once a term has been selected, the next step should be to confirm and extend my findings. Fortunately, the basics may be easily replicated by means of the methods described in this book, and no doubt additional methods can be devised that will check both my findings and the effects of my methods. Because the data presented in this book are very sensitive to interviewer effects, I have felt reassured that while I have been at work on this project several colleagues have generously done some such replication. Naturally the confirmation of these findings will extend and probably modify some of them.

I cannot stress too strongly that the replicability of these findings is a consequence of the empirical nature of the approach. Many of the generalizations that have been attempted in the past about belief have not been so easily susceptible to empirical verification. Symbolic interpretations, for example, vary dramatically with the theoretical preferences of the interpreter. With the Old Hag, either a pattern is present or is not. Is there immobility? Is the environment said to be accurately perceived? Do some subjects hear footsteps, and do some describe a pressure on the chest? Efforts to confirm and extend my findings should remain closely tied to discrete and substantial observations. Even features that are hard to describe, such as the "tinglings" or alterations of body image, are much clearer and more unequivocal than such abstract categories as "passivity" or "regression." Higher levels of abstraction should be approached carefully, one step at a time.

Among the most surprising aspects of the Old Hag is the frequency with which the experience seems to occur. As I have discussed in the course of this book, the question repeatedly arises as to how something so common can be so unknown. In 1975 Andrew M. Greeley published a study called *The Sociology of the Paranormal: A Reconnaisance.* Although he did not include the Old Hag among his data, his work underlines the significance of the question and extends it to more than a single phenomenon. Using far more sophisticated sampling techniques and statistical analysis than I have, Greeley examined the frequency with which the general American population claims to have had three classes of experience: déjà vu, extrasensory perception, and clairvoyance; communication with the dead; and mystical experiences. Greeley presents a thorough analysis of the figures for each, the number of experiences per subject, and the association of each category with the other. I quote only the following comment. "Almost a fifth of the American population reports frequent paranormal experiences, a finding that dazzles our social science colleagues as it does us. How could such an extraordinary phenomenon be overlooked for so long? Better yet, why has it been overlooked for so long?"[1]

I recommend Greeley's monograph to all who wish to go beyond the material presented in this book. Greeley supports my conclusion that such experiences are not ordinarily connected with illness, either physical or mental. He accompanied his questions with a measure of "psychological well-being" called a balance affect scale and found a strong positive correlation between the experiences he studied and a positive affect balance. The most crucial point raised by Greeley, however, may be his questions about how and why "such an extraordinary phenomenon" has been overlooked. Greeley's work, carried out in a scholarly fashion by a reputable sociologist, is tremendously important for the study of belief and experience. And yet five years after its publication, the book was out of print, and it is rarely cited even in those articles and books to which its contents are directly and obviously relevant. The reasons for this neglect are to be sought in the culture of modern academic research, and such an inquiry should be considered an important scholarly venture promising both theoretical and practical payoffs.

One of the chief implications of my findings about the Old Hag is that what I have called the cultural source hypothesis needs to be seriously reexamined. It has often been an implicit assumption and therefore has never received careful scrutiny and methodical development, all too often operating by consensus as representing common sense. The present opportunity to bring it into sharp focus and find that for some concepts it does not work at all well may lead to its rehabilitation. But the possibility in a reexamination that I find most intriguing is the location of other researchable phenomena that seem to have been explained out of existence. A reexamination of the cultural source hypothesis in folklore, anthropology, psychia-

---

1. Andrew M. Greeley, *The Sociology of the Paranormal: A Reconnaissance*, Sage Research Papers in the Social Sciences, vol. 3 (Beverly Hills: Sage Publications, 1975), p. 7.

try, religious thought, and other disciplines should result not only in the elucidation of historical points but also in important new directions for current research. An example of the need to reconsider scholarship that has assumed the validity of the cultural source hypothesis is Nicolas Kiessling's *The Incubus in English Literature: Provenance and Progeny,* published in 1977. In this book the author attempts to trace the development of what he takes to be essentially a literary theme reflecting universal forms of human fantasy.[2] As Joseph F. Nagy perceptively stated in a review in *Western Folklore,* "The basic problem with this book is that the author has accumulated too wide a range of folkloristic and literary material under the heading of incubus; the reader is ultimately left quite confused as to what exactly an incubus is and does."[3] I cannot speak for all of the varieties included by Kiessling, but the Old Hag is definitely ill treated. From the frontispiece, which is Fuseli's ubiquitous painting "The Nightmare" (the 1781 version), to the final page of the conclusion, the Old Hag—under a variety of titles—is treated as but one of the many forms of a single class of imaginative inventions. In his final paragraph Kiessling makes the following statement: "Certainly the incubus is enjoying an avatar at the present time in pretty much the same guise, if under different names. Poeple who dream that they are being possessed by the devil are probably tormented by the same imaginary being who stalked through the dreams of primitive man and was described centuries ago as the nightmare who 'leaps on, oppresses, or crushes.' "[4]

In treating as a single phenomenon the Old Hag, the incubus and succubus, the medieval wildman, Pan, Satan, and a great crowd of others associated with an enormous variety of activities and traits, Kiessling uses the cultural source hypothesis to the hilt. Essential phenomenological and cultural

2. Nicolas Kiessling, *The Incubus in English Literature: Provenance and Progeny* (N.p.: Washington State University Press, 1977).

3. Joseph F. Nagy, Review of Nicholas Kiessling's *The Incubus in English Literature, Western Folklore* 38 (1979):134.

4. Kiessling, *The Incubus in English Literature,* p. 87.

distinctions are disregarded, while cause and effect relationships between experiences and traditions are asserted without evidence.

A more general sort of error made by writers on the subject, however, may be more important. Countless articles and
books on supernatural belief have stated that such belief is irrational and, sometimes even by definition, not empirically
grounded. I think that the present study has amply demonstrated that at least some apparently fantastic beliefs are in
fact empirically grounded and that the empirical data have
been dealt with rationally by those who have assimilated
these experiences to their world views. One of the advantages
of having a reasonable description of the stable elements of
the Old Hag experience is that it should make possible a
more careful analysis of the logic employed in the inferential
processes used on those experiences most likely to be
thought supernatural. Such an analysis does not require the
scholar to share the conclusions of tradition, but it does allow
the reaching of such conclusions to be seen as other than stupid. The use of the cultural source hypothesis to attribute
profound stupidity, or at least a fundamental lack of critical
faculties, to those who hold supernatural traditions is well exemplified in the following passage taken from *Swedish Legends
and Folktales* published in 1978.

The nightmare was thought to be able to "ride" either humans
or cattle. The rationalistic explanation, long since offered, is that
the concept of the nightmare is the product of dreams and problems sleeping. A heavy featherbed settles over a sleeper's face,
or a sinus condition affects his breathing, and given the traditional belief in the nightmare, the difficulty is retroactively as-
signed to the nightmare. Unlike many other supernatural
beings, the nightmare is seldom encountered, except in migra-
tory legends; when the sleeper awakes to an empty room, it is
assumed that the nightmare has vanished or turned itself into
some small and insignificant object.[5]

5. John Lindow, *Swedish Legends and Folktales* (Berkeley and Los Angeles:
University of California Press, 1978), pp. 178–79.

For the study of careless thinking retroactively applied with little regard for evidence, we would be better advised to study these assumptions which abound in the literature of folk belief than the belief traditions themselves. And in fact "traditions of disbelief" make up a serious and researchable topic. It would be wrong, however, to be too harshly critical. The history of science is full of blind spots, and this is one in which most of the academic world has participated at least for the past century or two.[6]

As I suggested above in connection with the incubus, one of the important implications of this study is the possibility that the Old Hag is not unique. If one such stable and complex experience exists, apparently independent of cultural models in its etiology and distribution, but having a major role in the development of traditional beliefs, are there any more? The great advantage of the Old Hag for my research was that it involved an experience for which large groups of naive subjects were available. I was thus able to control for at least gross cultural variables in my comparison of the cultural source and experiential source hypotheses. There may well be other such classes of experience which are not well known in North American tradition but have a general distribution. Even more intriguing, however, is the possibility that some beliefs that are well represented in North American traditions, and have therefore been especially easily removed from serious study by means of the cultural source hypothesis, may in fact also be *causes of* belief rather than being *caused by* belief. Space will not permit a full consideration of the possibilities inherent in this suggestion. One, however, is worth mentioning.

The "near death experience" (NDE) is currently a popular topic for argument, and I assume that most readers are familiar with the form that these experiences are said to take. For those who are not, Raymond Moody's *Life after Life* outlines the pattern and most of the arguments begin and end with that pat-

---

6. I have discussed some of the reasons for this problem in folklore studies in "Humanoids and Anomalous Lights: Taxonomic and Epistemological Problems," *Fabula: Journal of Folktale Studies* 18 (1977):234–41.

tern.[7] The writings pro and con on this subject exemplify the effect of a common metaphysical red herring (if I may use such a phrase). Almost all editorializing and much of the research have focused on the question of whether these experiences consititute evidence of life after death. Those who oppose such a belief rush to provide alternate explanations that rarely fit the data currently available. Those who advance the experiences as evidence for the belief in life after death tend to dissipate energy that might better be spent in actual research than on counterarguments about life after death. As a result, very few have focused on a thoroughly empirical study of the experience itself to discover its distribution and frequency, its relationship to other experiences (for example, other out-of-body experiences as discussed at the end of Chapter 5), and its phenomenology. These are eminently researchable questions, and they do not require any particular metaphysical position.

It is perhaps inevitable that those who rushed to explain these experiences away turned automatically to the cultural source hypothesis. For example, an editorial in the *Archives of Internal Medicine* in 1977 acknowledged the existence of a pattern in the NDEs but stated that "the picture is not unfamiliar to those who have seen similar representations of the hereafter in filmed Hollywood fantasies."[8] Not only is the Hollywood statement inaccurate, but it implies that the pattern is a reflection of general themes and expectations in our culture.[9] Beyond the single idea of personal survival, this is incorrect. The experiences as reported by Moody and others do not include such popular images as pearly gates, streets paved with gold,

7. Raymond A. Moody, Jr., *Life after Life* (Atlanta: Mockingbird Books, 1975), pp. 23–24.

8. Samuel Vaisrub, "Afterthoughts on Afterlife," *Archives of Internal Medicine* 137 (1977):150.

9. The one film with which I am familiar that presents the pattern under discussion is Sunn Classic Pictures' *Beyond and Back* released in 1977. This production was clearly a response to the controversy touched off by Moody's book and related discussions in the press. Although the film has helped to render subsequent research more difficult by broad dissemination of the model, its timing prohibits its implication in producing the experiences presented by Moody and those who wrote immediately after the publication of *Life after Life*.

or angels with wings and harps. St. Peter is not said to greet the person and check for his or her name in the *Book of Life*. Conversely, many of the features of these experiences are conspicuously absent from the most commonly provided cultural images of life after death. Floating over the bed and watching resuscitation attempts would have struck most North Americans as incongruous before the popular dissemination of these accounts. Much more consistent with expectations would be an instant change of scene to Heaven or Hell.

But what is most consistently missed is that such critical appraisals of hypotheses need not be conceptualized as a part of the argument pro or con personal survival of death. Most who hold this belief do not need such evidence, and those who do not hold the belief do not want such evidence. The question itself is a red herring. Those who believe may reasonably assimilate such data to their beliefs, and those who do not believe are under no obligation to follow suit. But if those on either side wish to make any claims of scholarship on the subject, they must address those questions about the experiences that are researchable. For example, although I find the cultural source hypothesis to be a shaky explanation on the grounds already noted, the role of cultural models can be determined empirically. Some denominations have specific teachings about what will happen following death, and these teachings differ both from those of the mainstream denominations and those reported in connection with the NDEs. Examples would be the Seventh Day Adventists and the Jehovah's Witnesses, both of whom believe that from the moment of death until the Final Judgment at the end of time the soul experiences a dreamless sleep. Given this strongly preached expectation, if the experiences are a consequence of cultural models, resuscitated Adventists and Witnesses ought to report either nothing at all or a vision of the Final Judgment. If instead these people also reported the standard pattern, the cultural source hypothesis would be effectively ruled out as an explanation of the NDE. The study I have just outlined is not without difficulty. For example, those Adventists and Witnesses who have had the standard experience might either leave their denomination as a consequence or be unwilling to admit to such a dissonant set of observations. In either case, the most important subjects would be at least underrepresented in a retrospective study. However, I do not think that such obstacles would be impossible to overcome. At all events, the trick is to attend to the data and work on hypotheses that are open to empirical confirmation or disconfirmation. It should be unnecessary to issue such advice, but the subject of supernatural belief somehow leads to a lot of forgetting about what constitutes serious scholarship. Fortunately, not all authors who have mentioned the subject in print have lost their footing in this way. Russell Noyes, Jr., and his colleagues, for example, have published useful articles about these experiences under the rubric "depersonalization" without any of the metaphysical confusion that has marred the efforts of so many others.[10] Lewis Thomas briefly considered the experiences in his column in the *New England Journal of Medicine* and, though not undertaking their study, commented that "something is probably going on that we don't yet know about."[11] Thomas's remark may seem simple, but it represents precisely the attitude that has been lacking when potential metaphysical implications have been focused on rather than the observations that are obviously of considerable inherent interest. Thomas's comment suggests further study, whereas statements to the effect that, "Oh, that's just such and such," argue against investigation.

An excellent book on the subject is Kenneth Ring's *Life at Death: A Scientific Investigation of the Near-Death Experience*, published in 1980.[12] Ring takes his subject seriously and is

10. See, for example, Russell Noyes, Jr., and Roy Kletti, "Depersonalization in the Face of Life-Threatening Danger: A Description," *Psychiatry* 39 (1976):19–27; Russell Noyes, Jr., et al., "Depersonalization in Accident Victims and Psychiatric Patients," *Journal of Nervous and Mental Disease* 164 (1977):401–7; Russell Noyes, Jr., and Roy Kletti, "Depersonalization in the Face of Life-Threatening Danger: An Interpretation," *Omega* 7 (1976):103–14.

11. Lewis Thomas, "Facts of Life," *New England Journal of Medicine* 296 (1977):1464.

12. Kenneth Ring, *Life at Death: A Scientific Investigation of the Near-Death Experience* (New York: Coward, McCann & Geoghegan, 1980).

able to provide initial answers to some of the most tantalizing questions raised by earlier work. Of special interest to folklorists, and analogous to my own findings on the relationship between the Old Hag experience and cultural shaping, Ring found that prior knowledge of the near death experience showed no significant association with having the experience during a brush with death. What association he did find was negative. This book is an important addition to the growing literature on the relationship of experience and supernatural belief. Especially refreshing is the fact that although Ring suggests some unorthodox interpretations of his findings, he has kept his collection and presentation of data distinct from these interpretations. Whether or not one finds the interpretations plausible, the findings themselves remain of great interest and apparently free from bias.

Of course, the near death experience is not the only possible object of the kind of investigation I have performed on the Old Hag. Another possibility directly suggested by the material presented in this book is the incubus/succubus experience. I have noted above that this explicitly sexual experience has some elements in common with the Old Hag but also has some very different features. A list of further possibilities would be very long, and it is not necessary to begin their enumeration here. I hope, though, that other students of belief will seriously consider using this experience-centered approach to start the work. As I stated in the Introduction, I believe that what I have done in the present book constitutes the beginnings of a distinctive approach and that this approach can provide new means for the study of supernatural belief in a way that is systematic, empirical, and potentially useful for a variety of academic and practical ends.

I have called this book a beginning, and I wish to emphasize *beginning*. I recognize that everything involved from my survey techniques to my interviewing methods can be developed and improved. The same is true for my efforts at the analysis of the experience into stable components for both indexing and comparison. The means that I have used for deriving a pattern from these components by dividing them into primary and secondary features is still crude.[13] I hope that other investigators who agree that the data are interesting, that the subject is of importance, and that much of what has been observed about supernatural beliefs over the centuries still awaits serious and rigorous study will join me in bringing this approach to maturity. It will not replace the others now in use, but it can supplement them well.

In closing, I want to return to a point that I raised in the Introduction to this book. The subject of supernatural belief is enormously sensitive. Supernatural belief systems entail implications for all fields of human activity and thought, so it is natural that both believers and disbelievers hold strong opinions on the subject. Many readers of this book will in part respond to what I have reported in terms of its usefulness in reducing apparently supernatural events to physical explanations; other readers will be concerned with whether my findings can be used in arguing for a reality beyond the physical. Looking back over what I have presented, I feel that there are some grounds for each argument. A plausible hypothesis linking these attacks to a known psychophysiological state has been offered. On the other hand, the explanation of the contents of that state appears more difficult now than when I began. As I stated at the beginning, however, this book is not offered as an argument for reductive materialism, parapsychology, or any other general position on the ultimate nature of reality. It is instead an effort to gain a better knowledge of the experiences lying behind a particular supernatural belief and to begin to consider the role of those experiences in such belief. A major advantage of the experience-centered approach for carrying out this task is that it does not require presuppositions about the ultimate nature of the events investigated, although it can provide some information relevant to investigations of that nature.

13. For example, the results of my method could be compared with Ring's use of a weighted scoring method to decide whether to include a given experience as a genuine near death experience (ibid., pp. 32–38).

Appendix

The following is the Memorial University of Newfoundland Folklore and Language Archive "Nightmare/Hag/Old Hag Questionnaire" discussed in Chapter 1.

NIGHTMARE/HAG/OLD HAG

Recently, a Folklore student at MUN brought to light an interesting body of material from Newfoundland and elsewhere concerning nightmare/hag/old hag. We are anxious to learn more about this subject. If you know about this yourself or can get information from other people (especially older persons), would you help us by writing it down.

Please write down the descriptions exactly as you know them or have heard them. Detailed descriptions would be best but if you cannot give them, we would be glad to have you answer as many of the following questions as you can.

These questions suggest some points about which we need information. Please feel free, however, to write about any aspect of nightmare or hag even though it may not be covered by the questions.

In the following questions the word hag is used throughout. When writing your information please use the word which is known in your community.

Please write details rather than give straight yes or no answers.

1. In your community, do people speak of having nightmares? If not, what other word do they use (e.g., hag, old hag, etc.)? Whatever they call it, is it thought to be the same as a bad dream? If not, how is it different?

2. Describe the weather conditions under which the hag was experienced (e.g., when the temperature was hot and humid, etc.). Was the hag experienced most often by night or by day or at any special season? Was it generally experienced in one's home, on a boat or elsewhere?

3. What form does the hag take (e.g., human, animal, spirit, witch, object, etc.)? Can the hag be heard/seen approaching? Describe its approach. Please describe what the hag looks like giving a specific example if possible. What is the sex of the hag, if any? What is its age (e.g., always older/younger than the person beset, etc.)?

4. Who experienced the hag most often—men or women? Did a female hag always attack a male, a male always attack a female? Did children experience the hag? How could a person tell if an animal experienced the hag?

5. Would the person beset by the hag be asleep, half-asleep, sleepwalking, etc.? Was a person lying in a certain position when the hag came (e.g., lying on back, on side, sitting in a chair, etc.)? What was the physical and mental condition of the person beset (e.g., tired, under stress, etc.)? What did people say caused a person/animal to experience the hag (e.g., bad blood, going down the forecastle ladder of a boat the wrong way, etc.)? Was it sometimes brought by some outside power (e.g., magic, witching, curse, etc.)?

6. Describe what the hag would do to a person/animal whom it attacked. What parts of the body were most affected? Did the hag sometimes injure, inflict pain, take breath, etc.? Were there any other physical or mental reactions to the hag? Did it sometimes kill people?

7. How did people react to a person who had experienced the hag (e.g., teasing, fear, worry, etc.)? Was the person himself worried about his experience? Does he (or she) talk freely about it?

8. What were ways of gaining release from the hag (e.g., say name backwards, move forefinger, draw blood, etc.)? What information can you give about ways of preventing the hag from coming (e.g., block all openings in the house/on the boat, use of magic, use of mirror, word of God, salt, etc.)?

REMEMBER THAT A DETAILED DESCRIPTION OF A SINGLE EXPERIENCE WOULD BE BEST. REMEMBER TOO, TO SAY WHERE, WHEN, AND TO WHOM IT HAPPENED.

Bibliography

ASERINSKY, EUGENE, AND KLEITMAN, NATHANIEL. "Regularly Occurring Periods of Eye Motility and Concomitant Phenomena during Sleep." *Science* 118 (1953):273–79.

BEITMAN, BERNARD D., AND CARLIN, ALBERT S. "Night Terrors Treated with Imipramine." *American Journal of Psychiatry* 136 (1979):1087–88.

BLOOM, JOSEPH D., AND GELARDIN, RICHARD D. "Eskimo Sleep Paralysis." *Arctic* 29 (1976):20–26.

BREWSTER, PAUL G.; TAYLOR, A.; BARTLETT, J. W.; WILSON, G. P.; AND THOMPSON, S., eds. *Games and Rhymes; Beliefs and Customs; Riddles; Proverbs; Speech; Tales and Legends.* Frank C. Brown Collection of North Carolina Folklore, vol. 1. 7 vols. Durham, N.C.: Duke University Press, 1952–64.

BROUGHTON, ROGER J. "Sleep Disorders: Disorders of Arousal?" *Science* 159 (1968):1070–78.

BRUNVAND, JAN HAROLD. *The Study of American Folklore.* New York: W. W. Norton & Co., 1968.

———, ed. *Readings in American Folklore.* New York: W. W. Norton & Co., 1979.

BURCH, ERNEST, JR. "The Nonempirical Environment of the Arctic Alaskan Eskimos." *Southwestern Journal of Anthropology* 27 (1971):148–65.

CASON, HULSEY. *The Nightmare Dream.* Psychological Monographs 46, no. 5, whole no. 209. Princeton: Psychological Review Co., 1935.

ČIŽMAŘ, JOSEF. *Lidové lékařství v Československu.* 2 vols. Brno: Melantrich, A.S., 1946.

DAVISON, K. "Episodic Depersonalization: Observations on 7 Patients." *British Journal of Psychiatry* 110 (1964):505–13.

DE FELITTA, FRANK. *The Entity.* New York: Warner Books, 1978.

DEMENT, WILLIAM; HALPER, C.; PIVIK, T.; FERGUSON, J.; COHEN, H.; HENRIKSEN, S.; MC GARR, K.; GONDA, W.; HOYT, G.; RYAN, L.; MITCHELL, G.; BARCHAS, J.; AND ZARCONE, V. "Hallucinations and Dreaming." In Association for Research in Nervous and Mental Disease Research Publications, *Perception and Its Disorders: Proceedings of the Association, December 6 & 7, 1968,* 48:335–59. Baltimore: Williams & Wilkins, 1970.

———, AND KLEITMAN, NATHANIEL. "Cyclic Variations in EEG during Sleep and Their Relation to Eye Movements, Body Motility, and Dreaming." *Electroencephalography and Clinical Neurophysiology* 9 (1957):673–90.

DEMETRIO Y RADAZA, FRANCISCO, S.J., ed. and comp. *Dictionary of Philippine Folk Beliefs and Customs.* Museum and Archives Publication no. 2. 4 vols. Cagayan de Oro City: Xavier University, 1970.

Dorland's Illustrated Medical Dictionary. 25th ed. Philadelphia: W. B. Saunders Co., 1974.

DORSON, RICHARD M. *American Negro Folktales.* Greenwich: Fawcett Publications, 1967.

ELLIS, HAVELOCK. *The World of Dreams.* Boston: Houghton Mifflin Co., 1922. Reprint. Detroit: Gale Research Co., 1976.

EVERETT, HENRY C. "Sleep Paralysis in Medical Students." *Journal of Nervous and Mental Disease* 136 (1963):283–87.

FELDMAN, MARVIN J., AND HYMAN, EDWARD. "Content Analysis of Nightmare Reports." *Psychophysiology* 5 (1968):221.

FESTINGER, LEON, RIECKEN, HENRY W., AND SCHACHTER, STANLEY. *When Prophecy Fails.* Minneapolis: University of Minnesota Press, 1956.

FISHER, CHARLES; BYRNE, J. V.; EDWARDS, A.; AND KAHN, E. "The Nightmare: REM and NREM Nightmares." In *International Psychiatry Clinics.* Vol. 7: *Sleep and Dreaming,* edited by Ernest Hartmann, pp. 183–87. Boston: Little, Brown & Co., 1970.

———; BYRNE, J.; EDWARDS, A.; AND KAHN, E. "A Psychophysiological Study of Nightmares." *Journal of the American Psychoanalytic Association* 18 (1970): 747–82.

———; KAHN, E.; EDWARDS, A.; AND DAVIS, D. M. "A Psychophysiological Study of Nightmares and Night Terrors: Physiological Aspects of the Stage Four Night Terror." *Journal of Nervous and Mental Disease* 157 (1973):75–98.

———; KAHN, E.; EDWARDS, A.; DAVIS, D. M.; AND FINE, J. "A Psychophysiological Study of Nightmares and Night Terrors: Mental Content and Recall of Stage Four Night Terrors." *Journal of Nervous and Mental Disease* 158 (1974):174–88.

FREEDMAN, A., AND KAPLAN, H., eds. *Comprehensive Textbook of Psychiatry.* Baltimore: Williams & Wilkins, 1966.

FREUD, SIGMUND. *The Interpretation of Dreams.* In *The Basic Writings of Sigmund Freud,* translated and edited by A. A. Brill. Modern Library. New York: Random House, 1938.

GASTAUT, HENRI, AND BROUGHTON, ROGER. "A Clinical and Polygraphic Study of Episodic Phenomena during Sleep." *Recent Advances in Biological Psychiatry* 7 (1965):198–221.

GOODE, G. BROWNE. "Sleep Paralysis." *Archives of Neurology* 6 (1962):228–34.

GREELEY, ANDREW M. *The Sociology of the Paranormal: A Reconnaissance.* Sage Research Papers in the Social Sciences. Vol. 3, series 90–023 (Studies in Religion and Ethnicity). Beverly Hills: Sage Publications, 1975.

GUILLEMINAULT, CHRISTIAN; ELDRIDGE, F. L.; SIMMONS, F. B.; AND DEMENT, W. C. "Sleep Apnea in Eight Children." *Pediatrics* 58 (1976):23–30.

———; ELDRIDGE, F. L.; TILKIAN, A.; SIMMONS, B.; AND DEMENT, W. C. "Sleep Apnea Syndrome Due to Upper Airway Obstruction: A Review of 25 Cases." *Archives of Internal Medicine* 137 (1977):296–300.

———; DEMENT, WILLIAM C., AND PASSOUANT, PIERRE, eds. *Narcolepsy: Proceedings of the First International Symposium on Narcolepsy.* Advances in Sleep Research, vol. 3. New York: Spectrum Publications, 1976.

HADFIELD, J. A. *Dreams and Nightmares.* Baltimore: Penguin Books, 1971.

HAND, WAYLAND D. "Witch-Riding and Other Demonic Assault in American Folk Legend." In *Probleme der Sagenforschung,* edited by Lutz Röhrich, pp. 165–76. Freiburg im Breisgau: Deutsche Forschungsgemeinschaft, 1973.

———, ed. *Popular Beliefs and Superstitions from North Carolina.* Frank C. Brown Collection of North Carolina Folklore, vols. 6 and 7, 1961, 1964. 7 vols. Durham, N.C.: Duke University Press, 1952–64.

———, AND ARLT, GUSTAV, eds. *Humaniora: Essays in Literature, Folklore and Bibliography Honoring Archer Taylor.* Locust Valley, N.Y.: J. J. Augustin, 1969.

HERSEN, MICHEL. "Nightmare Behavior: A Review." *Psychological Bulletin* 78 (1972):37–48.

HISHIKAWA, YASUO. "Sleep Paralysis." In *Narcolepsy: Proceedings of the First International Symposium on Narcolepsy.* Advances in Sleep Research, vol. 3, edited by Christian Guilleminault, William C. Dement, and Pierre Passouant, pp. 97–124. New York: Spectrum Publications, 1976.

———, AND KANEKO, Z. "Electroencephalographic Study of Narcolepsy." *Electroencephalography and Clinical Neurophysiology* 18 (1965):249–59.

HOBBES, THOMAS. *Leviathan.* Edited by Michael Oakeshott. Oxford: Basil Blackwell, 1960.

HOED, JOHANNA VAN DEN, LUCAS, EDGAR A., AND DEMENT, WILLIAM C. "Hallucinatory Experiences during Cataplexy in Patients with Narcolepsy." *American Journal of Psychiatry* 136 (1979):1210–11.

HONKO, LAURI. "Memorates and the Study of Folk Beliefs." *Fabula: Journal of Folktale Studies* 1 (1964):5–19.

HUDSON, ARTHUR PALMER, AND MCCARTER, PETER KYLE. "The Bell Witch of Tennessee and Mississippi: A Folk Legend." *Journal of American Folklore* 47 (1934):45–63.

HUFFORD, DAVID J. "Ambiguity and the Rhetoric of Belief." *Keystone Folklore Quarterly* 21 (1976):11–24.

———. "Humanoids and Anomalous Lights: Taxonomic and Epistemological Problems." *Fabula: Journal of Folktale Studies* 18 (1977):234–41.

———. "A New Approach to 'The Old Hag': The Nightmare Tradition Reexamined." In *American Folk Medicine,* edited by Wayland D. Hand, pp. 73–85. Berkeley and Los Angeles: University of California Press, 1976.

————. "Psychology, Psychoanalysis, and Folklore." *Southern Folklore Quarterly* 38 (1974):187–97.

HUSON, PAUL. *Mastering Witchcraft: A Practical Guide for Witches, Warlocks, and Covens.* New York: G. P. Putnam's Sons, 1970.

JAMES, WILLIAM. *The Varieties of Religious Experience: A Study in Human Nature.* New York: Longmans, Green & Co., 1902. Reprint. New York: Modern Library, Random House, n.d.

JOHNSON, D. M. "The 'Phantom Anaesthetist' of Matoon: A Field Study of Mass Hysteria." *Journal of Abnormal and Social Psychology* 40 (1945):175–86.

JOHNSON, LAVERNE C. "Are Stages of Sleep Related to Waking Behavior?" *American Scientist* 61 (1973):326–38.

JONES, ERNEST M. *On the Nightmare.* International Psycho-Analytical Library, no. 20. London: Hogarth Press, 1931.

JONES, LOUIS. "Ghosts of New York." *Journal of American Folklore* 57 (1944): 237–54.

JOUVET, MICHEL. "What Does a Cat Dream About?" *Trends in Neurosciences* 2 (1979):280–82.

KEEL, JOHN A. *Strange Creatures from Time and Space.* Greenwich: Fawcett Publications, 1970.

————. *Why UFOS: Operation Trojan Horse.* New York: Manor Books, 1970.

KENNEDY, RAYMOND B., JR. "Self-Induced Depersonalization Syndrome." *American Journal of Psychiatry* 133 (1976):1326–28.

KERCKHOFF, ALAN C., AND BACK, KURT W. *The June Bug: A Study of Hysterical Contagion.* New York: Appleton-Century-Crofts, 1968.

KIESSLING, NICOLAS. *The Incubus in English Literature: Provenance and Progeny.* N.p.: Washington State University Press, 1977.

KITTREDGE, GEORGE. *Witchcraft in Old and New England.* New York: Russell & Russell, 1929.

KOLB, LAWRENCE C. *Modern Clinical Psychiatry.* New edition. Philadelphia: W. B. Saunders Co., 1977.

KRAMER, HEINRICH, AND SPRENGER, JAMES. *The Malleus Maleficarum.* Translated with introduction, bibliography, and notes by Montague Summers. New York: Dover Publications, 1971.

LA BARRE, WESTON. "Anthropological Perspectives on Hallucination and Hallucinogens." In *Hallucinations: Behavior, Experience, and Theory,* edited by Ronald K. Siegel and Louis Jolyon West, pp. 9–52. New York: John Wiley & Sons, 1975.

LEHN, W. H., AND SCHROEDER, I. "The Norse Merman as an Optical Phenomenon." *Nature* 289 (1981):362–66.

LIDDON, SIM C. "Sleep Paralysis and Hypnagogic Hallucinations: Their Relationship to the Nightmare." *Archives of General Psychiatry* 17 (1967): 88–96.

LINDOW, JOHN. *Swedish Legends and Folktales.* Berkeley and Los Angeles: University of California Press, 1978.

McDONALD, CARRICK. "A Clinical Study of Hypnagogic Hallucinations." *British Journal of Psychiatry* 118 (1971):543–47.

MACK, JOHN E. *Nightmares and Human Conflict.* Sentry edition. Boston: Houghton Mifflin Co., 1974.

MACNISH, R. *The Philosophy of Sleep.* New York: Appleton, 1834.

MATHER, COTTON. *On Witchcraft: Being the Wonders of the Invisible World.* Boston: N.p., 1692. Reprint as *Cotton Mather on Witchcraft.* New York: Bell Publishing Co., n.d.

MONROE, ROBERT A. *Journeys Out of the Body.* Anchor Books. Garden City, N.Y.: Doubleday & Co., 1971. Reprint. Garden City: Anchor Press, Doubleday & Co., 1973.

MOODY, RAYMOND A., JR. *Life after Life.* Atlanta: Mockingbird Books, 1975.

MORRIS, WILLIAM, ed. *The American Heritage Dictionary of the English Language.* Boston: Houghton Mifflin Co., 1978.

MULDOON, SYLVAN, AND CARRINGTON, HEREWARD. *The Phenomena of Astral Projection.* New York: Samuel Weiser, 1969.

NAGY, JOSEPH F. Review of Nicolas Kiessling's *The Incubus in English Literature. Western Folklore* 38 (1979):134–35.

NAN'NO, H.; HISHIKAWA, Y.; KOIDA, H.; TAKAHASHI, H.; AND KANEKO, Z. "A Neurophysiological Study of Sleep Paralysis in Narcoleptic Patients." *Electroencephalography and Clinical Neurophysiology* 21 (1966):140–47.

NESS, ROBERT C. "The Old Hag Phenomenon as Sleep Paralysis: A Biocultural Interpretation." *Culture, Medicine and Psychiatry* 2 (1978):26–28.

NOYES, RUSSELL, JR., AND KLETTI, ROY. "Depersonalization in the Face of Life-Threatening Danger: A Description." *Psychiatry* 39 (1976):19–27.

———, AND KLETTI, ROY. "Depersonalization in the Face of Life-Threatening Danger: An Interpretation." *Omega* 7 (1976):103–14.

———; HOENK, P. R.; KUPERMAN, S.; AND SLYMEN, D. J. "Depersonalization in Accident Victims and Psychiatric Patients." *Journal of Nervous and Mental Disease* 164 (1977):401–7.

OTTO, RUDOLF. *The Idea of the Holy.* Translated by John W. Harvey. London: Oxford University Press, 1953.

PAYN, STEPHEN B. "A Psychoanalytic Approach to Sleep Paralysis: Review and Report of a Case." *Journal of Nervous and Mental Disease* 140 (1965):427–33.

PURDUE, CHARLES. "I Swear to God It's the Truth If I Ever Told It!" *Keystone Folklore Quarterly* 14 (1969):1–54.

PHILOLOGICAL SOCIETY. *The Oxford English Dictionary.* 12 vols. London: Oxford University Press, 1961.

RAMOS, MAXIMO D. *The Aswang Syncrasy in Philippine Folklore.* Philippine Folklore Society Paper no. 3. N.p.: Philippine Folklore Society, 1971.

RASCHKA, L. B. "The Incubus Syndrome: A Variant of Erotomania." *Canadian Journal of Psychiatry* 24 (1979):549–53.

REAGAN, CHARLES E., AND STEWART, DAVID, eds. *The Philosophy of Paul Ricoeur: An Anthology of His Work.* Boston: Beacon Press, 1978.

RIBSTEIN, MICHEL. "Hypnagogic Hallucinations." In *Narcolepsy: Proceedings of the First International Symposium on Narcolepsy.* Advances in Sleep Research, vol. 3, edited by Christian Guilleminault, William C. Dement, and Pierre Passouant, pp. 145–60. New York: Spectrum Publications, 1976.

RICKELS, PATRICIA K. "Some Accounts of Witch Riding." In *Readings in American Folklore,* edited by Jan Harold Brunvand, pp. 53–63. New York: W. W. Norton & Co., 1979. Reprinted from *Louisiana Folklore Miscellany* 2 (August 1961).

RING, KENNETH. *Life at Death: A Scientific Investigation of the Near-Death Experience.* New York: Coward, McCann & Geoghegan, 1980.

ROBBINS, ROSSELL. *The Encyclopedia of Witchcraft and Demonology.* London: Bookplan for Paul Hamlyn, 1959.

RÖHRICH, LUTZ, ed. *Probleme der Sagenforschung.* Freiburg im Breisgau: Deutsche Forschungsgemeinschaft, 1973.

ROSCHER, WILHELM HEINRICH. "Ephialtes: A Pathological-Mythological Treatise on the Nightmare in Classical Antiquity." In *Pan and the Nightmare,* translated by A. V. O'Brien. Psychological introduction by James Hillman. Dunquin Series 4, pp. 1–87. Zurich: Spring Publications, 1972.

———, AND HILLMAN, JAMES. *Pan and the Nightmare.* Translated by A. V. O'Brien. Dunquin Series 4, pp. i–lxiii. Zurich: Spring Publications, 1972.

SCHNECK, JEROME M. "Henry Fuseli, Nightmare and Sleep Paralysis." *Journal of the American Medical Association* 207 (1969):725–26.

———. "Sleep Paralysis." *American Journal of Psychiatry* 108 (1952):921–23.

———. "Sleep Paralysis without Narcolepsy or Cataplexy: Report of a Case." *Journal of the American Medical Association* 173 (1960):1129–30.

SHEED, F. J., ed. *Soundings in Satanism.* New York: Sheed & Ward, 1972.

SIEGEL, RONALD K., AND WEST, LOUIS JOLYON, eds. *Hallucinations: Behavior, Experience, and Theory.* New York: John Wiley & Sons, 1975.

SLEEP DISORDERS CLASSIFICATION COMMITTEE, ASSOCIATION OF SLEEP DISORDERS CENTERS. "Diagnostic Classification of Sleep and Arousal Disorders." *Sleep* 2, no. 1 (1979): entire issue.

SOLDATOS, CONSTANTIN R., KALES, ANTHONY, AND CADIEUX, ROGER. "Narcolepsy: Evaluation and Treatment." *Journal of Psychedelic Drugs* 10 (1978):319–25.

STOKER, BRAM. *Dracula.* Garden City, N.Y.: Doubleday & Co., n.d.

SUMMERS, MONTAGUE. *The Vampire in Europe.* New Hyde Park, N.Y.: University Books, 1961.

SWETERLITSCH, RICHARD, ed. *Papers on Applied Folklore.* Folklore Forum Bibliographic and Special Studies, no. 8. Bloomington: Folklore Forum, 1971.

Taber's Cyclopedic Medical Dictionary. 12th ed. Philadelphia: F. A. Davis Co., 1977.

TAILLEPIED, NOEL. *A Treatise of Ghosts.* Translated with introduction, commentary, and notes by Montague Summers. London: Fortune Press, n.d. Reprint. Ann Arbor: Gryphon Books, 1971. Originally published in Paris in 1588.

TALLMAN, RICHARD, ed. *Belief and Legend from Northern Kings County, Nova Scotia.* A class project of II General English class of Cornwallis District High School, Canning. Canning, Nova Scotia: N.p., 1969.

TART, CHARLES, ed. *Altered States of Consciousness: A Book of Readings.* New York: John Wiley & Sons, 1969.

TAUB, JOHN M.; KRAMER, M.; ARAND, D.; AND JACOBS, G. A. "Nightmare Dreams and Nightmare Confabulations." *Comprehensive Psychiatry* 19 (1978):285–91.

THEVENAZ, PIERRE. *What Is Phenomenology? And Other Essays.* Edited by James M. Edie. Chicago: Quadrangle Books, 1962.

THOMAS, LEWIS. "Facts of Life." *New England Journal of Medicine* 296 (1977): 1462–64.

THOMPSON, D. P. *Cassell's New Latin Dictionary: Latin-English, English-Latin.* New York: Funk and Wagnalls Co., 1960.

THOMPSON, STITH, ed. *Motif-Index of Folk-Literature.* 6 vols. Bloomington: Indiana University Press, 1966.

TILLHAGEN, CARL HERMAN. "The Conception of the Nightmare in Sweden." In *Humaniora: Essays in Literature, Folklore and Bibliography Honoring Archer Taylor,* edited by Wayland D. Hand and Gustav Arlt, pp. 317–29. Locust Valley, N.Y.: J. J. Augustin, 1969.

VAISRUB, SAMUEL. "Afterthoughts on Afterlife." *Archives of Internal Medicine* 137 (1977):150.

VALLEE, JACQUES. *Passport to Magonia: From Folklore to Flying Saucers.* Chicago: Henry Regnery Co., 1969.

VOGEL, GERALD, FOULKES, DAVID, AND TROSMAN, HARRY. "Ego Functions and Dreaming during Sleep Onset." In *Altered States of Consciousness: A Book of Readings,* edited by Charles Tart, pp. 75–91. New York: John Wiley & Sons, 1969. Reprinted from *Archives of General Psychiatry* 14 (1966): 238–48.

WARD, DONALD. "The Little Man Who Wasn't There: Encounters with the Supranormal." *Fabula: Journal of Folktale Studies* 18 (1977):213–25.

WEST, LOUIS JOLYON. "Dissociative Reaction." In *Comprehensive Textbook of Psychiatry,* edited by Alfred Freedman and Harold Kaplan, pp. 885–99. Baltimore: Williams & Wilkins, 1966.

WHITE, JOHN, comp. *Burke's Ballads.* St. John's, Newfoundland: N.d. (1960?).

Workers of the Writers' Program of the Works Projects Administration of South Carolina, comps. *South Carolina Folk Tales: Stories of Animals and Supernatural Beings.* Columbia, S.C.: University of South Carolina, 1941.

Index of Features

The arrangement of the following categories is based on a combination of factors including the commonness, specificity, order of development, and apparent interrelationship of the features of which they are comprised. The result is somewhat impressionistic but should help in the location and comparison of the various elements of the "Old Hag" attack.

Page numbers in *italics* refer to descriptions of features in quoted materials. Page numbers in roman type refer to references appearing in the discussion portions of the book.

General Index

Publications of the American Folklore Society
New Series
General Editor, Marta Weigle